How to Build

CAMPS
AND
COTTAGES

How to Build

CAMPS
AND
COTTAGES

CHARLES D. WHITE

DOVER PUBLICATIONS, INC.
MINEOLA, NEW YORK

Bibliographical Note

This Dover edition, first published in 2020, is an unabridged republication of the 1946 revised edition of *Camps and Cottages: How to Build Them*, originally published in 1939 by the Thomas Y. Crowell Company, New York.

Library of Congress Cataloging-in-Publication Data

Names: White, Charles D. (Charles Danville), 1875- author.
Title: How to build Camps and Cottages / Charles D. White ; illustrated by
   the author.
Description: Dover edition. | Mineola, New York : Dover Publications, Inc.,
   2020. | Summary: "After spending seven years constructing the perfect
   family retreat, architect Charles D. White shares his methods in this
   comprehensive guide, which features tested plans for 14 camps, cottages,
   and guest cabins. The book covers everything from selecting the ideal site
   to acquiring the necessary materials to complete instructions for building,
   finishing, and painting. More than 100 detailed drawings complement the
   text"— Provided by publisher.
Identifiers: LCCN 2019039445 | ISBN 9780486841397 | ISBN 0486841391
Subjects: LCSH: Camps. | Cottages.
Classification: LCC NA8470 .W5 2020 | DDC 728/.370223—dc23
LC record available at https://lccn.loc.gov/2019039445

Manufactured in the United States by LSC Communications
84139101
www.doverpublications.com

2 4 6 8 10 9 7 5 3 1
2019

To the Reader

Books have been written about camps before and, no doubt, will be written in the future, but this is your book, about your camp, and it is written with the idea that you may derive real and practical help from our own actual experiences.

This all started in the actual building of a camp by a son (who wanted a camp) and his architect father. Into the planning and design of that camp went all of the eager enthusiasm of youth and the experience that is a partial recompense for age. Not only did they design but, with battered hands and blistered thumbs, they turned into a successful reality the pencil lines so easily run on the drawing board.

Season followed season, and in summer and winter many friends came as guests to enjoy the pleasures and comforts embodied in the camp. So many were the questions asked and so numerous have been other camps constructed by reason of these visits, that it became apparent that there might be many kindred souls with the same desire, to whom the catalogued details of our own experiences might be of real assistance.

To put as many of these practical helps into a book, to show you how and to tell you why, to explain in simple terms and by illustrated detail the proper and easy way to approach and complete each step has been the motivating spirit in writing this book.

THE AUTHOR

Contents

CHAPTER 1

The Evolution of a Camp

We had many hours of pleasure while planning our camp. If the dream had never come true, the planning and the anticipation of having a retreat from city life would have been some compensation. But, as we discussed the idea more and more, it became more and more real—and I found myself in deeper and deeper water.

Apparently it was not enough for me to draw up a set of plans. It became evident that I was expected to demonstrate how they should be properly carried out—with the hammer and the saw. Yet I can't say that I am sorry, for I honestly think that there is no pleasure more satisfactory than the pleasure of building for yourself some kind of a house. Perhaps it is some native, inborn instinct, common to us all.

At first we had a shack of small dimensions, with few conveniences, which grew a little with each season. Indeed, a camp that is completed the first year loses the really intriguing feature of the adventure—the anticipation of adding a new room, of fixing up the kitchen, of doing something more. Even if you have unlimited

1

funds and can build your cottage exactly the way you think you want it, the chances are you will have some new ideas after you have lived there a while. A sink, which first may have seemed high enough, may turn out to be a backbreaking nuisance. Often, in fact usually, you will find that you need more storage space than you had planned. When you engage an architect to design a home in the city, you have to look a number of years ahead and plan accordingly. But when you are building your own little place, let it grow. It's more fun.

We were extremely fortunate in the selection of the site. After months of patient search, our ideal spot was found in the glorious hills of New Hampshire—deep in the woods, not too far from a good road and only two hours drive from the office. Close at hand were several ski trails and within a few miles were lakes which would furnish excellent skating and iceboating. A more perfect setting could not have been found. A flat terrace, with the mountains in the background, sloped down to a quiet, natural pool where trout slapped at flies in the twilight and upon whose mirrored surface the hemlock and birches were reflected in ever-changing pictures.

A rough shack was constructed of native lumber purchased at a near-by sawmill and all the construction was done by the owner and friends inveigled out for holidays. The walls were framed of dressed studding (i.e., uprights) over which we nailed hemlock boards vertically. Three-inch battens—strips of wood 3 inches wide and nearly an inch thick—were tightly nailed over the joints. The roof was covered with two-ply composition roll roofing over the roof boarding.

How often it happens that things which are not valued at first may later become choice! It was with regret that we were forced to use hemlock boards at that time or pay through the nose for spruce from a distance. The local mill offered a rather fine quality of wide hemlock boards which had been seasoning for some time and could be had at a low price. The price decided the question and the hemlock lumber was accepted with good grace. We gave the inside of the camp a coat of light brown stain and the matter no more thought. Some three years later one of our enthusiastic camp-building friends, we found, was searching everywhere for suitable hemlock, as he was impressed with the appearance of our aging hemlock. Then we realized, perhaps for the first time, that the fading of the stain and the aging of the wood had produced a surface of amazing beauty.

The windows were small, single-sash, hinged at the side to swing in and secured by sash fasts (Fig. 14). The use of these sash fasts insures against leakage of cold and we found no need for weather-stripping; the windows could be closed as tightly as an icebox. Neither is there any leakage in storms, a fault which the usual

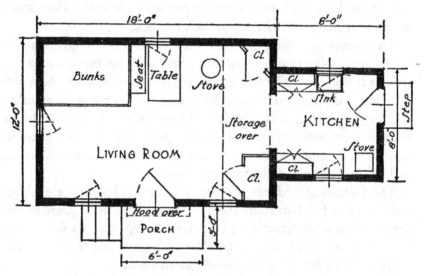

Fig. 1a. "Dunwurken"—plan of first unit.

inward-swinging casements may have. In passing, we can only say that after six years of week-end use in winter and constant occupancy in summer we would use the same type of sash were we to build tomorrow.

The camp (Fig. 1a) had only a main room 12' x 18' and a kitchen ell 8' x 8'. In one corner of the main room we built double bunks, one over the other, both being completely boxed in to avoid the circulation of cold air under mattresses (Fig. 103). A small balcony at the level of and resting on the wall plate, seven feet above the floor, was built for storage: a corner cupboard held dishes, and a closet in the opposite corner sufficed for clothes and equipment. In the kitchen a cast-iron sink (since replaced by an enameled one), a cook board with drawers and cupboard under and a cupboard above completed the equipment, for the time being.

The heating and cooking equipment consisted of a second-hand, pot-belly, cast-iron stove in the living room and a cast-iron laundry stove with stovepipe oven over it in the kitchen. Stovepipes were, temporarily we hoped, passed through sheet-metal collars in the roof, their tops fitted with shanty caps to prevent down drafts and entrance of snow or rain. We expect some day to have a brick chimney, but if we do we shall miss the extra heat thrown out by the long angle of the stovepipe up to the roof. Here again we see that makeshifts have their advantages.

The camp was christened "Dunwurken" and appropriate it surely was. Not that a name can make a camp but a camp *can* make a name. Many have been the guests endowed with the material things of this world who have enjoyed its rough hospitality and have unconsciously cast off all worries and business cares to relax and recuperate in this simple place, made with amateur hands but surrounded on every side by the perfection of Nature, and the handiwork of the Supreme Builder.

The following summer we added a screened porch, eight feet wide and the full length of the building. Many meals were served here—meals made appetizing by ravenous appetites. A Gloucester hammock on the porch invited afternoon naps and was a favorite sleeping place for whoever could get there first.

A fine tent platform and a frame, over which a large wall tent was erected with fly extended to make a porch, became the summer home of the three boys, or was used as a guest house at odd times. A permanent stone and concrete dam, blending into the natural ledges, together with some clearing of bushes and rocks, enlarged the pool to imposing dimensions. The addition of a small boat on the pool gave pleasure to children (and grownups) who delighted in exploring the upper reaches of the stream. A small concrete landing, with a stepping stone path from the cabin, lent a picturesque as well as a marine air to the landscape. Gradual clearing of the surrounding growth brought out the beauties of the spruce, pine, and hemlock trees and provided an ample supply of firewood.

Then came the addition of the two small bedrooms on the back of the cabin, with built-in bunks to make the beds snug and warm

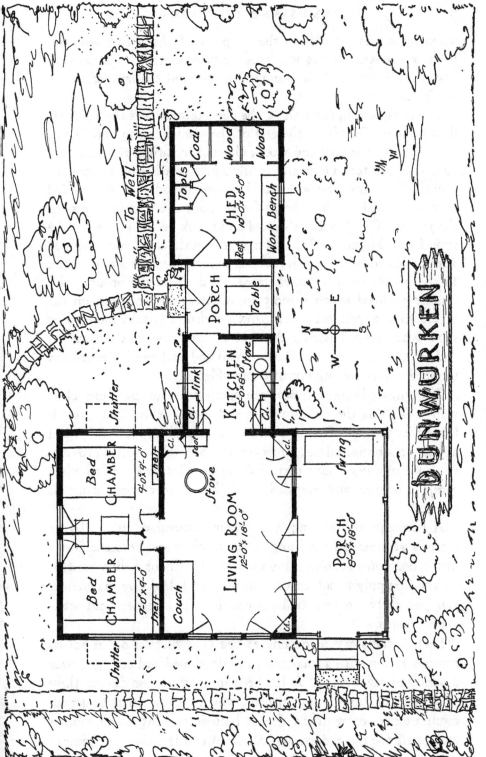

Fig. 1b. "Dunwurken" completed.

when open windows let in the crisp air of the winter months. Built-in dressers, shelves and hanging space in these bedrooms allowed the removal of the storage balcony and the large closet in the living room.

The next, and in some ways, the best addition was the 10′ x 15′ shed built six feet from the end of the kitchen wing and in line with it. Bins for coal and wood, closets for garden tools and for paints, ample tool racks and a substantial work bench were installed. The porch between the kitchen ell and shed was roofed over and closed in with screens for summer and with shutters for the winter. Overlooking the pool and brook, located between the stove in the kitchen and the refrigerator in the shed, and equipped with table and benches, this porch is an ideal summer dining room. In the winter months, when snow lies deep on the ground, this shutter enclosed porch is most appreciated. After a run on the ski trails it is a welcome spot in which to drop all packs and remove snow gear before entering the cabin. After the fires are started and the cabin is snug and warm, wood and coal can be reached in the shed without going out of doors (Fig. 1*b*).

A spring-fed dug well near the camp provides sparkling, clear water. We dug the well ourselves and rocked it in. The water is laboratory tested at frequent intervals. A small copper tank, open at the top, connected to a brass coil in the kitchen stove, provides an ample supply of hot water at all times. This tank is filled when camp is opened and emptied through a faucet when camp is closed.

A kerosene mantel lamp with chain suspensions in the living room, a gasoline lantern hung in the kitchen and kerosene lamps in the bedrooms furnish illumination. Open bookshelves contain an ample supply of adventure, mystery and detective magazines, and two shelves over a built-in couch in one corner hold well-chosen books.

Such is the story in outline of the construction of an actual camp, starting with a small unit and developed and enlarged over a period of seven years. It has been in constant use during these years both in summer and winter, which means a trial under all circumstances of weather. It has been interesting to all visitors and guests for the gadgets and details of construction. A summer home for a growing family and a cabin for the real enjoyment of winter sports.

We learned much in anticipation of the reality—we learned more in its construction. We learned that not all plans, attractive as they might seem on paper, would be satisfactory when constructed in permanent materials—that things which would be essential for convenience and comfort were not even shown— and that if a camp is to be satisfactory, every item of its proposed development must be studied and every possible use to which it might be put must be considered.

In other words we advise you to STOP, LOOK, and CONSIDER before proceeding with the construction of your camp. Just as important as showing you *how* to build your plan is it to guide you in the consideration of those plans with a view to eliminating, as far as possible, errors of judgment in how things will look. For instance: Do you want to discover that the only toilet opens off of a bedroom and you have guests who are not using that bedroom? Have you ever been a guest in a bedroom so small that one person had to remain in bed while the other dressed? Have you ever seen a living room so high that it looked like the Grand Central Station and would be as difficult to heat on a cold day?

We say again, STOP, LOOK, and CONSIDER.

CHAPTER 2

The Quest for the Ideal Site

In his delightful and comprehensive book, *The Real Log Cabin*, Chilson D. Aldrich advises the choice of a site that gives you a thrill. No better advice with which to introduce this subject could be found. If the location really gives you a thrill, there will be continued and increasing pleasure in your visits, and throughout the time between trips to the camp your mind will dwell on the anticipated pleasures.

There are, naturally, other and more practical signposts by which to be guided when in search of the ideal site. Time and thought expended in the selection will be repaid with compound interest, whereas a hasty and premature selection will result only in disappointment and disillusion. One seldom buys the first suit or dress shown by a salesperson even though it is expected that it will be discarded in a comparatively short time. Why, then, should not even more consideration be given to the selection of a camp site when, in the natural order of things, it is reasonable to expect that it will be in use for many years? The advantage of a good resale value is not without consideration, for it may be an important factor in the future. Perhaps it sounds like heresy to speak already about selling to some one else, but everyone likes to feel that he *could* get back what he paid. If you should have to move your home to another city, you might like to feel that you could change your week-end place. Also, consider that you may be obliged to buy a larger piece at first than you really need. There may be a good opportunity to sell or share a part of it. Then it is certainly a question whether it will cut to advantage, or whether in the entire portion there is only one logical location for a camp. It sometimes happens that you will find a number of acres for sale, on which the price per acre is surprisingly low. This may seem to be a bargain until you discover that because of the shape of the land there is actually only one decent place for the cottage.

In fact, when the element of cost is under consideration, a factor appears that applies as much here as in the consideration of relative values of city property; namely, *that a parcel of land is not always cheap because the price is low.* It is the development costs added to the purchase price which determine the actual capital investment. A piece of land has no value in and of itself. It is the value that can reasonably be expected to be realized from its use that measures its ultimate value. Of two or more pieces of property of different valuation, that piece is cheapest which will require the least capital investment. This would include the initial purchase price of the land plus permanent improvement costs: roads, grading, clearing, power and water and the cost of delivery of building materials to the site.

Of course, any site which is finally selected may lack some of the desired details, but perfection is rare in any situation, and some ideas must be sacrificed to the general average. The greater the number of people whose opinions are to be considered in the final selection, the more difficult it will be to make a final selection which will meet all of your requirements. The ultimate success of the camp and the degree with which it will be enjoyed will depend, to a large measure, not only on the location but on the surroundings.

Is the location to be on a lake or pond, at the seashore, among the mountains or in deep woods on some mountain stream? Must the camp be within a radius of easy travel from home and office or can it be at a more remote situation? Are there reasons for wishing to be near some group or particular location? All of these factors are of importance and should have intensive consideration.

When the general location within the desired radius from home has been established, the search for the ideal spot may be confined to definite areas. Weekend and holiday drives and rambles will disclose possibilities which can be carefully considered from every viewpoint. The maps issued by the U. S. Geological Survey at small cost are available for most areas and are particularly valuable in that they show roads, elevations, ground contours, streams and other useful information.

The location for our cabin was selected after a long and patient search during which many days were spent tramping in an apparent wilderness. In this search we were looking for a location in the mountains, on a brook or mountain stream, in the deep woods and not over a two hour drive from home. We found the geological map very helpful. A spot fulfilling all of our requirements was actually found and the time consumed in the search has been certainly repaid. After seven years of development, the real value of the selection is admitted even by the scoffing natives who at first questioned the sanity of anyone who would deliberately choose such an out-of-the-way and lonely spot.

If your camp is to be used only in the summer, a location should be selected where the prevailing breezes or natural drafts through a valley will assure relief from the heat of the summer months. A point projecting into a lake or the ocean, or a high ridge will be degrees cooler than adjacent sections. Be sure, however, that they are wooded lest there be a too abundant supply of glaring sunshine. In the deep woods you may find a valley which, because of the conformation of the land, will have a constant draft and, if combined with a running stream, will be much cooler than other nearby locations.

If your camp is to be used in the winter months, you should consider the extreme cold which may be expected and select a site that is well sheltered from the frigid northerly winds but open to sunshine. Our ancestors were far-seeing when they built their houses with living rooms to the south. During the winter months the sun was low, traveling a short course across the south and flooding these rooms with sunshine; while in the summer, with the sun high, these rooms did not get the direct rays of the sun but received the full benefit of the prevailing westerly winds.

In the selection of the site there are positive and negative points to be considered; the things which it is desirable to have and those things which should be avoided. Of the things which are desirable, the most important is that of accessibility. To the tyro this point may seem very trivial at first but it will assume astounding proportions in time. A spot which at first may have all the fascination of pioneering and back-to-nature appeal, will soon lose all that appeal when balanced against unnecessary drudgery.

Let it be clearly understood that we are not speaking of the type of camp built in the big woods, miles from the jumping-off place where everything must be carried in by pack or canoe. Many a camp has been built in just such situations where axes and saws

and the surrounding timber furnished everything for the construction. Our forefathers did this very thing and developed this
country, at the same time developing a sense of self-reliance and
thrift—which would not be out of place today. Modern pioneers
with ample resources of time and money still do it and no doubt
many delightful places have been developed.

That is an entirely different matter and has its place and its own
literature but has no place in this narrative. We are speaking here
of the sort of camp that thousands of modern cliff dwellers, in
their steam-heated apartments, dream about on hot summer
nights. The type of place that can be reached by automobile in a
reasonable length of time and to which one can slip away for a
weekend or a longer period at a moment's notice without turning
one's self into a pack mule to get a few provisions into the camp.

The writer has been in the big woods where one carried all be-
longings on the back, miles from habitation or road, in far-off
places where it required more time to get there and to return than
could be spent after he arrived. It is not as a tenderfoot or as one
who has never stumbled sorefooted over rocks and logs with the
load of Atlas on his shoulders that this attitude is taken. That sort
of thing is fine and we loved it and gloried in our ability to "take
it" and keep up our end. Now it is a relief to drive right into
camp and get the dunnage in without making trips like that long
hike over a portage with the second load.

Can the camp be reached without the necessity of carrying
everything for some distance? Can the elderly relatives or friends
reach the camp? Can your private road be constructed to your
door economically as to cost or labor? You can be assured by one
who knows that the beauty of the spot will never compensate for
the drudgery after the newness and appeal of the camp have worn
thin and only the work remains. It may seem that too much em-
phasis is being placed on the point of accessibility but if you will
STOP, LOOK, and CONSIDER, before the final decision is made, this
chapter will be much more to you than mere words and phrases.
In fact, after seeing some camps in wonderful settings, but unoc-
cupied because of *inaccessiblity*, we rewrote this chapter. The
owners won't go and others won't rent. Why? Because everything must be carried or dragged over an apology for a road nearly

a mile long. Exhilarating! After a three-day storm and the baby's milk has been left in the car?

An important and vital requisite is the matter of pure drinking water and plenty of it close to the camp. A nice spring or one that can be developed may be found on the site. If so you are fortunate. A brook or pond may be apparently a source of pure water and free from contamination but it is not safe to assume that it is pure until it has been laboratory tested.

The nature of the soil and the natural vegetation should be carefully considered. We can build our town houses in all sorts of locations which may have undesirable conditions but between public improvements and the expenditures of the owner, these conditions can be remedied. It is a different matter in the case of a camp site. The disadvantage of low-lying land on a lake or sour and unhealthy looking conditions in a wooded area cannot be easily overcome. Pine land is dry and well drained. Spruce and hemlock flourish in places with more ground water than pine can endure, but if no water-retaining spots are near, their healthy condition indicates a good location.

Many desirable locations are on a hillside and the camp must be built there. If this is true in your case, listen to a word of warning. Be sure that the camp is set well above grade, for if the drainage water, running down toward the house, is allowed to stand against woodwork or foundations, it can raise havoc. Put your building out of reach of any drainage water by setting it high enough above grade.

Check carefully for low or swamp ground in the near vicinity where the mosquito can rear its young. If the camp is to be on a brook or river, check for high water in past years and be absolutely sure that the spot is well above the reach of the highest possible water. Check for human surroundings. Undesirable neighbors, too near for comfort, can spoil the enjoyment and relaxation of your camp life. Even the nicest of people, if too near, can be a detriment to the isolation and quiet that you seek. Check for surrounding native inhabitants and the possibilities of malicious mischief or thievery. Camps have been abandoned because of the cost and annoyance resulting from such depredations.

And finally, be sure that you get an undisputed title to your land; and if it is necessary to cross some one else's land to reach yours from the highway, make sure that a right of way to your property is in the deed, also. Needless to say, it is much better to have your roadway on your own property, even if you are obliged to purchase a small extra piece.

When a person has agreed to buy a piece of land, it is customary for him to sign a contract with the owner. This contract states the price, the terms of the deed and falls due usually thirty or sixty days from the date of signing. On that day the purchaser will "take title," but in the meantime he has an opportunity to make sure that everything is in order. First there is usually a correct survey. Frequently the owner has this done, but the cost is borne half by him and half by the purchaser. Now the purchaser wishes to make sure that his title will be clear and it is advisable for him to have it investigated or "searched." The reason for this is that the land may have changed hands many times since the original grant years ago, and under obscure circumstances. Possibly there have been mortgage claims against it. At any rate, the buyer wants to know pretty well what he is getting. He can have the title searched by a lawyer, and usually it is sufficient to go back through several transactions. Better still, however, is to have this service performed by a title guaranty company, which, for an additional fee, will issue a policy insuring the title. These two fees are of course to be paid by the person who is buying the land, and he has two other fees to pay (the last): the fee for the recording of the deed in the office of the town or county clerk, and the U. S. Documentary Stamp Tax.

CHAPTER 3

Selecting the Type of Camp

The type of camp that you may build will depend upon a great number of factors involving cost (unfortunately), besides size and appearance. The number of people who will occupy the camp and the amount in the budget will determine, to a marked degree, the proposed size and accommodations which will be needed. The type of materials will also have a direct bearing upon the cost, although a difference in unit costs of materials has a surprisingly small effect upon the total cost of construction.

What is actually desired in the way of accommodations? Is it to be a small but snug camp for winter sports to which a few congenial souls will go for short periods, or is it to be a summer place in which the family and possible guests will be housed for a considerable length of time? It may consist only of a single room— serving for living quarters with bunks, stove and table in the one space. This type does not lend itself to parties of mixed genders or personalities, although a certain amount of visual privacy may be had with curtains or screens. It may be on a larger and more elaborate scale with living room, kitchen, bedrooms and bath or it may be a central cabin with detached guest cabins to be built at a later date.

Whichever type may be the final choice, it may be necessary, sooner or later, to add to the original structure and the planning for that possibility should be included in the general scheme.

An experienced woodsman once said that in making a pack for a trip into the woods, all the material that you *think* you will need should be made into three piles. The first pile should contain only those things which you cannot do without, the second pile the things that you think will be needed and the third those articles which you would *like* to take. When you have finished sorting, make up the pack from the first pile!

So it is in planning your camp. Put down on a paper a list of all the things which you would like to include and then eliminate, until the net result is within the budget. It is not necessary that you have all the desirable features at first. Once you are housed from the weather, many details can be omitted until time and your own ingenuity have made these features possible.

The general requirements as to size and facilities having been accepted for the time being, the general type of construction and the materials to be used should have careful consideration. The site and its surroundings should be somewhat of a controlling factor in the appearance of your camp. One would hardly build a Cape Cod cottage, with its white paint and green shutters, in the deep woods nor a log cabin on a city lot. Each is perfectly charming in its proper setting and equally out of place in other than its natural environment.

The type of camp and its general appearance will also depend, to a large extent, upon the materials which are available within a reasonable distance. This will necessarily be governed by the product of the local mills as it is hardly practicable or profitable to transport lumber to any great distance merely for the purpose of using some particular kind of wood.

There is the log cabin, the ancestor of all our wooden buildings which, in some spots, has an appeal that warrants its construction. It was developed as a necessity in times before sawmills existed when the only materials at hand were the trees and the only tools available an axe, perhaps a saw and an auger. With these simple implements, homes were literally carved from the wilderness which furnished all the materials. The modern log cabin, with its peeled and varnished logs and even its tiled bathroom, is a far cry from its ancestor, but it makes a delightful camp for those who prefer that variety. With log cabins we are not concerned. Several books are available that cover every phase of their construction and equipment in a thorough and charming manner and we will devote our entire discussion to the building of the framed camp.

For those who feel that they *must* have a log cabin, there is a fine opportunity to get much of the appearance of a log cabin by the use of sawed log sections, spoken of later in this book, used both on the outside of the framing and on the inside as well. This method gives all the appearance of the log cabin at a much lower cost and without some of the undesirable features of the real log cabin.

Whatever type is to be built, the framing or skeleton of the structure will be essentially the same and the methods of construction will only vary as required by the plan and the outside surface. Framing, boarding and roof material will be constructed from mill lumber and, with the exception of sash, frames and drawer sets, the entire structure will be dependent upon the kinds and qualities of the mill materials which are conveniently available. It is the material with which the skeleton, or framing, is clothed that determines the final appearance—as well as the comfort. It may look attractive to the eye but, if the heat in winter can pour out of it as easily as bugs in summer can pour in, only drastic measures will remedy the defect. If you have ever passed a night in a place where any light after dark brought myriads of merciless insects through every crevice, you will grasp the idea.

For outside covering, a wide choice of materials is available, each with its distinctive appearance and each particularly adapted to a special use. Some materials are sufficient in themselves and others are dependent upon additional materials to make their use practicable. The materials are described in this chapter from the standpoint of appearance, and as a help in your decision as to the general type (Fig. 2).

Batten Design

The simplest type of outside covering is vertical boarding with batten strips securely nailed over the joints between the boards. It has the advantage of ease of construction and low cost. Its appearance, either finished in stain or paint, is pleasing and is in perfect harmony in any setting. That it is an inexpensive covering is no indication that it is not practicable and attractive.

This style has years of duty to show for itself as can be readily seen if you will notice the many city houses that were constructed in the years of the last century with outside boarding and molded battens, frequently in the carpenter Gothic mode. This type was used in the construction of "Dunwurken." So tight and warm has it been that in zero weather and even at twenty below zero, the camp is snug and warm without any drafts or cold spots.

BATTEN CONSTRUCTION

SHINGLES

Paper

CLAPBOARDS

Paper

BEVELED SIDING

NOVELTY SIDING

LOG SIDING

TYPES OF SIDING

Fig. 2.

With the vertical boarding planed on both sides and the exposed wall framed of planed lumber, a coat of stain on the interior will bring out the natural beauty of the wood and is all that the interior finish needs. Judicious planning of outside trim around doors and windows in connection with the battens, produces a pleasing result. For the results obtained, the cost is very low.

Siding

For a summer camp in which heating is no problem, there are several forms of siding which can be nailed horizontally and directly upon the framing. As the siding is applied directly to the framing and is not usually supplemented by inside sheathing, there is the problem of making the surface tight and free from crevices which may develop from the shrinkage of the material. There are several good kinds of siding, as will be seen from the illustration.

Sheathing the frame with boards, either matched or square-edged, allows the use of shingles, clapboards or wide-beveled siding. Various combinations of these materials are easy to make, increasing the variety of surface treatments which can be made.

An example of the use of two or more materials is a camp made with vertical boarding and battens up to the level of the plate, and flitch sawed boards (described in the next paragraph) applied horizontally on gable ends. This will be very woodsy and delightful appearing.

One type of outside surface material which can be used alone or preferably with other materials is the flitch-sawed board. This is regular unplanned boarding with the bark, or waney edge, left on. One or both edges of the board are left without any trimming, thus showing a more or less beveled irregular edge of bark. Even if the bark falls off, the uneven edge will still retain the effect desired. The boards are laid overlapping in the same manner in which wide siding is laid. In gables and as a covering between sill and ground, instead of lattice work, a very effective appearance may be obtained with this material when other materials are used on the rest of the camp. Staining with oil and raw umber or other colors brings out the grain of the wood and improves the appearance.

As a compromise between a real log cabin and the more easily constructed frame camp, lumber cut to represent the face of a log, with edges cut to make a tight joint similar to shiplap, would give the general appearance of a log cabin and would appeal to many persons. Oiled or stained, with a properly selected roof surface, these walls can be a cheap and delightful answer to the desire for a log cabin appearance.

Size and Accommodations

We have discussed style and appearance of materials and outside finish. More important even than that is the type that will be determined by the number of rooms which are desired. It is one thing to plan for a simple one-room camp, but it is a different matter when only a number of rooms can possibly be sufficient. It is essential to remember that even the simple camp may be outgrown and additions may be necessary at some time in the future. This possibility should be foreseen and provided for in the original plan. It is possible that the one-room camp will be sufficient for your needs; at least you may think so now, but it is better to plan for extended facilities should you decide later that you need them.

The most simple arrangement—one which would serve for four people nicely as a hunting or fishing camp or for winter sports—consists of only one room in which are bunks for four people, a stove serving for both heating and cooking, a small sink and space for tables and chairs or benches. This was the usual type of cabin of our pioneer forefathers and many such cabins are still in use in parts of this country. In fact we have seen many permanent homes commenced with this unit, later perhaps to serve as a wing of a larger house (Fig. 3).

The next step may be the addition of a kitchen, perhaps with a small shed as part of the wing. This addition permits the removal of the culinary department from the main room and requires an additional stove to replace the cooking stove in the main room (Fig. 4).

The addition of a bedroom in the plan removes the necessity for bunks in the living room but leaves the problem of housing overnight guests (Fig. 5). This can be met by a couch in the main room or a separate guest house or tent.

The average camp, however, will probably later require two

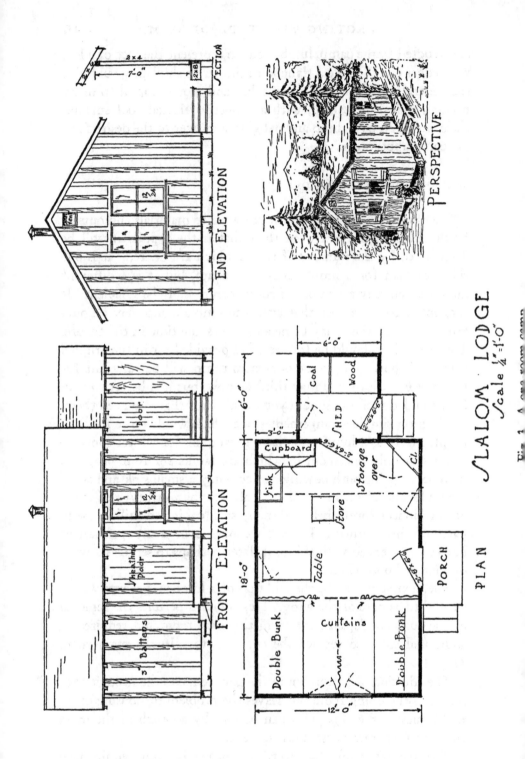

SECTION

2×4

7'-0"

2×8

END ELEVATION

PERSPECTIVE

FRONT ELEVATION

Roof

Sheathing
Paper

6" Battens

SLALOM LODGE
Scale ¼"=1'-0"

6'-0"

6'-0"

Coal

Wood

3'-0"

SHED

Cupboard

Sink

Storage
over

Stove

2-6×6'6"

Cl.

Table

2'-6×6'6"

Double Bunk

Curtains

Double Bunk

Porch

18'-0"

12'-0"

PLAN

Fig. 1. A one-room camp

20

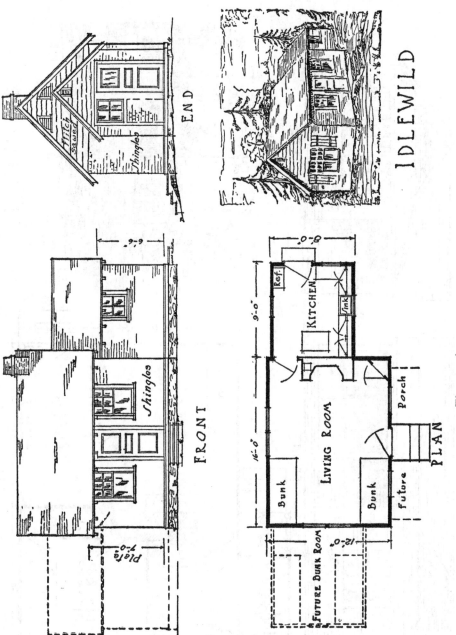

END

IDLEWILD

FRONT

PLAN

Fig. 4. A two-room camp.

21

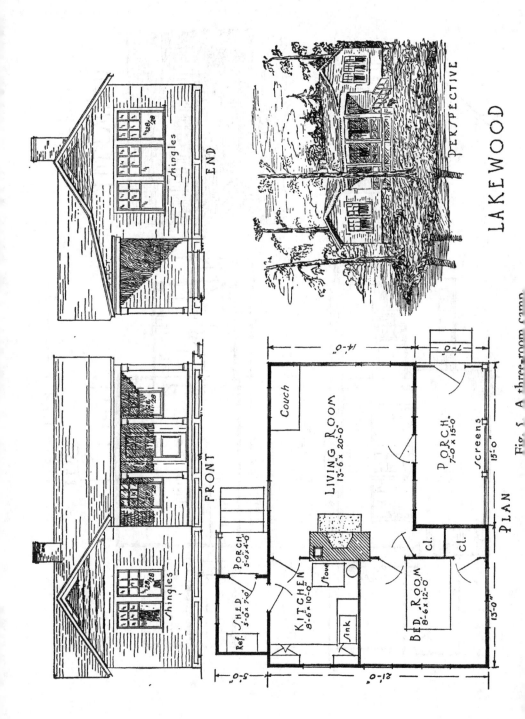

SHINGLES

END

28x28

PERSPECTIVE

SHINGLES

28x28

28x28

28x28

FRONT

LAKEWOOD

PORCH
5'-0"x4'-0"

Couch

14'-0"

SHED.
5'-0"x7'-0"

Ref.

LIVING ROOM
15'-6" x 20'-0"

PORCH
7'-0" x 15'-0"

7'-0"

KITCHEN
8'-6"x10'-0"

Stove

Screens

15'-0"

Sink

cl.

cl.

BED ROOM
8'-6"x12'-0"

5'-0"

21'-0"

15'-0"

PLAN

Fig. 5. A three-room camp.

22

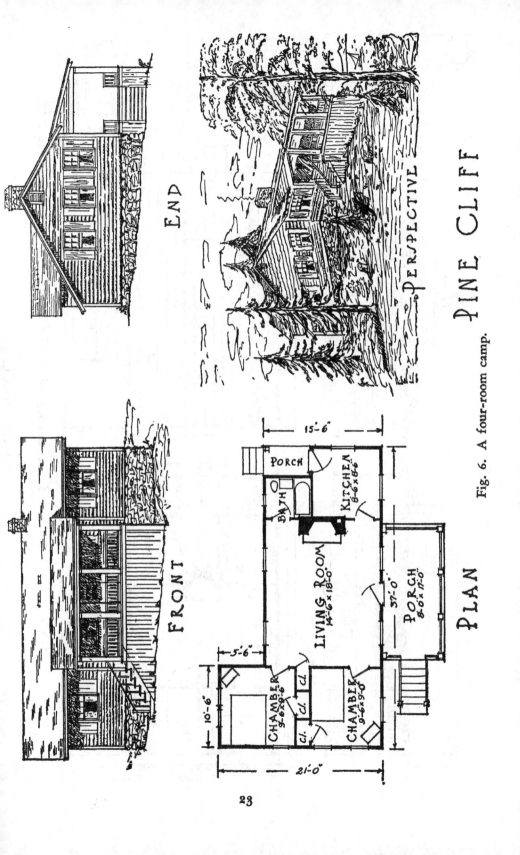

END

PERSPECTIVE

PINE CLIFF

Fig. 6. A four-room camp.

FRONT

PLAN

15'-6"

PORCH

BATH

KITCHEN
8'-6"×8'-6"

LIVING ROOM
14'-6"×18'-0"

37'-0"

PORCH
8'-0"×17'-0"

5'-6"

CHAMBER
9'-6"×9'-6"

Cl.

Cl.

Cl.

Cl.

CHAMBER
9'-6"×9'-0"

10'-6"

21'-0"

23

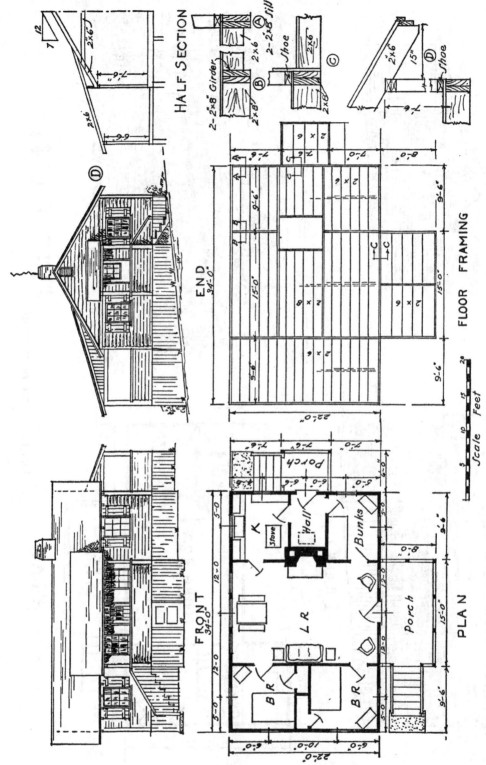

Fig. 7. Sunset Lodge.

24

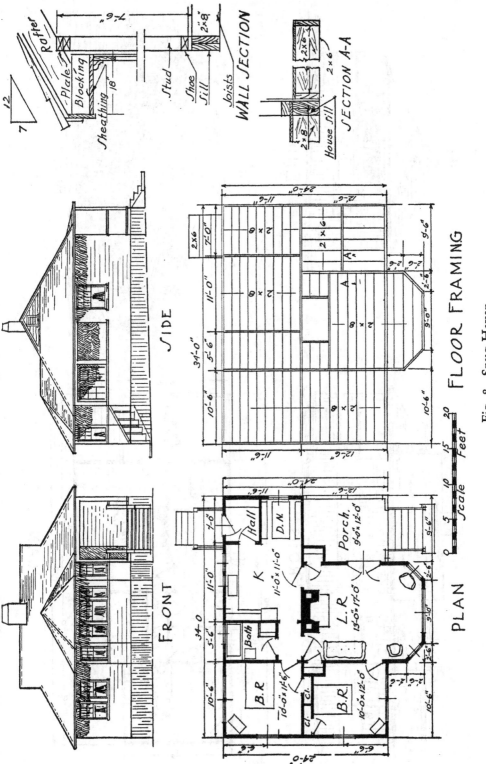

WALL SECTION

SECTION A-A

SIDE

FRONT

FLOOR FRAMING

PLAN

Fig. 8. Snug Haven.

25

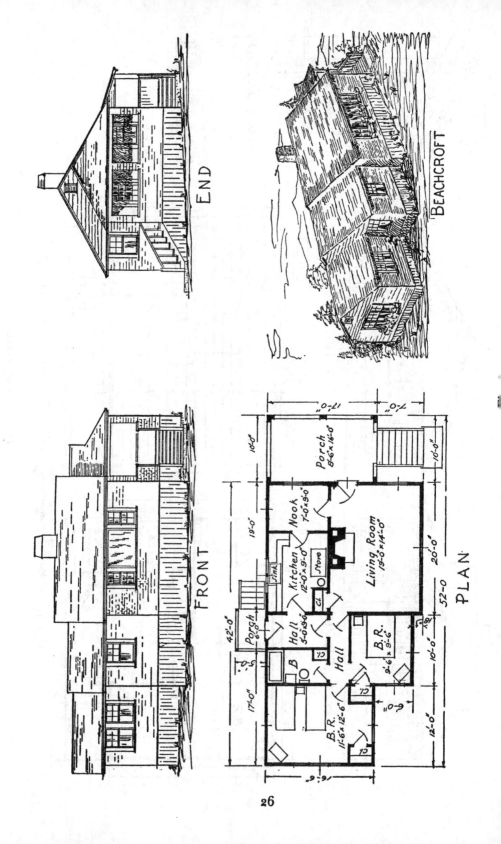

END

BEACHCROFT

FRONT

PLAN

Porch
8'-6" x 16'-0"

Nook
7'-0" x 9'-0"

Kitchen
12'-0" x 9'-0"

Living Room
19'-0" x 14'-0"

Stove

Sink

Hall
5'-0" x 9'-0"

Porch
6'-0"

B

Hall

B.R.
9'-6" x 9'-6"

B.R.
11'-6" x 12'-6"

Cl.

42'-0"

19'-0"

16'-0"

17'-0"

52'-0"

20'-0"

16'-0"

12'-0"

16'-6"

6'-0"

7'-0"

17'-0"

10'-0"

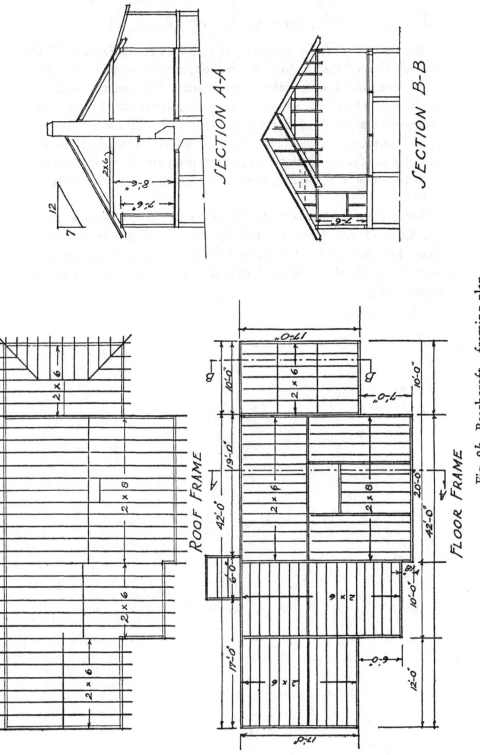

SECTION A-A

SECTION B-B

ROOF FRAME

FLOOR FRAME

Fig. 9b. Beachcroft—framing plan.

27

bedrooms at least for guests or extra members of the family. With the addition of two bedrooms (Fig. 6), a toilet or at least a separate washroom becomes almost a necessity. We met this problem at "Dunwurken" by installing enameled lavatories in the bedrooms with a practical waste pipe. Hot and cold water was supplied in pitchers. These lavatories were added to avoid the necessity of guests using the kitchen for morning ablutions, interfering with the cook and spoiling their breakfast appetite with pilfered morsels.

Three further developments are shown in Sunset Lodge (Fig. 7), Snug Haven (Fig. 8), and Beachcroft (Figs. 9a and 9b). These are, of course, much more complicated and are designed to meet the needs of the larger family or the family that does much entertaining.

CHAPTER 4

Materials

We have now reached the stage when it is advisable to consider the different materials on the basis of their use in construction. You have very definite ideas about the plan and general type of camp and have spent many pleasant hours drawing different sketches until the numerous ideas and requirements have been condensed and crystallized into the final, accepted plan.

It is now time to transpose this plan into terms of wood and brick or stone and select the materials to be used in the actual construction. It will be to your advantage both in convenience and cost, to purchase the lumber at the nearest possible source of supply, for the kinds of lumber and materials available locally will vary in the different sections of the country. It is advisable to take your sketches and lists of materials to the dealers in your vicinity and consult with them as to qualities and prices before your final decisions are made.

Several different kinds of lumber are usually available, each having certain characteristics which make it especially suitable for use in one part of the building and equally unsuitable in some other part, owing to peculiarities of growth or texture. Each variety is again divided into several grades, each grade suitable for some type of work and yet not necessarily required for all conditions. Underfloors and rough boarding do not necessarily have to be a select stock, while outside trim and inside finish should be selected from the best grade available.

No suggestions other than general can be given in this discussion that will apply equally in all sections because the types of lumber available and in common use vary so much in the different sections of the country. Local usage and the advice of the mill man will be your best guide in the selection of the several materials.

Posts which are to be set in the ground or any timber which is to be in contact with earth should be made from a wood which, from its natural resistance to decay, will not deteriorate. Chestnut, cedar, cypress, redwood or locust are preferable for such work. The hardwoods such as birch, maple, or oak are not so durable but will last a long time.

Framing lumber should be lightweight, free from defects which would impair its strength, straight and available in various usual lengths. Spruce, yellow pine, fir, and hemlock are the varieties most commonly available. The same species also come in board form for underfloors, wall and roof boarding. White pine, cypress, red cedar, and redwood are easily worked, take paint well, retain their shape without warping and twisting, and will withstand the deteriorating effect of the weather when used as trim and finish on the exterior.

All boards should be dressed two sides, except underflooring on first floor, which can be dressed one side to an even thickness. Boarding should have straight, square edges, free from bark or wane. By wane, we mean an edge of the board which has not been sawed and which shows the surface from which the bark has been removed. Boarding for roofs, if exposed on the interior, should be matched. The extra cost is not prohibitive and the added appearance is well worth the extra cost except for the roughest type of camp. If you decide to use roll roofing for the finished surface of the roof, the roofing material will lie much better and will be less subject to wrinkles and bulges if the roof sheathing is matched.

Walls sheathed with matched boarding instead of square edged boards are much stronger and far warmer than square-edge boards when used as sheathing under shingles, clapboards, or siding. The interior surface, if exposed, will naturally excel square edge boarding in appearance. For finished flooring which is to be painted, pine, spruce, and fir may be used. Southern pine, birch, maple, beech, and oak are the commonly used varieties for floors which are to be finished in the natural wood.

Species of Wood Commonly Available

Eastern Section: white pine, yellow pine, eastern spruce, hemlock, cypress, poplar, oak, maple, birch, gum.

Western Section: Douglas fir, redwood, red cedar, Sitka spruce, western white pine, western hemlock, larch.

Schedule of Uses

Interior Posts, Girders: spruce, yellow pine, fir.
Light Framing: spruce, yellow pine, hemlock.
Outside Finish: white pine, cypress, redwood, poplar, spruce.
Siding and Clapboards: spruce, cypress, redwood, cedar.
Shingles: cedar, cypress, redwood.
Sash, Doors, and Frames: white pine, fir, yellow pine.
Flooring (*painted*): pine, spruce.
Flooring (*natural finish*): oak, maple, birch, beech, yellow pine.
Interior Finish (*painted*): white pine, yellow pine, spruce, fir,
  redwood.
Interior Finish (*natural*): oak, chestnut, birch, cypress, redwood,
  gum, white pine, yellow pine.

White Pine

The pine tree, with its numerous species ranging from the white pine in the northern climates through the many varieties of pitch or southern pine, is common to all parts of the country and as a source of lumber is the most extensively used of all our native trees. White pine was formerly used for every purpose in construction but is now almost entirely reserved for finish or trim. It was the first lumber to be used by the settlers of New England and the North Atlantic states. It is light in color and weight with a fine, uniform grain, is easily worked and does not warp or twist. It does not shrink as much as the harder species of pine.

It withstands the deteriorating effects of time and moisture, especially if well protected by paint and it is the natural material for sash, doors, and outside trim. Much of the white pine now produced in the eastern part of the country is subject to many knots in direct contrast to western pine which can be obtained in wide boards, free from knots or other defects. Even the objectionable knot has now been glorified and the lowly "knotty pine" has become the choice material for inside finish and is lording it over the princely walnut and mahogany of earlier days. It has an undeniable charm and appeal and has a rare patina when properly finished. The origin of this type of finish was in the early American carpenter work and, ironically enough, the early craftsman would have been deeply chagrined had a knot been found in his wood-work.

Yellow Pine

We use this term in building to include all species of pine which are not white pine. Their names are legion and a complete category is not within the scope of this book. In the central and southern parts of the country these pines are used as general pur-pose lumber including framing, sheathing, and finish.

The wood varies from the lighter toned color of white pine to the darker and heavier Georgia pine. It has strength for framing, can be procured in long lengths and any reasonable size. It is worked into all forms of finish and finished flooring so that in sec-tions where it constitutes the principal local supply, practically every piece on your bill of materials will be furnished from this wood.

Spruce

Is an admirable wood for framing, boarding, cheap flooring, and even inside trim, although not so desirable for trim as pine or the hard woods. It is light in color, straight-grained, and strong. In sections where it is commonly available, it is considered the best timber for framing, sheathing, and boarding. It is not satisfactory for outside finish as it is not very durable when exposed to the weather.

Fir

There are two general species of fir: one common to the east and the other produced in the west coast country. The lumber bears a marked resemblance to spruce, and the western or Douglas fir, much in use for framing, is difficult to distinguish from long-leaved pine for which it is a substitute with almost equal strength. It can be used for interior finish, finished floors, and general inside work or where it is not exposed to the weather.

It is comparatively light in weight, fairly soft to work, and has a coarse grain, especially when used as plywood. This type of veneer takes on an interesting but splashy appearance under stain and natural finish.

Hemlock

While hemlock is a durable wood, it shrinks and checks freely, is coarse-grained, brittle, and splits easily. It has an unusual holding property for nailing and is not attacked by mice and rodents as they do not relish its sharp, brittle splinters. The lumber should be handled carefully, for edge splinters have a way of entering unprotected hands. It is used for framing and general boarding when it is available in place of spruce which may not be in the local market.

Cypress

Somewhat like cedar in its appearance and qualities, cypress is an all-enduring wood. For wood gutter stock it has no superior and for any exposed situation such as outside finish, etc., it is most suitable. It has been extensively used as interior trim and can be finished in attractive effects.

Unique panels can be made from curly or wavy grained cypress by scorching the surface with a blow torch flame and then scrubbing the charred portions with a wire brush. Owing to the alternate hard and soft grain, an effect of low-relief carving is obtained.

Gum

Peculiar to some sections, this wood has somewhat the appearance of walnut when stained and finished in shellac or varnish. It is used for interior trim, as veneers and sometimes as finished flooring. However, if it is to be used successfully as trim and flooring it must be properly selected and cured.

Redwood

Redwood is to the West what white pine is to the East and the yellow pine is to the South. It is used where locally available as a universal building material in its native West. The entire bill of materials, from framing to finish, can be filled with this wood. It is reasonably light in weight, easy to work, takes a fine polish and has a natural resistance to fire.

Chestnut

Once abundant over a large section of the country, chestnut is now almost extinct owing to a blight which swept over a large area. It has a natural resistance to decay and is unsurpassed for posts or timbers in contact with the ground. Used as an interior wood, it is easily mistaken for oak and its distinctive grain and general appearance under proper finish, make it very suitable for some types of trim and cabinet work.

Locust

While locust is not commonly available, if it can be obtained, is especially suitable for posts.

Oak

Heavy and strong with coarse, open grain, oak is used mostly for flooring, trim, and furniture. It was once much used for timber framing. Native oak can be used for posts under sills.

Birch

Fine and even with close grain, hard and strong, birch takes a beautiful finish either stained or natural. It is used for finished flooring and trim and as a veneer on doors, panels, and cabinet work.

Poplar

This is a soft, even-grained wood noticeably free from defects. It makes a good material for paneling and can be finished natural. In some sections it is known as whitewood.

Commercial Sizes

The various sizes, length, thickness, and width of all commercial lumber have been very thoroughly standardized throughout the country and with the exception of the products of the smaller sawmills, are much the same everywhere. Small local mills are apt to produce lumber varying from these sizes but usually on the side of increased dimensions.

Several common terms should be noted at this time. Common boards comprise lumber which has been sawed to inch thickness. "Dimension stuff" is two inches thick and from four to twelve inches wide. Studding and light framing are usually termed "scantlings," and if over six inches in width are called "planks." Lumber over four inches thick and six inches in width is designated as "timbers."

Stock Lengths

It is of prime importance in the cost of the camp that all framing be so designed that the usual stock lengths can be used without excessive and wasteful cutting. In most lumber yards stock lengths are available by even feet from eight feet up. Seven-foot lengths may be found; or, if they are not, the fourteen-feet stock length may be cut into two seven-foot sticks. If floor joists are commercially available in twelve, fourteen and sixteen feet as yard stock, your plans should be made to use one of these stock lengths without cutting to waste. For example: A twelve-foot stock plank for floor joist with the usual trimming to square the ends, plus the thickness of the double sills at each side, would make a camp with an over-all width of twelve feet six inches.

If you should plan a camp exactly thirteen feet in width, it would be necessary, usually, to pay for the fourteen-foot joist and then waste at least a foot in length from each joist. The same principle is true in wall studding. Figure the total height of the top of the plate above the rough floor, deduct the thickness of the partition shoe and the double cap and then plan for a stud length nearest to a stock length.

Sizing

It is quite important that you know the exact dimensions of these different commercial sizes of lumber, especially when laying out or detailing any part of the work. Finished lumber for trim, inside work, window casings, etc., is commonly thought of as one inch thick but actually it is only thirteen-sixteenths and even that is reduced to twenty-five thirty-seconds of an inch in some cases. Two by four scantlings are actually $1\frac{5}{8}''$ x $3\frac{5}{8}''$, three-eighths of an inch less than the nominal term for the size. All dimension stock is at least three-eights of an inch less than the nominal or catalogue size.

When lumber is first sawed from the log, the various sizes and types of material are cut so that they use to the best advantage all the wood in the log.

Objectionable rough-sawed surfaces on lumber are smoothed by running the lumber through power planers which somewhat reduce the actual size. The treatment is called "dressing," and the terms used in a bill of materials indicate how extensively lumber should be dressed. For example, "D4S" means "dressed four sides"; "S1S1E" means "surfaced one side and one edge."

Lumber is always spoken of and listed in all billings by the "nominal" size, that is, the size by which it is known and the size that was actually furnished in the early days of sawmill practice. The "actual" size is the final size of dressed lumber in use today, with a slight tolerance.

AMERICAN STANDARD LUMBER SIZES

Nominal	Actual	Nominal	Actual
2″ x 3″	$1\frac{5}{8}''$ x $2\frac{5}{8}''$	3″ x 4″	$2\frac{5}{8}''$ x $3\frac{5}{8}''$
2″ x 4″	$1\frac{5}{8}''$ x $3\frac{5}{8}''$	4″ x 6″	$3\frac{5}{8}''$ x $5\frac{5}{8}''$
2″ x 6″	$1\frac{5}{8}''$ x $5\frac{5}{8}''$	4″ x 8″	$3\frac{5}{8}''$ x $7\frac{1}{2}''$
2″ x 8″	$1\frac{5}{8}''$ x $7\frac{1}{2}''$		

Grading

In order to utilize every available portion of the product of the sawmill, lumber is also divided into several grades which also have been standardized to a large degree. The cost of the camp can be kept to a minimum by a wise selection of these grades in keeping with the purpose for which they are intended.

As rough-sawed lumber comes from the saw and all during the various processes of manufacture, it is graded by well-defined and commonly adopted standards, a subject complete in itself. But for our purposes it is enough to know in a general way what the more common grades are. Most of our framing and finish materials can be roughly divided into "yard lumber" and "finish stock."

Yard lumber is given five separate grades but the three better grades are all that we shall use for anything but the very roughest types of work.

No. 1 Common: Sound and light knotted; may be considered watertight lumber.

No. 2 Common: Of same general quality but less restricted in quality than No. 1.

No. 3 Common: Prevailing grade characteristics larger than in No. 2.

Finishing Lumber

Grade A: Practically clear.

Grade B: High quality, clear in general.

Grade C: Good for best-quality paint finish.

Grade D: Intermediate between Grade C and No. 1 Common.

Most specifications for finished material read "Grade B or better."

Definitions

Cap. A piece of lumber, usually 2" x 4", nailed on top of a line of studing to complete the wall or partition framing. Always formed by nailing one piece flat on top of the upright studs and usually, except in interior partitions, by spiking another line on top of the first, breaking joints in the two layers, that is, having the joints in the upper member as far from any joint in the lower layer as possible (Fig. 10).

Girder. Intermediate timber support used when a floor span is too long for a single length of joint without one or more extra bearings (Fig. 34).

Girt. Short horizontal piece of framing cut in between studs to make nailing bearings for vertical boarding or sheathing.

Joist. One of the timbers which support the wood flooring (Fig. 10).

Plate. Same as cap.

Rafter. One of the timbers which support the roof boarding (Fig. 10).

Shoe. A piece of timber, usually 2" x 4", laid and spiked flat on the floor or framing, upon which the upright studs for walls and partitions may be spiked (Fig. 10).

Sill. The timber or joists forming the outside perimeter of the first floor framing and to which or on which all the floor joists are spiked and the outside walls rest (Fig. 10).

Building Papers

By this general term we include all those forms of paper or felt which are used between a supporting material like underfloors or wall boarding and the finished surface material like finished floors, siding, shingles, etc., on walls or roofs.

Building papers are used for additional protection from the weather or changes in temperature and are a vital part of the structure. The materials between which the building paper is placed may be of mediocre quality but the heart of the sandwich, the building paper, should be the best that the budget will allow. For this reason the very best quality, waterproof preferably, should always be used however rigid an economy may be practiced in other respects. Just because the material is completely hidden from sight and its quality cannot be seen, there is no reason for skimping on this item. We saw one camp practically torn to pieces and rebuilt because the owner was more interested in the appearance of the flitch-sawed boards with which it was attrac-

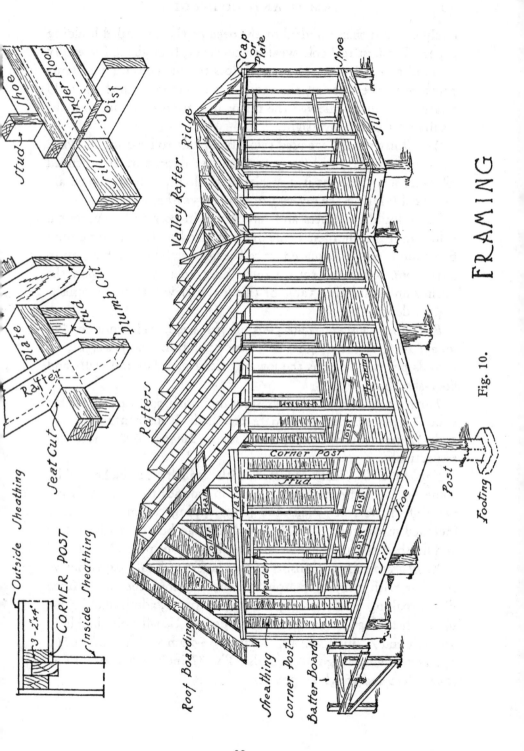

FRAMING

Fig. 10.

Stud
Shoe
Under Floor
Sill
Joist

Outside Sheathing
Plate
Rafter
Seat Cut
Stud
plumb Cut
CORNER POST
Inside Sheathing
3-2"x4"

Cap or Plate
Valley Rafter Ridge
Shoe
Sill

Rafters
Roof Boarding
Sheathing
Corner Post
Batter Boards
Corner Post
Stud.
Header
Corner Post
Plate
Sill
Shoe
Joist
Joist
Joist
Girder
Bracing
Post
Footing

39

tively covered than mindful of the need of the concealed building paper. The first real cold weather, however, brought it forcefully to mind and after ineffectual attempts to change the frigid temperature of the interior, the camp was abandoned until the mild weather of spring allowed the major operation of remedying the results of a simple oversight.

At "Dunwurken" we used two-ply asphalt roll roofing between the rough and finished floors to the utter disgust of experienced kibitzers who thought it a species of madness. But the floors are never cold during the severest of winter weather.

These building papers and felts range in cost and in practical value from the cheapest grade of rosin-sized paper weighing only five pounds per 100 square feet to the heavier felts weighing up to sixty pounds per 100 square feet. Every penny spent upon the quality and insulating value of this material will return astonishing dividends.

Red Rosin Paper. Thirty-six inches wide, rolls contain 500 square feet. Light weight, 20 pounds per roll, heavy weight, 40 pounds per roll. This is the lowest priced paper of the wall- and floor-sheathing type.

Tarred Felt Sheathing. Felt saturated with coal tar; 32 inches wide, 15 pounds per 100 square feet laid. Rolls containing 216 and 432 gross square feet, actually laying 200 and 400 square feet respectively.

Asphalt Felt. Felt saturated with asphalt; 36 inches wide; comes in a variety of weights from 15 pounds to 60 pounds per net 100 square feet. Nails and joint-lapping cement are usually included in the roll. The 15-pound felt can be used under siding and finished flooring but the 30-pound would be much better.

Reinforced Paper. Consists of two layers of Kraft paper bound together with a layer of asphalt, in which are imbedded crossed fibers, making a very tough, waterproof paper, admirable for use under sheathing and under finished floors. Usually obtainable in 36-inch and 72-inch widths. Rolls of 36-inch width contain 500 square feet and weigh 30 pounds. The 72-inch rolls contain 360 square feet and weigh 24 pounds.

Floor insulation

Best of all for floor insulation is the commercial asphalt roll roofing with a talc surface, not slate-coated, which can be purchased in several weights. The rolls are 36 inches wide and contain 108 square feet laying a net 100 square feet. The lightest grade weighs approximately 35 pounds per roll, medium weight, 45 pounds, and the heavy weight 55 pounds.

Roll Roofing

This material, when the cost, ease of application, and duration of service is considered, is without doubt the cheapest form of roof surfacing. It is not necessarily cheap looking and if one of the slate-surfaced, concealed lap joint types are used, is not without value in the appearance of the camp.

Roll roofing is sold in rolls 36 inches in width. Each roll contains 108 square feet and will lay 100 square feet including the two-inch lap. Complete instructions for laying, together with nails and joint cement, are included in each roll. The slate surface is available in dark green, deep red, or black. Either color is in good taste in any location.

The important point to remember is that the weights and quality vary and the price is a sure index to the relative value. The heaviest and best grades will weigh 90 pounds per roll and a life of at least fifteen years is assured by the manufacturers. The heaviest grades are lapped three inches at the joints. One-inch nails are used when roofing is applied directly to sheathing and one-and-three-quarter-inch nails if applied over old shingles or heavy insulation.

Asphalt Shingles

These are similar to roll roofing in composition and are made both in strips and as single shingles (Fig. 11). They are applied in the same manner as wood shingles but with special bung-head roofing nails.

The single shingles measure 9″ x 12″, are packed in bundles, each one of which will cover 25 square feet when laid with four-inch exposure to the weather. It takes four bundles to lay a square (100 square feet) and the shingles to cover a square weigh 240 pounds. A jumbo, or extra size, shingle is 12" x 16" and, with five-inch exposure, each bundle will cover 25 square feet. Four bundles, enough to cover a square, will weigh 325 pounds.

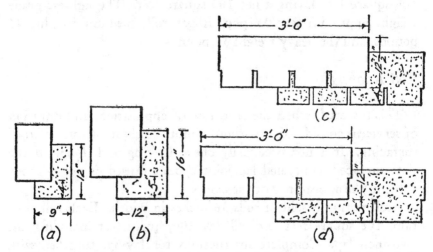

Fig. 11. Asphalt shingles: (*a*) standard individual, (*b*) giant individual, (*c*) 4-in-1 strip, (*d*) 3-in-1 strip.

The strip shingles are made in the four-in-one type, twelve and a half inches wide by thirty-six long. Three bundles will lay 100 square feet, with four-inch exposure, and weigh 262 pounds per square. The three-in-one type are twelve inches wide and thirty-six inches long, two bundles to lay 100 square feet, five inches to the weather, and weigh 220 pounds per square (Fig. 11).

Both the single and the strip shingles are secured with large-headed, zinc-coated roofing nails, one inch long on new roofs and one and three-quarters inches when laid over old roofing material.

NAILS REQUIRED PER 100 SQUARE FEET

Shingles	1" Nails		1¾" Nails	
9" x 12"	4	pounds	7	pounds
12" x 16"	2½	"	3	"
4-in-1 strip	2	"	3½	"
3-in-1 "	1	"	1½	"

Asbestos Shingles

These are made of asbestos fiber and cement and are strictly fireproof but more expensive than the other types. They are made in several shapes and sizes and in various colors. Several brands are on the market which closely resemble worn wood shingles and make a very artistic roof surface, perfectly fireproof, and with unlimited life.

Asbestos shingles and clapboards for side-wall covering which weather to a soft, neutral gray and are fireproof are now available. The shingles are 12" x 24" x ⅜₆", self-aligning by ready punched nail holes and packed three bundles to the square or 100 square feet laid. Included are cadmium non-rusting nails for exposure nailing. Additional 1½" galvanized nails are required for head-nailing, one pound per square.

Wood Shingles

Wood shingles are the most commonly used and most familiar type of roof and wall covering. The commercial, or common type of shingle, is sawed from cedar, sixteen inches long and of random width. They are put up four bunches to the thousand, which is the equivalent of one thousand shingles four inches wide. The standard grade will measure five butts to two inches in thickness. One thousand shingles will cover from 80 square feet for four-inch exposure to 100 feet for five-inch exposure.

Shingles are classed in several grades. The names vary in different sections, but the requirements of the grading are the same. The best grade is clear and free from knots, the second grade may be laid four inches to the weather with no exposed knots, while the lowest grade permits exposed sound knots. The clear grade should be used for roofing while the grade which will lay clear to the weather will be economical for the sidewalls.

The appearance and durability of wood shingles can be materially improved by dipping in a stain, either creosote or oil base, before application. A thousand shingles will require two and a half to three gallons of stain and one man can dip about six thousand shingles per day. The method of dipping is described on page

130. Pre-stained shingles of excellent quality and many shades can be obtained in most localities.

Wood shingles are laid with an exposure to the weather varying from four to five inches and should be fastened with four-penny cut or coated nails, using four to five pounds per thousand shingles. On roofs the usual exposure is 4 inches and on side walls 5 inches. These dimensions may be varied somewhat depending upon the quality of the shingle and on the pitch of the roof. The steeper the pitch, the greater the exposure can be. Extra-size shingles, made to resemble the old hand-split type can be obtained and make a surface with more character than the regular shingle and are especially attractive on side walls (Fig. 2).

To estimate the number of shingles required for roof or side-wall areas, figure the total surface of the roof or the total surface of side walls with no deductions for openings. The following table shows the approximate area covered by four bundles (one square) of 16-inch shingles when laid with various exposures:

Exposed	Area Covered
4″ to the weather	80 square feet
4½″ " " "	·90 " "
5″ " " "	100 " "
5½″ " " "	110 " "
6″ " " "	120 " "

No allowance need be made for waste.

Shakes

Another modern adaptation of an old necessity are the long split units that are a copy of the original shakes which the pioneers split from three- or even four-foot long sections of cedar or cypress logs and used as cover for their cabin roofs. These are laid with an exposure of a little less than half their length and with a slight space between shakes. It is necessary to use roofing felt under the shakes to prevent the entrance of snow and rain.

Clapboards

Clapboards date from the development of the earliest frame

houses and are still a favorite surface treatment of many homes. They are usually made from pine or spruce in four-foot lengths, one-half inch thick at the butt, six inches wide and tapering to one-eighth inch thick at the top edge. Clapboards are sawed from a round section by running it over a saw to cut from circumference to core. This gives the same result as quarter-sawing and reduces the liability of shrinkage (Fig. 2).

They are usually laid from three and one-half to four inches to the weather and are secured with a special clapboard nail through the butt. Clapboards are always painted, while shingles are usually stained (Fig. 2).

Beveled Siding

This material resembles overgrown clapboards in shape but is not quarter-sawed and varies in length from six to sixteen feet with a width of eight to ten inches. It is made from several varieties of wood, chiefly red cedar, cypress and white pine. Redwood is also used but is liable to split from shrinkage if not properly nailed (Fig. 2).

As a sidewall covering to be painted, it has more character than clapboards due to the larger scale produced by wider surfaces and thicker butts. On garages it is sometimes applied directly to the studding but it should be used only over sheathing if entrance of cold or bugs is to be prevented.

To estimate clapboards or beveled siding required, figure area to be covered, deducting large openings. To this total, add as follows:

Siding	Exposure	Add
½″ x 4″	3¼″	25%
½″ x 4″	3″	33⅓
½″ x 4″	2¾″	50
½″ x 5″	4¼″	20
½″ x 5″	4″	25
½″ x 5″	3¾″	33⅓
½″ x 6″	5¼″	20
½″ x 6″	5″	22
½″ x 6″	4¾″	25%

Novelty Siding

Novelty siding is milled in a variety of shapes of a uniform thickness but molded in patterns with either a lap joint or tongue and groove at the edges. It is also made from boards which are left as they come from the saw with only a bevel and the tongue at the edges. Because the siding is of full thickness and not beveled to a thin edge, it is possible to apply it directly to studding without any under sheathing. This should only be done on a camp for summer use and care must be used when installing the siding to prevent shrinkage from opening the joints (Fig. 2).

Log Siding

A material, now very popular as an outside covering for the frame cabin is log siding which is pine, redwood or even cypress planks milled with a rounding surface on the outside and flat on the back. The joint is a form of ship lap, each piece lapping over the one below. It has been developed as a compromise between the cabin built of logs and the frame camp. While it will not deceive even a greenhorn into the belief that it is a real log cabin, we must admit that some delightful examples of its use may be seen.

We saw one perfect little gem this summer, but the otherwise charming little cabin was completely ruined by a Joseph's Coat of many colors on the roof—not a blend of soft shades almost melting into each other, but a perfect blaze of outrageous and glaring contrasts.

Log siding is available in six-, eight-, and ten-inch widths, cut from two-inch stock and ranging in length from six to sixteen feet. It can be laid with uniform or random widths or alternate narrow and wide sections. Random laying is much better as it avoids a regularity of pattern (Fig. 2).

Plywood

One of the most useful of camp construction materials is the plywood of various types now available. It is made in several sizes up to a maximum of four feet by eight feet with three-ply ⅜" thick and five-ply ¾″ thick. It comes in a variety of surface woods and can be used in many situations. The type made with waterproof binder will withstand weather and dampness.

The usual stock has a fir surface and is the one in common use. It is now possible to get this plywood with a "knotty pine" surface finish.

Wall Board

Various forms of wall board are now commonly available and are useful in many ways as construction material. These wall boards are made of some fibrous material and a binder compressed under great pressure. They are made in different thicknesses and commonly in four-foot widths and eight-foot lengths. Some types have high insulating value and the degree varies inversely with the density of the material.

The sturdier and thicker types, if damp-resisting, can be applied directly over framing as a weather backing for beveled, novelty or log siding, making a finished appearing surface on the interior. This should be done only when the studding can be used as nailing grounds. During the war years much construction was done with specially-manufactured board of this type which was used entirely in place of wood sheathing.

There are so many varieties and products of this material that we will not attempt to describe them. The varieties for interior decoration include, in addition to plain surfaces, imitations of knotty pine, vertical plank designs of soft color, paneled effects, and even glazed-tile patterns.

On the interior of the camp, the outside boarding can be covered with panels of wall board cut in between the frame members or the sheets can be applied directly to the face of the studding as an inside sheathing.

Hardware

With the exception of the rough hardware, nails, bolts and screws used in the construction of the camp, the actual amount of hardware is small and can be very inexpensive. As the number of items is small and the cost of real hardware is not large, it is a good idea to select fittings that increase the charm of the camp.

The cheapest type that can be purchased at any chain or country general store will serve the purpose and, if given a coat of flat black paint will look like a different article. In fact the dull black of properly treated iron work is the fitting type to use in any camp. Brass or bronze belongs to the finished house in company with plaster and white paint. The real handwrought iron-work, product of the forge and expert craftsmanship, may be excessively out of proportion in cost but has a character and finished peculiarly its own. Fortunately, charming imitations of this old wrought hardware are now commercially made and a reference to a catalogue or visit to a hardware store will demonstrate the artistic value of such products and their surprisingly low cost.

The hardware used in construction is classified as "staple" or "builders'" and as "finished" hardware. The first includes such materials as nails and spikes, screws and bolts, sash weights and other materials of this nature which are not generally exposed or have finished surfaces. "Finished" hardware includes locks and latches, hinges, door and window fittings, and in general is exposed and has finished surfaces.

Nails

Nails are divided roughly into cut nails, wire nails and clinch nails. The cut nail is made from sheet steel and in appearance most closely resembles the old hand-made nail. Cut nails are made in common, flooring, finish, casing and shingle styles and are used as the names indicate. Wire nails are made in corresponding styles and types. Common nails are used for framing, rough flooring, boarding and sheathing. Finish nails are used for finish and trim where the small heads can be sunk or set for puttying to be inconspicuous in woodwork (Fig. 12).

Cut nails have great holding power and are used in exposed positions in preference to wire nails. They are heavier than wire nails and, weighing fewer to the pound, are more expensive at equivalent pound prices. They are made in wedge shape, so they should always be driven with the chisel point across the grain of the wood to prevent splitting (Fig. 12).

Wire nails, as the term expresses, are made from steel wire by pointing one end and upsetting a head on the other. Brads are slender species of the wire nail. Flooring brads are made of heavier gauge wire with a type of head that allows for severe draw without splitting the tongue of the flooring board. Wire nails are easier to use than cut nails and are somewhat cheaper, but are more liable to rust and are not so durable in exposed positions. They also have less holding power.

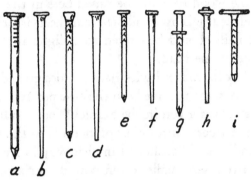

Fig. 12. Nails: (*a*) common wire, (*b*) common cut, (*c*) wire finish, or flooring, (*d*) cut, (*e*) wire shingle, (*f*) cut shingle, (*g*) double head, (*h*) clout, (*i*) roofing.

When wire nails are to be driven into hardwood, they should be rubbed on a cake of soap or wax which makes them more easily driven and prevents bending. In some hardwoods it is advisable to drill for the nail. On southern pine finish, always drill for nailing; otherwise the nail may follow the curve of the softer part of the grain, and the point will look you reproachfully in the eye where it is least expected. Brads and finish nails should be carefully driven and set home with a nail-set to avoid hammer marks on the finished work.

The clinch nail has the appearance of the cut nail but is made of a softer grade of steel so that when a back-up iron is held on one side of the joint as the nail is driven home, the point will turn over and clinch into the wood. Clinch nails serve the same purpose as the old style wrought iron nail in the construction of batten doors, etc. In the batten construction of camps, they should be used between studs or nailing supports to draw the batten and board tightly together. In this case, the nails should be driven from the outside while a smooth iron is held by an assistant against the point on the inside.

Clout nails are cut nails which are excellent for use where an Early American effect is desired. This type is made with a broad, flat head with a raised boss in the center of the head. It looks very much like a hand-wrought nail. Due to the raised boss on the head, the last hammer blow sets the head well into the wood without marring the wood because the raised boss in the center of the nail head receives the blow while the nail head is driven into the wood. Clout nails should be driven at a slight angle to improve the appearance of the head.

The sizes of both cut and wire nails are designated by the term "penny," said by some to have been the cost per 100 nails. A more logical explanation is given in the Stanley Tool Catalogue: "Nails have been made a certain number of pounds to the thousand for many years and are still reckoned in that way in England, a ten-penny being a thousand nails to ten pounds, a six-penny a thousand nails to six pounds, a twenty-penny weighing twenty pounds to the thousand; and, in ordering, buyers call for the three-pound, six-pound, or ten-pound variety, etc., until by the Englishman's abbreviation of 'pun' for 'pound,' the abbreviation has been made to stand for penny, instead of pound, as originally intended." The following table shows actual length of nails and their descriptive sizes. "Penny" is always indicated by the letter *d*.

2d	1	inch	10d	3	inch
3d	1¼	"	12d	3¼	"
4d	1½	"	16d	3½	"
5d	1¾	"	20d	4	"
6d	2	"	30d	4½	"
7d	2¼	"	40d	5	"
8d	2½	"	50d	5½	"
9d	2¾	"	60d	6	"

NAIL SIZES AND USES

Framing, Joists, Sills, and Plates	20d common wire
Framing Sills to Joists	30d " "
Studding, Toe Nailing	10d " "

Studding, Nailing Through	12d	" "
Boarding, Sheathing and Under Flooring	8d	" "
Wood Shingles	3d shingle cut	
Asphalt Shingles	Special roofing	
Roll Roofing	" "	
Finished Floors, surface-nailed	8d common wire	
Finished Floors, ¾ through tongue	Flooring brad	
Siding	6d coated	
Clapboards	5-6d gal. box	
Clinch for Battens	6d clinch nails	
Interior Finish	8d finish wire	
Moldings, Small Trim	Brads	
Outside Casings	6d casing cut	
Outside Casings, if into studs	8d	" "

Finished Hardware

Hinges are divided into two classes by the trade. Those that are screwed on the face of a door or shutter are called "hinges" while those that are cut into the edge of the door and the jamb are called "butts." Hinges are applied directly to the face of the work, require no cutting, are entirely exposed and can be easily removed from the outside. Butts are concealed except for the small part projecting from the door and cannot be removed from the outside when the door or shutter is closed. In camp construction, hinges are very satisfactory for inside doors and for outside doors which swing in because the hinge cannot be removed from the outside, allowing easy access to intruders. They are now available in various styles which resemble real handwrought iron. They are reasonable in price and add a beautiful touch to the batten doors and cabinets (Fig. 13).

Shutters which are put on for protection should be hung on butts with sufficient projection or clearance to allow shutters to swing back flat against the outside wall.

Strap hinges and T hinges are made in sizes varying from three to sixteen inches for the length of each leaf of the strap hinge or of the long leaf of the T hinge. For doors hung in a frame, it is generally necessary to use T hinges. For cabinets and small closet doors, plated hinges which come complete with screws, are now

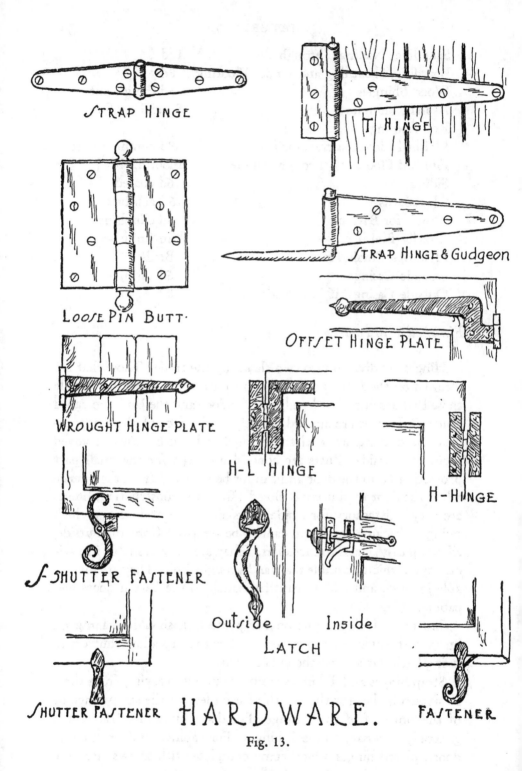

STRAP HINGE

T HINGE

STRAP HINGE & Gudgeon

LOOSE PIN BUTT

OFFSET HINGE PLATE

WROUGHT HINGE PLATE

H-L HINGE

H-HINGE

S-SHUTTER FASTENER

Outside   Inside
LATCH

SHUTTER FASTENER   HARDWARE.   FASTENER

Fig. 13.

packaged on set cards. This also applies to cupboard catches and latches.

Crescent sash fasts are just the thing to use on a casement sash that swings in—two to a sash, with the socket part on the jamb and the movable member on the sash. These not only secure the window but draw the sash weather-tight into the frame (Fig. 14).

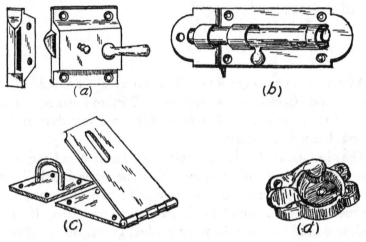

Fig. 14. Catches: (*a*) screen-door catch, (*b*) barrel bolt, (*c*) hasp, (*d*) sash fast.

Door latches go with a camp like bacon with eggs, are inexpensive and have a natural fitness for the surroundings. We recommend only latches in your camp for knobs have no place there (Fig. 13).

All exterior doors, but one, need barrel bolts only—two to each door, as these doors can always be secured from the inside (Fig. 14). For the one door to be used as locking entrance and exit, a heavy hasp with good padlock on the outside, will be secure and inexpensive. If you use the hasp, be sure to get the type with the folding plate that covers the screws when the hasp is closed (Fig. 14).

If you decide that you must have a good Yale lock on the camp, be sure to buy the dead-bolt type without the spring latch which can be set by push button to lock when the door is shut. The former type can be locked only by turning the key and will insure against possibility of being locked out in the cold. If you use the spring latch type which locks automatically when the door is closed, you may sometime find yourself locked out with the keys on the inside.

Shutters should be securely fastened from the inside with heavy hooks and eyes. If hinges which can be removed from the outside are used on the shutters, be sure to use enough hooks and eyes on the inside to prevent removal of the shutter if the hinges are removed by intruders.

Concrete

As you will be using more or less concrete, we should discuss it at this time. Concrete is a mixture of Portland cement, sand and crushed stone or gravel. It sets, or jells, in a few days and, after curing, becomes rock hard.

The sand should be clean, coarse, varied in size, not too fine, and free from dirt and other impurities. The stone should be clean, hard rock not too large to pass through a two-inch ring when used for mass concrete, foundations, piers and floor slabs. If gravel is used, it should be clean, bank or washed gravel, screened to separate the smaller sizes.

For mass concrete for foundations, piers, etc., one part cement, two and one-half parts of sand and five parts of crushed stone or large gravel, with fine portions screened out, will make excellent concrete. If good gravel, varying in size from coarse sand to pebbles is available, use one part cement and six parts of the unscreened gravel. For finished surfaces on walks, steps, etc., use a mixture of one part of cement to three parts sand or fine gravel, which should be spread about one inch thick over the base concrete before it has set and then troweled to a smooth, even surface.

Only enough water should be used in mixing concrete to make a plastic material, as the strength of the concrete varies inversely with the amount of water used. The more water used—the more cement should be added. The proportions of cement, sand and stone can be varied somewhat as the materials themselves will vary. It is an easy matter, after some of the work has hardened and the forms have been removed, to judge just what proportions of available materials will make a concrete suitable for the purpose intended. As the strength of the concrete depends entirely upon the ratio of cement, sand and water, and the stone or coarse gravel serves only as a filling material, stone can be added to almost any degree without weakening the concrete if the quantity of stone does not prevent the mass being dense without voids or does not allow contact of stone to stone.

When mixing concrete in large amounts, it is best to construct a mixing box with sides from six to ten inches high and with a tight bottom. It should be at least five feet long by three feet wide. For small batches, the metal wheel barrow will serve admirably. All the materials, except the water, should be thoroughly mixed by turning with a shovel until the mass shows an even, gray color. Then the water is added, a little at a time, and the batch is thoroughly mixed to an even consistency. Remember that any water escaping from the box is carrying cement with it and weakening the mixture. For this reason we repeat—the box should be water-tight.

The quality of the concrete is improved by the length of time during which it is being mixed after the water is added. The longer the mix can be agitated or stirred to prevent initial set, the better will be the concrete, for the continued hydration of the cement makes a smoother and more plastic material. This is especially important in mixtures used for finishing surfaces. In foundations or piers, or in any mass concrete, quite a saving can be made by dropping in small boulders and rocks, taking care that they do not touch each other or the forms, and that they are well imbedded in the concrete. The stones thus used must be clean. When pouring concrete into the forms, use a beveled board or a spade to agitate the mixture next to the forms forcing any large aggregate away from the surface and the plastic material against the form.

Mortar

To lay up separate units such as brick or stone, a mixture of sand, lime and cement, called mortar, is commonly used. A mixture of sand and cement alone makes a harsh material to handle and one which will shrink and crack. To make the material more plastic and better in every way, a certain amount of lime should be added. Some mortars are made of sand and lime tempered with a little cement, but generally speaking, better results are obtained by the use of lime to make cement more plastic, not only easier to work but less subject to shrinkage.

For fireplace and chimney work, a mixture of nine pounds of dry hydrated lime or one-fourth cubic foot of slaked lime putty with one bag of Portland cement and three times this volume of clean, coarse sand should be used. Add sufficient water to make an easily-worked paste which will stay in place under the weight of the brick or stone.

For general work, a mixture by volume of one part lime paste, one part cement, and six parts of sand will work admirably.

CHAPTER 5

Tools and Their Uses

To the amateur carpenter there is no more important subject than that of tools. The skilled craftsman has learned the value of good tools from necessity; the amateur has it to learn. The average city dweller may have a hammer and a saw, even a real kit of tools acquired over a period of time because of the love for making things. There is, however, a vast difference between making a hope chest or a sewing cabinet and the framing of a camp. Tools that would serve in the home hobby shop would be hopelessly inadequate on rugged timber.

There will be plenty of good hard work under the best of conditions without making the job unnecessarily difficult by trying to make that old home kit serve the purpose. From choice or necessity, the most rigid economy may be practiced in other details, but in the matter of tools it is false economy to attempt the job with inadequate or poor tools. After you have gnawed off a few floor joists with a home saw which was used previously only to saw a hambone, this point will be more evident.

A pair of heavy duty framing saws will cost about ten dollars, but the expenditure will pay unexpected dividends and the interest upon the investment, at present savings returns, amounts only to three cents a month. You can figure that one out for yourself as compared with the cost of liniment. This is not intended in any way to discourage the undertaking, but is to emphasize facts as proven by our own experience. We tried the home saw and the last time it was seen it was in whining flight into a gully. We now have a pair of real saws that completed one camp, assisted in the building of a second and are still as good as new. After you have let a good crosscut saw bite through a 2"x8" floor joist almost by its own weight, the five dollar investment will be written off the books.

No doubt many of the tools needed in the construction of the camp are already available and are suitable for the work intended, but unless the amateur builder is a carpenter, he will probably not have a real husky saw and suitable saws will have to be purchased.

Saws

The cross-cut saw is used for cutting across the grain of the wood and has teeth in the form of a V which are sharpened with a bevel on the edge. The teeth are bent out sideways alternately called the "set" and if you look along the cutting edge of the saw, a valley can be seen between the lines of the points (Fig. 15). These points are like a double row of knife points which cut out the width of the saw cut.

The rip saw, on the other hand, is made for cutting with the grain and the teeth form a row of chisels with only a slight set and are sharpened almost straight across. The reason that the teeth of the saws are bent out to the sides is to form a cutting edge that will cut a channel wider than the thickness of the saw blade to prevent the blade sticking and binding in the saw cut. This bending, or "set" as it is called, varies with the different types of saws and the work to be done.

The back saw is designed for use on fine work and where close-fitting joints are required. It will not be needed except for clapboards on the exterior and for moldings and trim on the interior. It is commonly used with a miter box (Fig. 15).

Miter Box

When you start to work on trim and finish you will need a miter box (Fig. 15) to enable you to make close joints either on a bevel or as a butt joint. Miter boxes can be purchased at all prices and if you were to do a lot of joinery you would need a good one. But for most of the work considered herein you can make a good one as shown by the drawing. The piece forming the bottom must have edges absolutely parallel, then with the try square mark lines straight across the top of the sides of the box and continue those lines down on each side (*a*). Now, very carefully saw these cuts down to the top of the base board. A piece of stock laid **in**

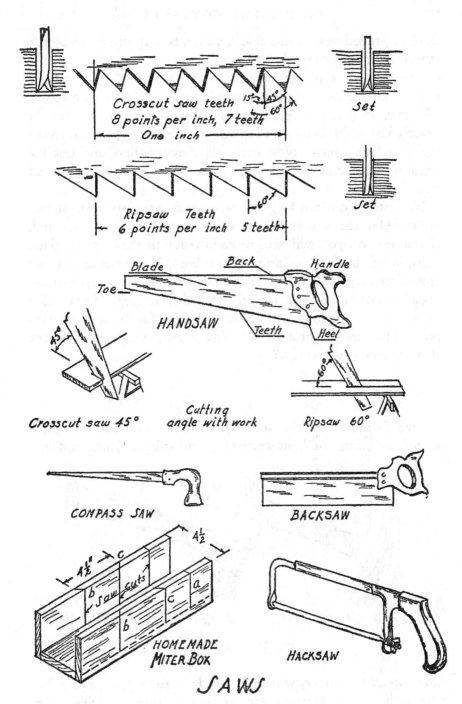

Crosscut saw teeth 15° 45° 60°
8 points per inch, 7 teeth
One inch

Ripsaw Teeth 60°
6 points per inch 5 teeth

Blade Back Handle
Toe
HANDSAW
Teeth Heel

45°

Crosscut saw 45°

Cutting angle with work

60°

Ripsaw 60°

COMPASS SAW

BACKSAW

4½" c 4½
b Saw cuts
c
b a
HOMEMADE
MITER BOX

HACKSAW

SAWS

Fig. 15.

59

the box pressed against one side can then be cut off square by the saw running in the saw slot.

The diagonal cuts which will give a cut of 45° and make a mitered corner are laid off by marking straight across the box at (*b*) then at (*c*), the distance apart of these two marks must be exactly the width between the two outer faces of the sides, forming a perfect square. Now draw the diagonal lines and test the angle with your bevel or try square and make the two diagonal cuts.

No instructions can be given here for sharpening saws. If you are skilled in that art, and an art it is, you will not need them and, if you are not, you will need more instruction than can be given space in this book. The instant a saw binds in the cut or requires any effort to make it bite, take it to someone who makes sharpening a business and have it properly set and sharpened. If you value your saws do not use them indiscriminately for sawing and ripping. They are set for a certain definite purpose, so use them for that purpose and no other.

Hammers

Two hammers will be actually needed: one medium weight with bent claws for light carpentry and cabinet work and one

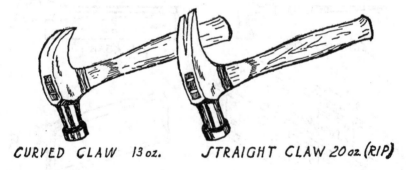

CURVED CLAW 13 oz.   STRAIGHT CLAW 20 oz. (RIP)

Fig. 16. Hammers.

heavy weight hammer, with straight claws for ripping and splitting, to be used in framing. Fig. 16. After trying to drive spikes in the framing with a light household hammer, the real advantage of a husky framing hammer that will do its work almost by its own weight, will be appreciated. The medium hammer should have a rounding rather than a flat face. When using the claw to draw nails, use a block of wood under the hammer for increased leverage and to prevent damage to the woodwork.

On all work where surface marks would be unsightly, use a nail-set on the nail to set it below the surface of the wood rather than driving the nail all the way home with the hammer and making a bad mark on the wood.

Drill a one-quarter inch hole about 1½ inches deep into the end of the light hammer and keep it filled with wax or paraffine. When driving finish nails into hard wood, plunge the nail into the wax before driving and the nail will be driven much more easily.

You will also need a fairly heavy wooden or rawhide mallet when using chisels. Don't use your hammer on chisel handles unless you wish to ruin them.

Planes

Planes, like saws, should be of the best quality and should be kept sharp at all times. A plane should not be allowed to rest on the face nor should it be left where other tools can damage the cutting edge (Fig. 17).

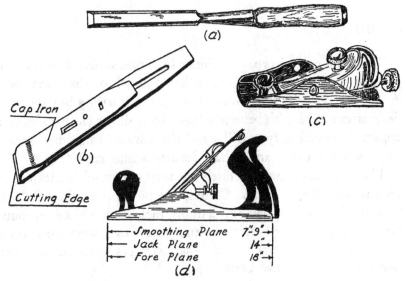

Fig. 17. Planes and chisel: (*a*) firmer chisel, (*b*) double plane iron, (*c*) block plane, (*d*) smoothing plane.

All planes are made so that the cutting iron can be adjusted for the amount of shaving to be removed. Every plane iron, except the block plane, has an iron cutter cap secured over the plane iron which can be adjusted in its relation to the cutting edge of the cutter iron. On soft wood or where a course cut is to be made by the plane, the cutter cap is moved back from the cutting edge. On hard or cross grained woods, the cap iron almost covers the cutting edge, preventing the tearing of the wood.

The plane should always be used in the direction of the grain. On some pieces of wood, the direction of the grain will vary and the piece must be reversed to prevent roughing up of the grain by the plane. The grain in wood may be compared to the hair on a dog, rubbing one way smooths it down, but rubbing the wrong way roughens it. The only difference is that the wood won't bite.

The block plane cutter has no cap iron and is used to plane across the end grain. When planing the end of a board, the block plane should be worked from both edges or one edge should be slightly beveled. Otherwise the edge will be splintered as the cutter reaches the corner.

The cutter irons should be kept sharp at all times and one trick that you should learn is to use the plane irons and chisels on an oilstone.

Chisels

There are several types of chisels in common use, but for your purpose we would recommend socketed chisels of the firmer type. A "firmer" chisel is not so-called because it is strong but the name designates a type with beveled edges which allows close up work in angles. The socket type will stand the misuse of hammer or mallet, especially if the handles have leather washer caps (Fig. 17).

The large-sized firmer chisels are used for rough smoothing of tenons and other surfaces. Chisels, like plane irons, should always be kept sharp and, when accidentally nicked, should be reground. One word of caution—NEVER HOLD THE WORK WITH ONE HAND AND THE CHISEL WITH THE OTHER. ALWAYS KEEP BOTH HANDS BACK OF THE CUTTING EDGE.

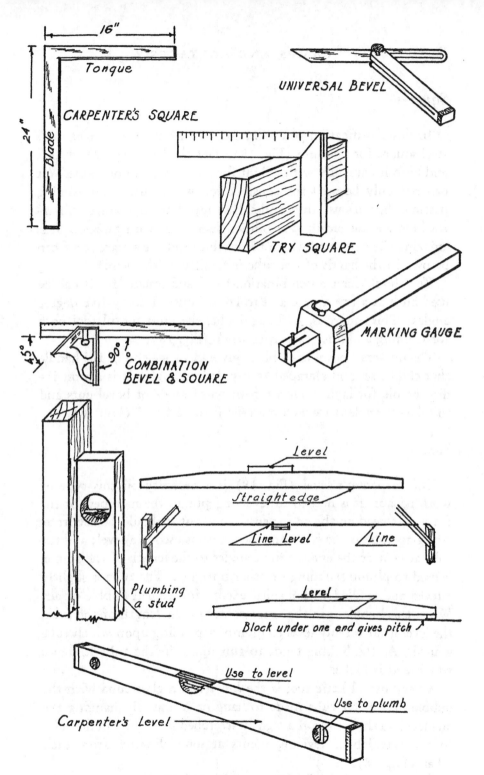

Fig. 18. Squares and levels.

Squares

In this classification you will need, first of all, a real carpenter's steel square for framing (Fig. 18). Get the large size, 24″ x 16″, and keep it carefully with a light film of oil when not in use. (It can not only be used for construction work but, as an evening pastime the various tables and aids stamped on its surface will afford more entertaining possibilities than cross word puzzles. It is amazing the extent to which these tables and the square itself can be used in the hands of one who is familiar with them.)

You should have a combination bevel and square, for it can be used both as a try square and to lay off cuts at forty-five degree angles. This square is, without doubt, the most useful tool both for framing and finer carpenter work (Fig. 18).

The universal bevel has a blade pivoted at one end of the handle that can be set and clamped at any desired angle. It is almost indispensable for laying out a repetition of angle or bevel cuts and to take off angles to which material is to be fitted (Fig. 18).

Levels

The carpenter's level (Fig. 18) is a necessity on this type of work because it is needed to level and plumb the members of the frame. It need not be an expensive one but it should be accurate. The glass tube at the center of the length is used as a level; and the tube at or near the end, at right angles to the length of the frame, is used to plumb studding or other uprights. The tube is slightly curved and is filled with a spirit except for a small bubble of air. When this bubble is in the exact center of the length of the tube, the level itself is truly level or plumb, depending upon which tube is used. As the bubble tends to run uphill in the tube it shows which end is higher.

A very useful little tool is the *line level*, a glass tube with the bubble in a metal tube made to hang on a line. By hanging the line level on the center of a tightly stretched line, one can do quite an accurate job of leveling points at some distance from each other (Fig. 18).

As a carpenter's level is comparatively short, between one foot and three feet long, and a mason's level is four feet long, a *straight edge* is often used in long lengths. The two edges of the straight edge must be absolutely parallel, at least at the center where the carpenter's level will be used. By setting the level on the top edge of the straight edge, the straight edge becomes a longer level (Fig. 18).

When we tell you to give a porch floor, for example, a pitch or slope of ⅛ inch to the foot, this straight edge will do it for you. Suppose that your porch is 8 feet wide; ⅛ inch for each foot in width would be 8 x ⅛, or 1 inch for the total drop of the floor. Now place a block one inch thick on the under edge of the straight edge at the end, and place the level on the top edge. If the floor has this slope the bubble will be in the center of the level tube.

Boring

The most necessary tool for this work is the ratchet brace or bit stock in combination with an assortment of auger bits and if possible, an expansive bit for larger holes. The ratchet brace has adjustable jaws to take the various sizes and kinds of bits and a ratchet action allows it to work where the complete circular sweep of the brace cannot be made. It need not be expensive so long as it is strong and well made.

The simplest tool for boring the smaller holes is the common gimlet which is cheap and useful. The better type, however, is the hand drill with rotary handle and gears in combination with a set of drills from ¹⁄₁₆″ to ¼″.

When boring wood where damage to the underside is to be avoided, stop boring when the point or worm of the bit penetrates the under surface. Then turn over the piece and complete the cut from that side. As you do, reverse turn the bit in a backward move until the spurs which define the cut have sufficiently cut the wood to prevent a sideslip when the cutting edges start to bite into the wood when the bit is turned in the cutting direction.

Wood should be drilled or punched for all screws. When flat-head screws are used, the hole should be countersunk so that the head of the screw will be below the surface of the wood.

When setting hinges and other hardware you will find that it is difficult to start the screw in the exact center of the screw hole in the fitting. One of the most useful tools for this purpose is the self-centering punch. This is a vest pocket do-funny with a pointed plunger which slides in a tube beveled at the end to fit the countersunk hole in the hardware. All you do is set the beveled head of the gadget in the screw hole of the hardware, give the plunger a wallop with the hammer and there it is—your starting hole is made for the screw in the exact center.

Screw Drivers

Have one husky ratchet screw driver and one smaller size and keep the ends of the blades straight and flat. A spiral drive screw driver costs very little and is in constant use when hanging doors, screens, etc. Keep the spiral shaft well oiled and screws can almost be pushed home.

Marking Gauge

This tool is almost indispensable, costs almost nothing and should wear for life. We are using one that has served through three generations and still is in fine condition. This tool is made of a square stick approximately eight inches long with a chisel pointed brad in the end. A sliding head which can be tightened to stay at any point on the bar, serves as a guide. If one wishes to rip a three inch strip from a board, the guide is set at three inches and with the guide held firmly in contact with the edge of the board and moved the required length, the chisel point marks the desired line. It is also used to lay out mortises, tenons, hinge seats and various similar items. Keep the marking point sharp and in a chisel edge (Fig. 18).

Chalk Line

This, truly, is one of the most useful friends on the job. Buy a good line wound on a spool and also a brad awl. When an absolutely straight line is wanted, be it 3 feet long or 50 feet, a loop is tied at the free end of the line and the brad awl is put through this loop into the work at one end of the needed line. Walk the required length of the line, rubbing the line with a blue or white chalk cake with a rotary motion to prevent cutting a deep groove in the cake. By holding the other end of the line tightly against the work and lifting the center of the line, a straight line will be printed on the work when the line is allowed to snap back on the work.

List of Tools

No list of tools could be given as minimum because one person's idea may differ from another's. One man will build a ship model with a razor blade and some sandpaper while another might think a complete set of modelmaker's tools indispensable. Our ancestors built their early homes with no other tool than the axe which they carried on their shoulders, later supplemented with saws and screw augers. Some of their descendants have more tools for amateur hobby work than the average craftsman uses in his trade.

The following list of tools suggests a happy medium, each one on the list constantly useful and none of them included as desirable luxuries. Not only will they be in constant use during the actual construction of the camp but, properly cared for and conveniently arranged in connection with a work bench, will be in frequent use every day.

For Framing and Common Carpentry

Cross cut saw, 26", 8 point
Rip saw, 26", 3½ point
Carpenter's steel square, 18" x 24"
Combination square and bevel, sliding arm, 12"
Universal bevel gauge
Spirit level, 24"
Curved claw hammer, 13 oz.
Straight claw hammer, 20 oz.
Marking gauge
Folding boxwood rule, 2'-0"
Socketed firmer chisels, ¼", ½", 1"
Wood mallet (rawhide or fiber)
Carpenter's pencil
Chalk line, chalk, spool, and brad awl

Wrecking bar (goose neck), 24"
Half hatchet
Carpenter's apron
Carpenter's horse

For the Finish and Finer Work

Cross cut saw, 24", 10 point
Back saw, 12", 14 point
Compass saw, 12", 8 point for cutting curved lines
Miter box
Nail sets, $\frac{2}{32}$", $\frac{4}{32}$"
Self-centering punch for screw holes in hardware
Jack plane, 14"
Smoothing plane, 9"
Block plane, 6"
Ratchet bit stock (or brace), 10"
Auger bits, $\frac{1}{8}$", $\frac{1}{4}$", $\frac{3}{8}$", $\frac{1}{2}$", $\frac{3}{4}$"
Expansive bit
Screw driver bits, $\frac{1}{4}$", $\frac{3}{8}$"
Wood countersink
Hand drill
Drill points, $\frac{1}{16}$" to $\frac{1}{4}$", by 16ths
Ratchet screw driver
Spiral drive screw driver
Half-round cabinet file

Additional Tools

Oilstone (double-face, two grades)
Oil can
Hack saw and blades
Pliers, with wire cutting jaw
Draw shave

We only wish that space would permit us to include additional directions for the use of the various tools. Many people have an instinctive knack in learning while others acquire the knowledge by painstaking effort. One can gradually learn by experience, but by profiting from the experiences of others, time and energy—to say nothing of epidermis—can be saved.

Unless the amateur builder is thoroughly familiar with the various tools, their use and proper care, helpful assistance can be obtained from books prepared especially for that purpose. Several books of this nature are available in the library or bookstores. *How to Work With Tools and Wood,* issued by The Stanley Rule and Level Company, New Britain, Connecticut, is very helpful and very comprehensive.

For the work in clearing away the bushes and trees and for general work about the place you will need a few more implements, which we list here:

Clippers, heavy duty with long wooden handles and short curved cutters

Mattock, a double-blade implement with one edge in the form of a narrow axe parallel with the handle, and the other edge at right angles to the first

Brush knife or cutter

Shovel

Rake

Hoe

Spade, long handle

Wheelbarrow

Paint all handles a bright red or orange. When you leave tools lying in the grass or bushes this brilliant color against nature's green makes them plainly visible.

A wheelbarrow will be needed not only during construction but for the many uses around the camp. There are several types available, but the steel barrow body type used by contractors is adapted to general work and can be used as a mixing box for small batches of concrete or mortar.

CHAPTER 6

Preparing the Site and Starting the Construction

It is assumed that you have selected and purchased the site and are now a land owner, free to roam over your own domain and to select the exact spot on which the actual camp will be built. This selection is of extreme importance and every hour spent in its consideration and rechecking thoroughly will be well repaid.

What are the best views? Where shall the camp be placed to take every advantage of the natural vistas? How best benefit by the prevailing breezes in the summer or obtain the full benefit of the sun and shelter from cold winds in the winter? Where can the building be located to avoid cutting trees that are part of the natural beauty of the location? A slight difference in location may be sufficient to save trees that will furnish refreshing shade and add to the charm of the camp.

Study the natural surface drainage. If the camp is to be built on a sloping surface, careful provision must be made to prevent damage to grading and building by the flow of surface water. It may be not only advisable but necessary to construct drainage ditches on the hill slopes to divert the flow of surface water away from the camp. Each location has its own problems which can only be solved by its own method.

After a tentative location for the camp has been selected, it is advisable to outline the proposed building with stakes and cords. From the inside of this enclosure, consider carefully the views, the prevailing winds and the travel of the sun. From various points outside the enclosure, visualize just how the camp will fit into the surroundings when the project is completed. If this location is not entirely satisfactory, do not hesitate to try a different position or location until the results are satisfactory. This work costs nothing but time, and a little effort may save future regrets.

In all of this experimental work in locating the spot for the camp, bear in mind the location of any other structure which may be built at once or later. It may be a boat house or landing dock, ice house, garage or guest cabins. If these are all carefully considered in relation to the completed project they will make a successful combination and a choice view will not be eclipsed by some utility structure which could have been located at some other point.

Of paramount importance to the entire job is the provision for sink drains and possible toilet drainage. These must have sufficient slope away from the camp and some type of disposal system must be provided. If a septic tank is to be installed, it must be located to provide the necassary slope for drain lines and soil suitable for outlet field seepage or for a cesspool. If a Chic Sales Specialty is the only type of toilet possible in the situation, it should be located conveniently but not too conspicuously and, above all other factors, so located that no seepage from the vault can possibly contaminate the water supply.

When you have selected the site that passes all tests, the space needed for the camp and adjacent grounds should be at least partially cleared. For the time being, only those trees and shrubs should be removed which would actually interfere with the construction work. Do not make the mistake of ruthlessly clearing a large area on the site if you are fortunate enough to have a thick growth of trees. There will be ample time to remove undesirable growth after the camp is completed and too much cutting at first may only lead to regrets.

In all clearing work now and in the future, do not glean too closely. It will be to your advantage to leave some of the smaller bushes and ground plants to form a natural shade and mulch for the ground. Too close cropping of this natural protection will only result in the drying-out of the ground, a detriment to the trees and, on hillside slopes, an invitation to the forces of erosion.

Check for any dead trees or limbs that might fall on the camp or for any shallow-rooted trees too near the camp for safety in a hard blow. If there are large evergreens, pine, spruce or hemlock and any gray birch are near enough to touch the limbs of the evergreens, cut those birch into firewood at once. Wherever the birch swings against an evergreen it will keep the limbs from growing and they will look as if a knife had pruned them. Those hard, dry limbs of a gray birch are a constant source of irritation to any evergreen.

Roadway

If you find it necessary to construct a private roadway into camp, it should be one of the first things planned, and the work of clearing the roadway and making it passable for trucks should be started at once. The exact line of the roadway may be easily plotted or it may require considerable study and consideration, depending upon the nature of the land and the length of road required. Here again, as in the choice of building site, a little work and foresight will pay dividends.

The most important factor in the location of the road is the presence of water, either ground or surface. Ground water must have provision made for drainage and surface water must have means of leading its erosive forces into the ways of the least damage. A slight grade is an advantage as it helps drainage.

Stake out the general course of the road. Cut a stick equal in length to the clear width of the proposed roadway and use this as you walk along the proposed center of the road to show just which trees or shrubs must be removed to make a uniform width. Be sure to include a circle, or turn-around at or near the camp so that cars may be driven in and make the turn without backing and filling. The road and the circle may require a little study to avoid the necessity of cutting nice trees. After you have established the location of your road, drive stakes throughout the length of the road, within sight of each other. These will establish the center of your road.

We suggest that at this point you cut out all trees and brush and remove stumps and rocks to make the road passable for the lumber trucks. Postpone any further road work until the trucking is completed, for the passing and travel of trucks and cars, at this stage, will cut up the road and will show you just how much corrective work will be needed for the completed roadbed.

While recommending that you discontinue your road work until the trucking is finished, we will complete our discussion of the road work itself. The success of even a rough camp road is in its proper drainage. All low spots that will hold water or in which water may stand, should be drained and filled with rocks and gravel. All low places where surface water will run across the road should be remedied by digging a ditch or drain across the road to a lower spot and filling the ditch with rocks or culvert pipe over which the finished surface is placed.

If you come across a rock that is too heavy for you to handle, it is an easy matter to bury it. Dig a deep hole alongside, roll the rock into it and grade off with dirt. There are two methods of disposal of trees and shrubs which must be removed. If the tree or large bush roots must be removed, the tree should be cut so that three or four feet of trunk is left above the ground. A chain is set around this stub which supplies the proper leverage for removal by tractor or a set of falls. If it is not necessary to remove the roots, the trunks should be cut off close to the ground, preferably with a saw, and not be cut with a jagged, pointed stub.

Do not cut in haste. Remove only such growth as may be actually necessary, leaving any further cutting and trimming for future consideration. Trees always look better and more natural in groups than as single specimens. Do your pruning with caution and if in doubt, do not cut until it is certain that the cutting is necessary or will result in an improvement.

All trees and sapling removed in clearing the roadway or site should be limbed and cut into lengths of not over eight feet. Stack these lengths near the camp and work them into firewood as you have the opportunity. Birch and maple will burn well with but little drying. Green alders if placed on a good base fire, will burn with almost as much heat as coal. Pine, if any, should be split into small pieces for kindling.

All limbs, brush and small bushes should not be left where cut, but should be stacked in piles and burned as soon as dry, and as soon as rain or snow conditions make it safe. Be careful about brush fires and remember that in most localities a permit from local authorities is required for the burning of brush or any fires. Slash, as it is called, left to dry where cut is only an invitation to serious trouble from the first cigarette carelessly tossed away.

The outline of the camp has been indicated by driving stakes to represent the four corners, and the final location has been approved. These stakes are not necessarily set accurately either for measurements or for square corners. Except for small structures, it is necessary to locate the lines exactly to dimensions, with all angles square and all points level. This work, for a building of any size, is done by the carpenter and an engineer with his instruments. In our own case, the job can be done, as it must be done in most cases, with our own hands and the simple tools required in the construction work.

Batter Boards

Even if the corner stakes could be set to the exact dimensions and at the proper heights, they would necessarily be disturbed and

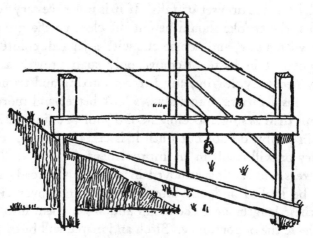

Fig. 19. Batter boards.

their exact location be lost as soon as any digging was done or the framing was started. To preserve these points, until they are no longer needed, by markers which will not interfere with construction work, a set of light timbers and bracings, called "batter boards," are set up back of each corner (Fig. 19).

On these boards, saw marks are made to indicate the points on which cords are drawn to locate the exact face of the structure. The point at which any two cords intersect is the exact corner and can be shown by hanging a plumb bob at that point.

Four to six feet behind any one of the temporary corner stakes, three posts (two by fours) are driven into the ground and on these posts two boards are nailed horizontally and exactly level from the corner post to each of the other two in the group. These horizontal pieces are parallel with the two adjacent sides of the plan. Using the front line of the building, a second set of batter boards is erected and on the horizontal boards a stout cord is stretched to show where the front of the structure will be.

The posts in each group should be braced with small stuff from the lower part of the corner post to a higher point on the other two stakes. The tops of the horizontal boards should be set exactly level and at the height of the floor framing. The boards forming the two sides do not have to be at exact right angles, as the squaring of the corners is done with the cords and the saw cuts in which they rest.

The two other corners should now be constructed and the boards should be brought to a level either with a line level or by use of a long straight-edge and the carpenter's level. Starting now with the corner batter board first erected, the cord representing the end wall of the building should be stretched and be squared with the front line by use of a triangle or measurements. Then the opposite end is squared and finally the rear wall.

You now have four cords tightly stretched over the top of the batter boards which indicate the four sides of the camp. They intersect at the corners inside the batter boards and a plumb bob, hung from any intersection will show the exact corner. After a careful recheck of exact dimensions, the accuracy of the square corners and the level of the floor, the exact spot where the cords cross the top of the batter boards should be carefully marked and a shallow saw cut be made. The cords can then be removed if they interfere with the work and can be accurately replaced to check or lay out the work.

To square these corners or to use for other work, when a large square is needed, we utilize the principle that a triangle, which has sides of three, four and five feet or any multiple of these dimensions, will have for one of its angles, a perfect right angle or square. If a frame is made of light stuff with sides which are exactly three, four or five feet or even six, eight and ten feet, it can be used to square the corners. The cords can also be used to give square corners by measuring the two shorter distances on two adjacent cords and then, with the tape set at the third dimension, swinging the end cord until this dimension corresponds with the other two (Fig. 20).

If foundation walls are to be built, the location of the inside and outside face of the wall should be marked on the batter boards by saw cuts, and all such cuts should be lettered in heavy pencil notations. Any projection from a plain rectangle should be laid out in the same manner as described for the four corners. Plumb bobs hung on any of these cords give the exact face of any part of the foundation work.

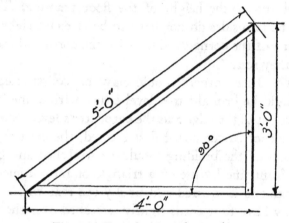

Fig. 20. Forming a right angle.

In the construction of a very small camp, these batter boards are unnecessary. The sills can be cut to the exact dimensions, set up on temporary posts or stones, the floor joists nailed in place and the framework squared and braced. Then it is an easy matter to set the permanent posts in line with the frame.

Elevation of Camp

If the camp is to be built on a hillside, and many of them are, let us emphasize the need for extreme foresight when establishing the height of the floor above grade. Few buildings are set too high, but many a building has been set too low. A floor level that may appear at first too high will be found to be too low at the back after a few years.

A hillside which, under natural conditions shows no sign of erosion, will start to slide downward the moment a spade is put into the soil or little feet commence to travel. This is because the natural wash and grading on a slope always tends to bank against construction, and all too soon the sill is buried in earth. It is better to have several steps, if necessary, at an entrance on the bank side of the camp and then grade, than it is to find that constant digging must be done to prevent earth and moisture destroying the sills on that side.

Sloping land is very deceiving to the eye. Until the space to be occupied by the building and the height of the floor is established, it is not possible to realize just how much difference in level there may be between the two sides of the building. A line level is very useful at this stage because differences in level can be easily determined by its use (Fig. 18).

A side hill site allows valuable storage space for wood and tools, dressing rooms for bathing and even space for a car which could never be utilized if the building were set too low.

Foundations

However well a structure may be built, a poor or inadequate foundation will ruin the best of super-structures. Any movement in the supports will result in binding doors and windows and uneven floors. Much depends upon the type of soil and the climatic conditions. If freezing temperatures are natural to the location, the supports must be such that any heaving of the soil will not lift the structure and the foundations must be designed and installed to prevent such trouble. If no freezing weather is to be expected, any old foundation will suffice if it is sufficient to bear the weight of the building.

If the soil is firm and not subject to frost movement, the simplest and cheapest method is the use of large, flat stones at the corners and intermediate points to support the sills above contact with the earth. Next in order, cost and labor considered, are wood posts, either natural round material or square-sawed timber. These should be cut from timber which has a natural resistance to decay caused by contact with damp earth. Cedar, chestnut, redwood and cypress are the most efficient for this use. The hardwoods, birch, maple and similar woods should not be used as they are short lived under this condition and would soon have to be replaced. Bark should always be removed from the round woods and all wood should be coated below the ground line with asphalt or creosote to preserve the timber. If you desire a rustic appearance, use cedar posts with the bark left on above grade and panel work between the posts (Fig. 21).

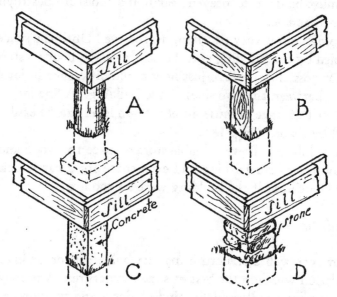

Fig. 21. Posts: (A) natural post, (B) square-sawed hood post, (C) concrete post, (D) stone and concrete post.

Square-sawed posts lend themselves to framing and are preferable if lattice or sheathing is to be used to fill the space between the sill and the grade. Posts should be set not less than three feet into the ground, and where danger from freezing exists, should be set well below any possible frost line. If the ground is soft or of low bearing value, a large stone, well bedded in the bottom of the post hole, should be set to support the post. Posts extending more than four feet above grade should be securely braced to prevent any movement when the ground is soft or the frost is coming out of the ground.

Commercially treated post material is available in some locations and makes most excellent supports. The treatment is applied under a vacuum or pressure condition with the result that the preservative penetrates the pores of the wood to a great depth.

Post material can be treated by hand and will be much longer lived as a result of the treatment. All bark should be removed and the creosote applied with a wirewound paint brush or brush made especially for the purpose. The liquid should be heated before application and care taken that it does not boil over and catch fire.

Apply a heavy coating worked well into every crack and crevice. When the first coat is dry, a second coat should be applied which will flow on more easily than the first. The post should be well dried on the surface before the treatment is applied and any damage to the treated surface should be recoated before the post is set.

In some sections of the country it is imperative that some protection be considered to prevent damage by termites and other wood-eating pests. When wood posts are used, a protection can be made by placing inverted pans of zinc or copper, with edges projecting downward at an angle to prevent the passage of the pests from the damp ground, where they live, to the wooden parts where they feed. There are many types of termite-preventing liquid treatments on the market, the merits of which should be investigated. All wood steps should rest on masonry or concrete platforms. Those portions in contact with or near the platform should be treated with creosote or heavy paint.

One very important principle always to keep in mind is the deteriorating effect of standing water. We speak of it at this time and shall continue to speak about it in other sections of the book. Its importance cannot be too much emphasized. All posts whose tops are exposed to the damage caused by standing water should be cut on a bevel and the grain be filled with paint. If supporting posts project beyond a protecting material, water standing on the end grain will penetrate the natural channels of the grain and decay will commence at once.

If an ample supply of rocks is available, rock piers can be built by excavating to a depth of four to five feet and filling the pier holes with large stones, well bedded and laid without cement below grade. If the camp is to set low, a large cap stone resting on the pier, will elevate the sills sufficiently above the ground. If piers are to extend above the ground, the stones above ground should be laid in cement.

For any camp, except a small cabin, concrete posts are a saving in the long run for they are impervious to decay and the actions of termites. It is not a difficult job to cast them in place by constructing rough lumber forms to make posts 8″ x 8″ or 10″ x 10″ at the top. They should extend well below the frost line, have a slight taper, and the foot of the post should be enlarged by setting the form one foot above the bottom of the post hole and allowing the concrete to spread out to form a footing. Remember that the forms will have to be removed, so do not be too generous with

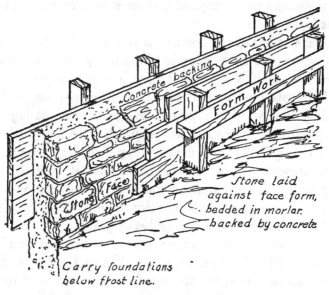

Fig. 22. Stone-faced, concrete foundation.

nails. For all concrete form work there is available a double-headed nail which allows the nails to be securely set. With the projecting secondary head the removal of the nail is easily done with the claw on the wrecking bar or the framing hammer.

Solid walls of rock or concrete, or of rock backed with concrete are of course, more in the nature of residential work, but sometimes are used (Fig. 22). If a solid wall is used, a few latticed or screened openings should be made to allow circulation of air under the floors and prevent timber rot. Such openings should have weather-tight shutters if camp is to be used in cold weather. Unless all dampness can readily dry out by circulation of air, decay of sills and floor construction sets in rapidly and will soon be a source of trouble and considerable expense.

Whatever type of piers or posts is used, it is essential that the spacing be in proportion to the weight to be carried and the type of sill. Less than six feet apart is not needed and over eight feet requires a strong sill. So use the happy medium—not under six feet nor over eight feet between supports. Supports should not be used directly under outside doors for the reason that the settlement between supports will tend to bind the door. Do not fill in solid rock between grade and sills but leave a small space above rocks or freezing will raise the ground and lift the sills above the supports.

When laying out posts or foundations, study carefully and sketch out the exact relation of the face of the sill to the face of the supports. A post extending beyond the sill line may have to be hewn off to allow the installation of lattice work or sheathing. In fact, it always pays to sit down with a piece of board or paper and sketch any detail before it is framed. After you have cut your last piece of rafter stock two inches too short, with the nearest supply twenty miles away, you'll see what we mean.

CHAPTER 7

Framing

Many people may have had the desire to build some kind of camp or cottage but have been deterred by the fear that they could not build it with their own hands and the cost of hired, skilled labor would make the desire impossible of realization. Let us hasten to assure you that the framing and construction of a camp presents no difficulties which the amateur carpenter cannot readily overcome with a little patience, study and planning.

It is for that very purpose that this book has been written for you. Step by step we shall endeavor to tell you just what to do and the simple way to do it. There is nothing especially difficult to do.

As for physical help, it is sometimes more difficult to limit the number of those willing to help in the work than it is to increase the volunteer working force. One always has acquaintances who may be able and glad to give practical suggestions and there are always those who will be only too willing to help in the actual work. But, if at any point you are doubtful as to the proper procedure, stop and think it through before you ruin good lumber and your own disposition.

Before you are ready to start on the actual construction work, we shall explain a few of the more common methods used in framing.

Carpenter's Horse. Before a start is made on the framing, at least two carpenter's horses should be available. These are simple and easy to make and will be in constant use. One horse can be perfectly plain with just the four legs, cross piece and top; the other should have the top made with a projection at one end in which a V-shaped cut is made to be used when starting to use the rip saw (Fig. 23).

To Cut off Boards. Always use a square and mark a heavy pencil line on the top and front edge of the board. Start the saw

cut with an upward movement of the saw and follow the line
carefully. Always saw on the *waste* side of the pencil line, so that
the line barely remains after the cut is made (Fig. 24).

To Cut off Studs or Joists. Mark top face and edge that is away
from you; keep the saw following these two lines and be careful

Fig. 23. Carpenter's horse.

to prevent the saw from slanting off on the last part of the cut
at the lower corner. The piece being cut off must be supported at
the last few saw strokes to prevent it breaking off with a long
sliver at the finish.

Ladders. You will need one ladder 10 or 12 feet long, or better
still, two ladders—one 10 feet long and an extension ladder.

To Rip a Board. It will frequently be necessary to reduce the
width of a board to fit a definite space. Establish a point at each
end of the board for the cut. Drive a nail or brad at one end, hook
a well-chalked line to this nail and stretch it tightly over the point
at the other end of the board. Then lift the line at the center and
let it snap against the board which will make a clear, straight line
as a guide for the saw. Always use a rip saw for this purpose—you

can tell it by the fact that the teeth rake sharply forward. As the length of the saw cut increases it tends to bind the saw and this can be remedied by setting a small wedge in the saw cut to force it slightly open. The saw blade will run more easily if rubbed with a piece of hard soap or pork rind.

Toenail. This is done by driving a nail or spike at an angle

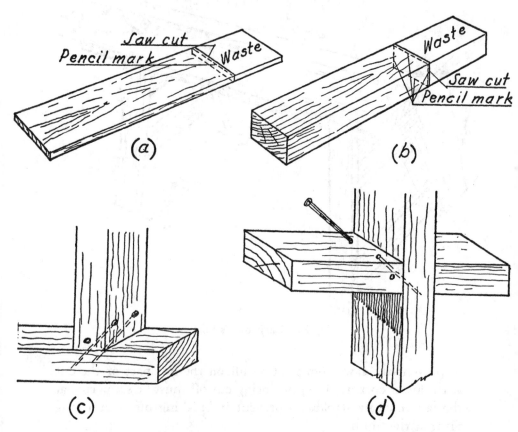

Fig. 24. Sawing and toenailing: (*a*) sawing off a board, (*b*) sawing off a stud, (*c*) toenailing studding at shoe, (*d*) toenailing a girt.

through one member into another when it is not possible to drive directly through one member into another. Where studs stand on a shoe, it is necessary to drive nails into the face of the stud at an angle, to penetrate the stud and into the shoe. However, in nailing on a cap, nails can be driven directly through the cap into the stud. When it is necessary to toenail a stud to the shoe, it is advisable to back up the foot of the stud by a brace or block temporarily nailed down to prevent the stud being driven out of position. After two nails have been set well home, the stud will not be moved by driving additional nails (Fig. 24).

Framing

You are now ready to start the framing so slip into a carpenter's apron which will hold your pencil, rule, two sizes of nails, etc., sharpen your carpenter's pencil, put a folding rule in the pocket, and *keep them both there when not in use.*

First, sort over your lumber and pile the different kinds and lengths by themselves. Boards should be stacked with cross sticks between the layers to permit circulation of air and prevent curling and warping. If the lumber schedule has been carefully prepared, there will be just about enough of each kind for the purpose intended. So stop, look and think before cutting a three foot length from a twelve foot joist. As you use the lumber, keep all the short pieces in some sort of order. When you need a piece only a foot long it is quite a pleasure to cut it from a waste piece which has been discarded instead of spoiling a long piece.

Sills

First in order are the sills or outside framing of the floor. The sills and floor joists form the chassis of the building so build them with care. There are several ways of constructing the sills but for the average camp the box type is easy to build, is inexpensive and, when properly constructed, will last as long as any type. In this type of construction, joists of the same size as the floor joists are set up on edge over the foundation or posts on each side and are spiked together at the corners. The floor joists are then set in place inside this frame and are secured to the sills by spiking through the sills into the end of floor joists (Fig. 25).

If the camp is larger than the single-room type, especially if the main room is over ten feet in width by twelve feet in length, it is advisable to spike a second joist onto the face of the first sill,

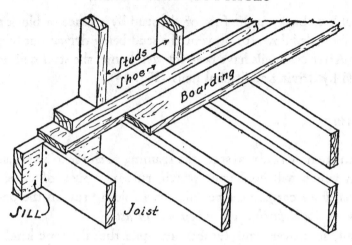

Fig. 25. Single-joist sill.

making a sill four inches thick. In this case, floor joists are securely spiked in place through the first or inside sill before the second joist is spiked on. This type of construction provides a very rugged sill and is easily made (Fig. 26).

Still another simple and strong type of sill can be made by using one joist on edge securely spiked to a joist laid flat-wise. This is called the box sill (Fig. 27).

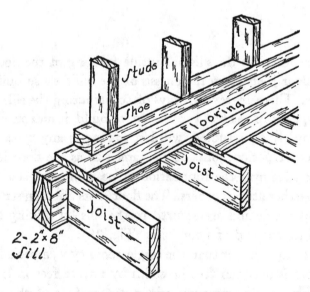

Fig. 26. Double-joist sill.

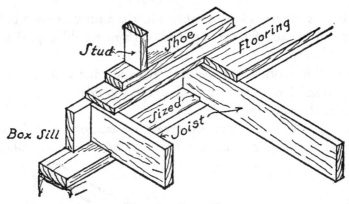

Fig. 27. Box sill.

Sizing

Because all joists of the same nominal size may not be uniform in width, it is necessary to "size" them at the ends where they rest on a support, so that the top edges which receive the flooring shall all be level.

To size joists, a distance is measured down from the top edges that will allow all of the joists to be cut to the same dimension. For example, if you are using 2" x 8" joists, you may find that the actual width may vary from 7½" to 8¼". This is not true of all lumber, but it is typical. If you should set all these joists on the

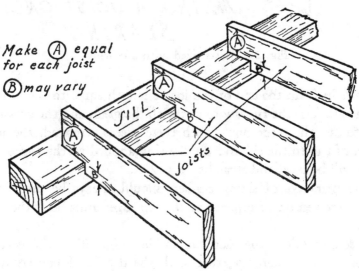

Fig. 28. How to size a joist.

same level support, like a timber sill, the upper edges would all be out of level and flooring applied to them would appear full of sags and humps.

If you will work from the proposed top edge and cut the surplus material from the lower edge, the top edge of all the joists will be at the same level (Fig. 28).

On a 2″ x 8″ joist, measure seven inches, for example, down from the top edge and draw a line parallel to the top edge and

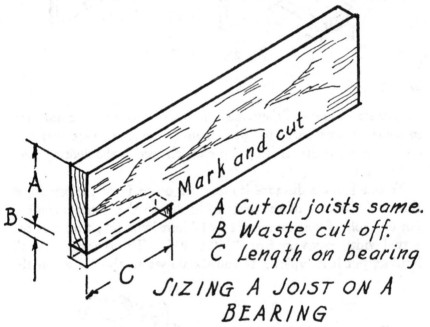

Mark and cut

A Cut all joists same.
B Waste cut off.
C Length on bearing

SIZING A JOIST ON A BEARING

Fig. 29. Joists sized onto a bearing.

measure in from the end of the joist a length equal to the bearing on the sill. Use the rip saw to cut with the grain and the cross-cut saw to cut the piece out. With these pieces removed, the joists will all fit onto the sill and the flooring applied to the top of the joists will be level and straight (Fig. 29).

This principle of sizing timbers should always be used when they are to rest on a support and the top edges must be at the same level.

In some sections the solid timber sill (Fig. 30) is the favorite and it is shown here together with the details of construction. Note that pieces of two-by-four stuff must be cut in at the floor level to close the pocket between flooring and outside boarding. This type of sill uses heavier lumber which may not always be straight. The built-up sill, using two pieces spiked together, can be made to a straight line, for one piece can be set to correct the defects in the other.

The solid timber sill is made by the use of solid timbers, 4" x 6" or 6" x 6" usually. The timbers are halved together at the corners

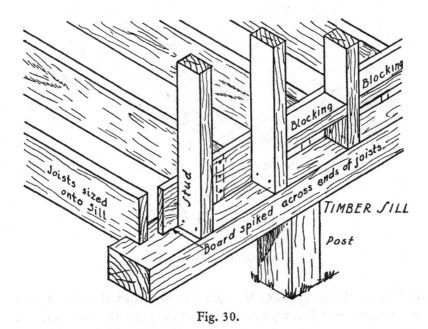

Fig. 30.

(Fig. 31), placed on the supporting posts, and then well spiked together at the corners.

The floor joists are then sized at each end to rest on the top of the sill.

The sized joists are set on the sill in their proper positions, projecting onto the sill two or more inches, depending upon the width of the sill. Space must be left to allow the wall studding to be set on the sill with a ⅞" upright board between the ends of the joists and the wall studs, nailed to the ends of the joists before the studs are set.

This board should be of sufficient width to cover the ends of the floor joists as they rest on the sill, and is continuous for the length of the sill.

The purpose of the board is to hold the ends of the floor joists from twisting as they shrink, to close the openings between the joists, and to provide a surface against which the wall studding can be nailed.

The wall studs are set in place on the sill and against this vertical board and can be spiked to both. At the ends of the building, because the floor joists are parallel with the end sills, there will be

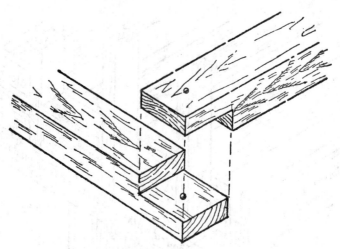

Fig. 31. Halving sills at corners.

no need of this piece. The first joist is set against the sill. It may be necessary to fill in a piece of timber between this joist and the wall studs to provide nailing for the ends of the floor boards.

Floor Joists

Many joists will show a slight curve up or down when set up on edge and should be selected and set so that the crowned or *upward* curving edge is uppermost. Those joists which show the most crown should be used in the center portions of a space because the center portion of a floor area will usually carry the most load and the natural settlement will be more in the center. Floor joists should not be over twenty inches on centers, the usual spacing for good construction being sixteen inches. Never, never under any circumstances, use floor joists that are too light for the work because it is false economy. The difference in cost between six-inch

joists, too frequently used, and the eight-inch joists is a mere baga-
telle.

To estimate the number of joists required, when spaced 16
inches on centers, add 1 to ¾ of the length of the building. For
example, your camp is 20 feet long; ¾ of 20 equals 15 + 1 equals
16, number required. Any framed openings in the floor will require additional joist.

As all floor joists may have a slight curve to left or right between the sills, it is advisable to hold them to an even spacing at
the middle of their length or, as it is called, *the center of the span.*

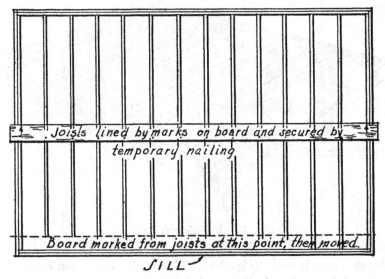

Fig. 32. Temporary alignment for floor joists.

To do this easily and accurately, use a long piece of 1″ x 6″ or
smaller stock, placed along the length of one sill to which the
joists are framed. The exact position of the ends of all the joists
is marked on this piece, and the piece then moved to the center of
the span parallel with the sill. Each floor joist is then moved into
position directly under the markings and is held in place with a
nail driven through the temporary spacer into each joist (Fig. 32).

This spacer will hold the floor joists parallel, with the proper
distance apart at the center of the span until the rough flooring
has been laid to that point. Needless to say, the nails are not driven
home on the spacer board but enough of the head is left project-

ing to allow removal when the rough flooring has been laid to that point, or a double headed nail may be used.

All openings in the floor, if of any size, should be framed with joists doubled around the opening. If a fireplace is to be built, the front of the hearth may be supported by floor joists which should be double. The sides of the opening will be also framed with double joists. If a fireplace is omitted at first but there is a probability that it will be built at a later date, the framing for the opening should be done now. The opening should be filled in with temporary joists and flooring which can be removed if and when

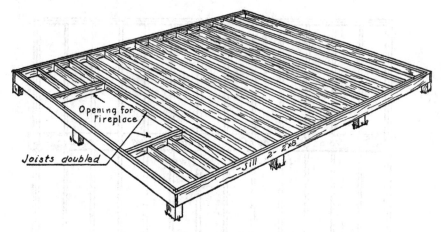

Fig. 33. Framing for fireplace.

the fireplace is built (Fig. 33). This is all easier than cutting out finished flooring and the framing later.

Girders

If the span, or length, of the floor joists is over twelve feet, it is advisable to run a girder or intermediate support to prevent the inevitable sagging of the floors. Years ago dance floors were built to have a spring but no one today wants a floor which springs and pitches when walked upon.

Girders, being intermediate supports for floor joists, must themselves be supported about every eight feet on posts or piers.

The girder may be below the floor joists with the joists sized upon it (Fig. 34). This is called a "drop girder." If the floor joists are framed to the girder so that the top of the girder is flush with the top of the floor joists, it is called a "flush girder."

Where no head room is required under the floor, the drop girder is used because it is much easier to frame and the extra shrinkage caused by the thickness of the girder plus that of the joist is negligible.

The drop girder can be a single timber which has a tendency to twist as it seasons or it can be made by spiking two or three 2" joists together.

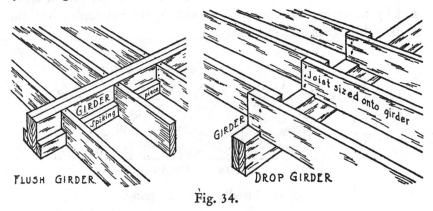

Fig. 34.

The flush type of girder is only needed when the projection of a drop girder below the floor timbers would be objectionable in any space below the floor. It is made preferably by spiking together two 2" joists and then spiking on each side flush with the lower edge 2" x 3" sticks on which the floor joists will rest.

The ends of the floor joist are cut to butt against the face of the girder with the lower corner of the joist cut out to fit on the 2" x 3". Each joist is solidly spiked to the girder by toenailing from each side of the joist into the girder.

A piece of one-inch board should be used as a pattern from which the ends of all the joists can be marked, always working from the top edge of the joist.

Cross Bridging

If floor spans are over eight feet in unsupported length, cross-bracing or bridging should be cut in to stiffen the floor and prevent an annoying vibration under walking.

This bracing is made from 1″ x 2″ or preferably 1″ x 3″ rough stock and easily cut to proper bevel by holding a piece of stock with one end just under a joist and the other end resting on the top of the next joist. Using the face of the first joist as a guide for the saw cut, the correct bevel for that end is made. Holding that cut end against the face of the joist and making a saw cut using the face of the second joist as a guide, cut the piece to the right length and with ends at the proper angle nail between the joists. The end bevel for the second piece is already cut by this method and by repeating the operation at each space between joists, the stock will be properly cut (Fig. 35).

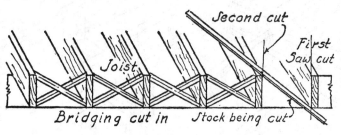

Fig. 35. Installation of bridging.

Nail the ends of the bridging at the top edges of the joists only at first, the bottom ends are to be nailed in place only after the rough floor has been nailed in place and has drawn the joists to a level. If the space under the floor allows this final nailing, the rough flooring can be completed and then you can nail the lower ends of the bridging. Two nails at each end are sufficient. If there is no working space under the floor, and the flooring is laid at right angles with joist, several boards on the line of bridging can be left off at the time the rest of the rough floor is laid, the line of bridging securely nailed and the few boards nailed in place.

Checking of Floor Framing

After the floor joists are all in place and thoroughly spiked to the sills, check the floor framing to see that the sills are straight and all corners are square. To check square corners, see Fig. 20. Check each sill with the carpenter's level and make any adjustments by wedges under the sill to make the frame level at all points. All openings should be properly framed and every joint thoroughly spiked. Nail some diagonal braces across the corners of the building so that the floor frame cannot be racked out of square while the rough flooring is laid.

Rough Flooring

You are now ready to lay the rough or under flooring. It is well to check one side of the floor framing with a cord stretched along the top and outer edge of the sill. Nail on the first width of rough flooring to keep that elge straight. Then the entire rough or under flooring can be laid, cutting all joints over a joist and using boards of the same width in the same continuous line. As you approach the opposite side and there are only two or three more widths to lay, check the remaining space and the width of the boards and avoid using a very narrow piece as the final width. The above method refers to the running of the boarding parallel with the sills.

A more satisfactory method for the benefit of the upper or finished floor is to lay the boarding diagonally at an angle of forty-five degrees. Let the ends of the boards project beyond the sill line and cut off flush with the sill. Set your bevel square to the proper angle, mark and cut off the other end of the board to center on a joist. This method, it is true, wastes a little lumber and requires cutting the ends of all boards at an angle but it is well worth this extra work even in smaller camps. The advantage of this method of laying is that the upper flooring will cross the under flooring at an angle and any defects in the underflooring or any warping of the boards will not affect the finished floor.

To set boards tightly against the one previously laid—into the far edge of the board at each bearing drive the first nail at an angle almost home (see Fig. 87); then, standing on that board on your toes, hit the nail a couple of real wallops. Your weight on the board holds all the effect of the hammer blows and prevents it from bouncing back after each blow. Then drive the second nail near the inside edge straight into the joist; and, if boards are over six inches wide, put one nail in the middle for luck. Just because this is an under floor and will be covered is no reason to skimp on nailing or quality of work.

Wall Shoe

You have completed the laying of the rough floor and are sure that you have not been niggardly with nails. Now trim any edges of boarding that may project beyond the face of the sills and spike a 2″ x 4″ shoe flat on the floor around the outside with its edge perfectly flush with the face of the sills (see Fig. 40). Be sure of this fact by using the blade of the steel square, held upright against the sill and the shoe. The shoe is omitted only at exterior door openings and even those can be left to be cut out later if you desire.

At all times, keep that chalk line, level and square always at hand and, what is more important, use them. If you were to build a wigwam with natural materials, these tools would not be needed but in this case you are dealing with materials which should be plumb, level and square.

Porch Floor Framing

The framing for porches is essentially the same as that required for the main part of the camp (Fig. 36). The joists supporting

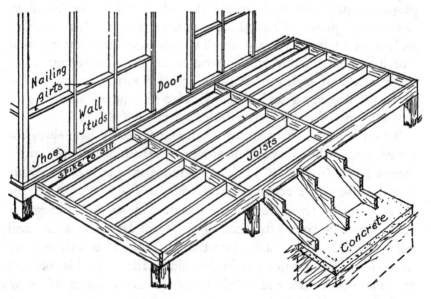

Fig. 36. Porch-floor framing.

the flooring should always be parallel with the wall of the house because the flooring, always single thickness, should run at right angles to the camp. The porch floor should be from two to four inches below the camp floor level to prevent water being driven into the living quarters from the porch floor. If the porch is permanently glassed-in and is a part of the house, this is not necessary. The floor of the porch should pitch or slope about ⅛th of

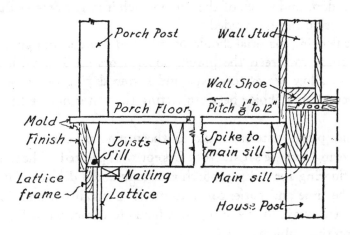

Fig. 37. Porch-floor section.

an inch for each foot in width to allow water to drain off quickly (Fig. 37).

As porches on camps are seldom over eight feet in width, six-inch joists are usually sufficient for strength and stiffness. Intermediate girders are framed in and the floor joists, usually twenty inches on centers, are framed in between them. A 2″ x 6″ joist should first be spiked against the camp wall, the end and front joists are spiked together and to the house joist. The intermediate girders are next spiked in and finally the secondary joists are put in place (Fig. 36).

If you value the life of the porch, soak the tops of all floor joists and timbers, and we mean soak, with oil paint or asphalt. Some even recommend the use of narrow strips of roll roofing on top of the joists before flooring is applied.

Porch Flooring

You might start to lay the porch flooring immediately but it is much better practice to lay a few loose boards for the time being and not lay the floor until the rough work on the camp is completed. The floor is not needed until the general construction work is done and much of the abuse which it might receive during construction can be avoided.

The flooring material should be matched, tongue and groove, if you expect to screen the porch. Some floors are laid with open joints to allow water to escape and hasten drying out after wet weather. It is a choice between letting the water out or the bugs in.

White pine, western fir and southern pine are commonly used for flooring and are satisfactory if kept well painted. The natural finish flooring for a camp porch is a snare and a delusion. If you have the time and patience to keep one in condition and do not have better ways of spending your hours in camp, we will say no more on that subject.

Nowhere in your camp will the use of paint pay larger dividends than on that porch floor. It is not sufficient to paint the top surface after it is laid, for the trouble will be below that surface. Start by giving every board a heavy priming coat on the under side. Paint both edges of the boards as you lay them and especially the groove. Then drive the boards together so that the paint fairly bursts out of the joints. When the floor is finally laid, give it a good priming coat on the surface. Now you can take your time with the finish coats and you will have a floor that will last.

Framing the Walls

In the construction of the type of camp described in this book, there are only two methods of framing the walls. If the walls are to be covered with boards put on vertically, and the joints covered with battens, they will be nailed at the plate and sill and will require additional nailing grounds at intermediate points. For this type of construction, the studs will be set from two to three feet

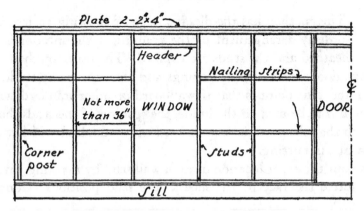

Fig. 38. Framing for vertical boarding.

apart and horizontal lines of 2″ x 4″ material will be cut in between the studs as additional nailing grounds (Fig. 38).

In the other type of framing, the boarding will be applied horizontally and nailing grounds will be provided by the studs themselves without the need for any additional horizontal members. Inasmuch as all the camps considered herein are of one story in height and no great stresses occur on the walls, the studding can be spaced on twenty-four inch centers instead of sixteen inches as in residential work (Fig. 39).

In this second method there are two ways of setting the studding. One, called the full frame, is made by spacing the studding sixteen or twenty-four inches on centers regardless of door and window openings and then cutting and filling to provide for

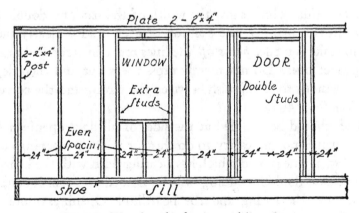

Fig. 39. Framing for horizontal boarding.

them. This method has the disadvantage of showing an irregular and disorderly arrangement of the framing if the interior is not to be sheathed and the studs are exposed. The other method is to lay out door and window openings and then space the studding. The important point is that if wallboard or other standard-width material is to be used on the inside, the spacing of the studs should be such that the material can be used in its standard width without wasteful cutting.

Lay out the exact location of each wall stud by marking parallel lines across the face of the shoe at the stud positions. Connect

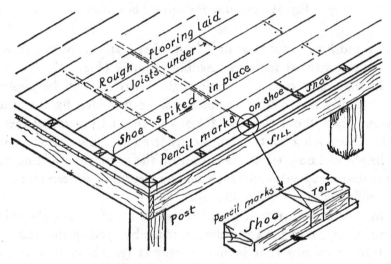

Fig. 40. Preparation for studding.

these two lines which show the width of the stud, by double cross lines. In this manner, the position of each stud is clearly shown. If a mistake is made, *plane off* the lines made in error and draw in the proper ones. Do not merely cross them out and then depend upon memory to distinguish between the wrong and the corrected position (Fig. 40).

Studs should be doubled at the sides of all door openings (Fig. 41), but it is not necessary to do this for window openings unless a window frame is used which has a casing flush with the boarding. In that case double studding will be needed to furnish sufficient surface for the casing and the boarding. Openings more than three feet wide should be trussed. In other words, the window header is cut in as usual; then diagonal pieces of 2" x 4" are cut in a triangle from between the corners above the header and the center point under the plate (Fig. 41).

Keeping the future appearance of the interior in mind, space the studding carefully, for the interior side of the outside wall will look much better if the panels formed by the studs are uniform

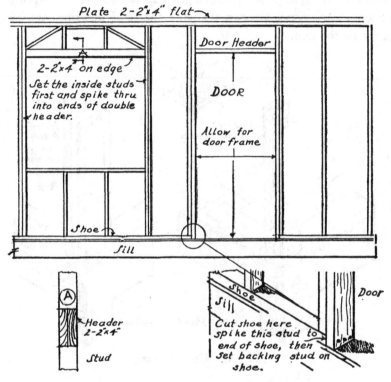

Fig. 41. Framing for wall openings.

and well-spaced. It is better to increase or decrease the spacing than to have narrow panels adjacent to windows or corners. This care is not necessary, of course, if the interior is to be sheathed.

When the shoe for the outside walls is put in place, a space must be figured for the outside door openings. To do this properly, draw a full-size detail for the doorway on a board, allowing for the width of the door plus the net thickness of the finished frame, ⅜" for clearance between each jamb and the stud and the thickness of two studs at each side. Then saw off the shoe so that the outside of the outer stud can be spiked against the sawed end of the shoe. This is repeated for the other side of the opening (Fig. 41).

We now have the shoe for the outside wall in place and the position of all the wall studs clearly marked. As the cap to be nailed on top of the studs is an exact duplicate of the shoe, except for door openings, we should get out the stock for this double-cap member. By laying each piece of the cap beside the corresponding section of the shoe, we can transfer the stud location marks directly to the cap.

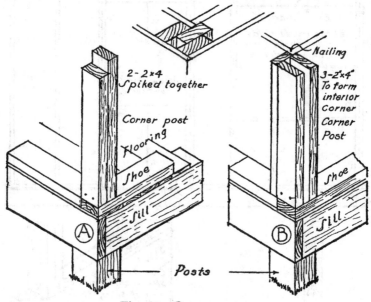

Fig. 42. Corner posts.

Lay the cap material aside and cut the studs for corner posts and for the wall framing. These will be cut six inches shorter than the height established for the top of the plate, allowing two inches for the thickness of the shoe and four inches for the double cap or plate. If the camp is not to be sheathed on the inside, the corner posts are made by spiking two studs together, making a solid square post. If the walls are to be sheathed on the inside, the posts should be formed of three studs, spiked together to form an inside corner in which sheathing can be nailed (Fig. 42).

At this point let us pause for a moment and plan ahead to make our work easy. We have all the corner posts and wall studding nicely cut to size and neatly piled ready to be set in place. Perhaps you are eager to see those walls in place; but, after the walls are in place, comes the hardest job of all, the roof framing.

Here we have a nice level and firm platform on which to work. The wall shoe spiked in place occupies the same position on the floor that the wall cap will on which the roof rafters will rest. That being so, imagine that the shoe is the cap and go ahead with cutting the roof timbers now while there are no wall studs in place to interfere.

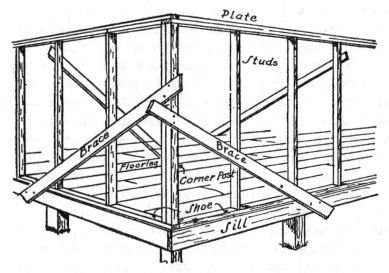

Fig. 43. Bracing for corner posts.

If you are wise you will now jump ahead in the book, see how we advise the framing of the roof, proceed to get out the rafters, and then come back to this point and proceed with the erection of the exterior walls.

Set the first corner post upright with both outside faces flush with the face of the sill at the corner—then toenail the foot of the post. Hold the post in position by nailing a brace near the top (Fig. 43) and drive a temporary nail into the other end of the brace and into the side of the sill. Nail a similar brace on the outside face of the post but not yet into the sill. While a helper plumbs the post with the level against the face of the post, let the foot of the brace slide along the face of the sill until the post is perfectly plumb in that direction—then nail the brace securely.

Loosen the nail in the foot of the other brace at the sill and do the same thing on the other side. This will make the corner post plumb in both directions. Check the post carefully and nail the braces securely to prevent movement. All the corner and any angle posts are erected in the same manner.

Now spike on the cap, which has already been cut to length and marked, to the corner posts upon which it will rest. It will be necessary to support the center of long lengths of cap until studs can be put in place. It may also have to be spliced to make the needed length by making a butt joint over a stud.

A sufficient number of studs should be cut to proper length and it is then an easy job for two persons to set each stud in place on the marked spots on the shoe. One person standing on a carpenter's horse can adjust each stud under its marking on the cap and nail through the cap into the stud. The other person adjusts the foot of the stud to the marks on the shoe and toenails it into the shoe. Be certain that the corner posts are well braced during all this work and check them for any movement out of plumb.

As soon as all wall studding has been set in place and securely spiked through the plate into the top of the studs, a second course of 2″ x 4″ studs is spiked flat on top of the cap to form the double plate. Where a joint occurs in the lower member, the top member should lap well over the joint. At the corners the butt joints alternate in each course. Any curvature in the lower member tending to curve the wall framing from a straight line should be corrected by using an upper member with an opposite curve and spiking thoroughly together. In this way, the pull of one is always corrected by the pull of the other. Check the straightness of the plate with a stretched cord and correct any curvature by long braces nailed to the plate and to the floor at some distance (Fig. 43).

If the walls are to be boarded vertically, horizontal members must be cut in between studs as nailing pieces. Two lines of these nailing girts will be required between shoe and plate, dividing the height of the wall into three panels. If the outside boarding is put on horizontally, these girts will not be necessary.

Before actually locating the position of these girts, let us do a little planning. The exact location, if not too widely spaced, will make no difference in the strength of the building. It is the interior appearance which is to be considered and the final result should look shipshape and orderly. As the lower strip will be about the height of the window sills, can it run in a line around the camp and the window sills be set on this strip? Is there a sink or work shelf to be supported? Is there a closet to be built and will these girts be in the wrong place when shelves are put in? All these and other details should be thoughtfully considered before installing these pieces to prevent unnecessary ripping out later on.

When you have decided upon the exact height of the lower line of girts, cut two pieces of 2" x 4" to the exact length to support the nailing strips between the studs while they are being nailed into place. Starting at one corner, cut a piece of 2" x 4" the exact length between two studs, measured at the shoe. Be sure to cut the ends perfectly square. Set this piece between the studs and support it at each end on the two hold-up pieces set against the studs. The girt is now at the exact distance from the shoe and can be spiked in place through one stud into the end of the piece. At its other end, due to its location, it will have to be toenailed into the side of the stud (see Fig. 24). This is where the two supporting pieces are of such help to the amateur carpenter; without the supports, the toenailing would drive that end down out of place. Continue to cut pieces and complete the lower line around the outside walls, moving the temporary supporting pieces as each panel is completed. The upper line is then cut in by the same method.

Always measure for the exact length of these girts at the shoe and not at the middle of the height. If measurement is made at the location for the girt, the spring of the studs will result in incorrect lengths and consequent bending of the studs. Now go over all the wall framing carefully, for it as an easy matter to make any changes or corrections at this point. All corners should be plumb, plates straight and every joint well nailed. Put on plenty of temporary braces to hold walls in proper position while boarding is done and rafters are put in place.

Roof Framing

Give a carpenter a steel square and a pencil, tell him the width of the building and the pitch of roof desired and he will cut rafters and never have to see the building. But he had to learn to do that. As these suggestions are to amateur craftsmen who may wish to build that roof the easiest way, a method is outlined here that is simplicity itself.

As we suggested earlier, lay out and cut the rafters before the studs are erected, using the shoe as the model of the plate. They can be laid flat on the floor with the ends projecting out over the shoe and the exact cuts at the ridge and plate can be laid off. Then a pair of trial rafters can be cut, nailed together and tested in the upright position on the shoe without even leaving the floor. Simple enough!

Rafters should be spaced evenly and not exceed thirty inches on centers. If excessive snow loads are to be expected, spacing should not be more than twenty-four inches. Just remember that a camp will be left to itself many times when a heavy snow fall would cave in a roof that was not properly framed.

Lay off the position of the rafters on the plate, marking as described for spacing studs on the shoe. Rafters at the ends of the camp will be flush with the end plate. Decide on the pitch or slope of the roof and the length and type of overhang at the eaves. The type of camp will determine, to some extent, the overhang or projection. A roof that projects well over the walls is a great protection to the wall surface and to open windows. Paint and stain last much longer when walls are well protected. A projection of the rafter ends of 12 inches beyond the wall surface is the minimum. If rafter ends are to be sawed as an ornament, 18 inches to 24 inches is even better.

At one end of the floor establish the exact center of the building on the shoe and make a heavy pencil line on the top and inner face of the shoe (Fig. 44). This is the center of the building and corresponds to the ridge line of the roof. Nail a piece of 2" x 6" on the floor in front of this line to support the ridge end of the rafters at the level of the shoe while framing them. Now lay one of the rafter joints on this block with the other end resting on the shoe at the side of the building and at the angle which has been selected for the pitch of the roof, letting the excess length of the joist extend beyond the outside wall. At the end which is to form the ridge, lay one leg of the steel square against the inner face of the shoe; the other leg of the square, lying on the joist and in exact line with the center line marked on the shoe, will give the exact line on which that end is to be cut for the "ridge" cut. At the other end of the joist which is lying on the shoe—where the lower edge of the joist meets the inner face of the shoe—draw a line square to the inner face of the shoe. This is the "seat" cut. Measure in four inches or the width of the plate, *plus* the thickness of the wall boarding, and draw a line square with the first line to the

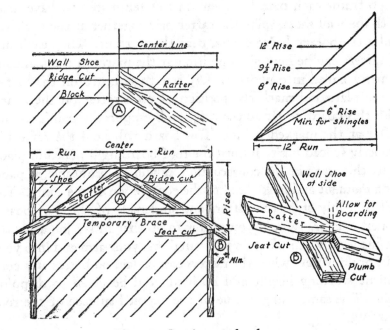

Fig. 44. Cutting roof rafters.

edge of the rafter. Mark these lines plainly on the surface of the rafter, and with the try square carry the line on one edge as a saw guide and make these saw cuts.

If the rafter is now raised to its proper angle, this seat cut will just fit over the shoe with allowance for boarding and will also fit the plate on which it is to be nailed. Mark the end of the rafter for the length of the overhang, either with a square end or with a line parallel to the shoe, so that the end of the rafter will be plumb when erected. Make all cuts marked and, with this rafter as a pattern, cut one to complete the pair. This pair should be framed together with a temporary tie brace and be set up on the shoe to check before cutting the remainder of the rafters. Lay the rafters flat, with the ends together at the ridge line on the inner face of the shoe and the two ends resting on the shoe at each side of the floor. Measure from the end shoe down each side to the seat cut in the rafter and be sure that these dimensions are exactly alike.

Do the rafters meet at the peak line in a fine joint? Does the seat cut fit neatly over the shoe on each side of the floor at the exact mark? If so, proceed to cut all rafters to the one pattern.

To frame each pair, lay them on this template you have made with the wall shoes, spike the rafter pair together at the peak and nail a temporary brace across, near the seat cut. Then each pair of rafters can be hoisted to position at the mark on the plate and securely nailed into position. Lay a narrow board on the rafters at the plate and mark the position of each rafter on the board. Slide this board nearly to the ridge and temporarily nail it to each rafter at the marked points. This board will hold the rafters in properly spaced position until the roof boarding is nailed in place.

At this stage in the construction, it will be profitable to pause for a moment and look ahead to the completion of the camp. You will probably stain the rafters and underside of the roof boards sooner or later. Would you prefer to do that messy job after the roofing is on when the stain will run down your arm and into your hair, or do it now when the rafters can be laid on horses at a convenient working height and no heed need be given to dripping stain? The same thing is true of the exposed surface of the roof boarding.

However, you will probably be in such a hurry to get the roof on that you will ignore this suggestion and leave it all for a later day. We did—but our excuse is that no one warned us and it did not occur to us until dripping stain, stiff necks and dirty dispositions forcibly drove the idea into our minds. You can take off the two lower edges of the rafters while they still can be worked on the horses. Not a large chamfer but enough to show a slight bevel.

There is a space between the rafters as the plate which must be filled before the roof boarding is applied. The job can be done more easily now than later. This space should be airtight and you can use 7/8″ boards, or, better still, pieces of 2″ x 4″ joist tightly fitted between the rafters and projecting somewhat above the line of rafters. Then plane them off on a bevel to the line of boarding. When the roof boarding is applied, it can be nailed through the

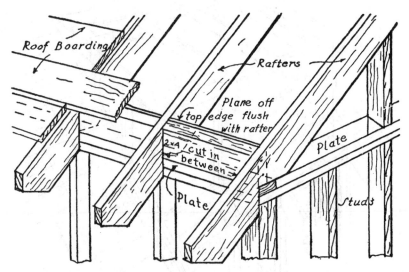

Fig. 45. Filler piece at plate.

boards into these filler pieces making weather-tight joints at the roof line (Fig. 45).

Dormers

The more simple the plan and the less the roof is cut up, the easier it will be to build and maintain. There are conditions which justify the addition of dormers to the roof construction. Light and air may be needed for the roof space which may be used for additional sleeping quarters or storage. The camp may be in thick woods and light may be needed in addition to the wall openings.

Under such conditions, a dormer on the roof may be a great help if properly located and constructed. Do not face it to the west or your room will become a fireless cooker in the late afternoon. A south exposure will not bother in the summer and the sun will be welcome in the winter.

An opening of the required size should be framed in the roof (Fig. 46), and, after roof boarding has been completed, the side walls of the dormer can be framed by notching the dormer side-wall studs one inch onto the joists and roof boarding where they form the sides of the opening in the roof. If the dormer is large, these side wall studs should extend down to the floor level and be spiked to a partition shoe. This will strengthen the roof and make

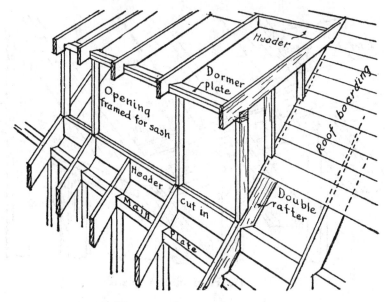

Fig. 46. Dormer framing.

the walls of the dormer rigid. In other words, the side walls of the dormer actually are framed as if the dormer were supported on the floor. This side wall framing for a dormer is necessary only where a large dormer is built and the second story is used.

Porch Roof Framing

The porch roof may be an extension of the main roof or it may be a lean-to added to the main structure and its framing will be similar to the framing of the main roof (Fig. 47). The posts can be plain 4″ x 4″ timbers with a plate made of a 4″ x 6″ on edge. This plate is halved together at the corners and wherever, due to length, it requires a splice. The rafters are cut over the plate and the space between rafters over the plate should have a filler piece cut in between the rafters (see Fig. 45).

Hip-Roof Framing

All the methods for roof framing thus far in our instructions have been for gable roofs. Gable roofs are those in which all rafters are in pairs and the end rafters are directly over the end

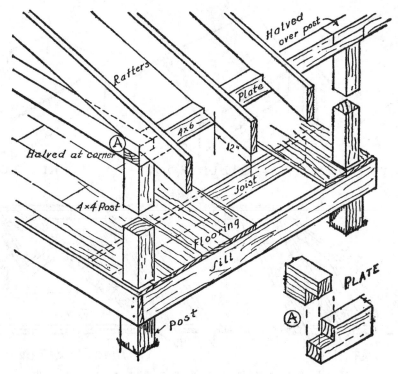

Fig. 47. Porch framing.

plates with the end walls of the camp extended in a triangle to the roof rafters. It may be that your plan requires or is improved by a hip roof, or an extension joining the main roof may require a valley construction where it meets the main roof.

A hip roof is one which shows a slope on all four sides of a simple oblong building or on two sides and an end if it is an extension from the main structure (Fig. 48). On a hip roof the framing is begun by setting up the hip rafters from each corner to meet the ridge rafter which will be necessary in this case. To lay out these hip rafters exactly by the use of a steel square is a trade in itself. However, we can go back on that floor again and, with a little trial and error method, get fairly close results.

As a hip rafter is the diagonal of a square, we lay off this diagonal from each of the two corners at one end (A, Fig. 49). The point where the two lines meet would represent the end of the ridge rafter against which the two hips would rest. But this line

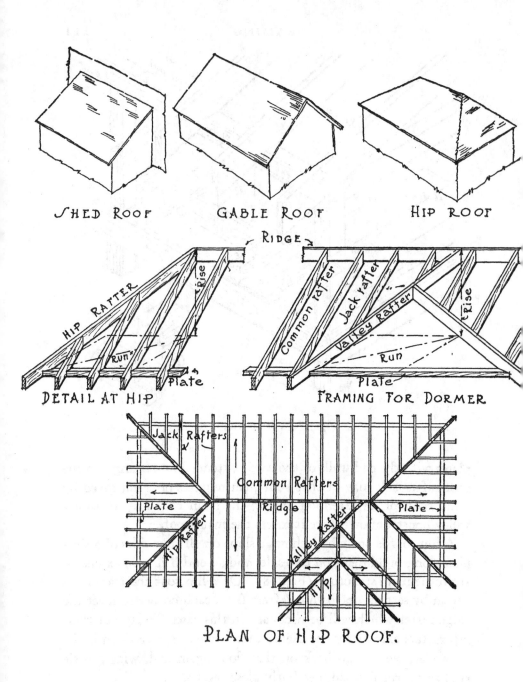

SHED ROOF   GABLE ROOF   HIP ROOF

DETAIL AT HIP   FRAMING FOR DORMER

PLAN OF HIP ROOF.

HIP ROOF FRAMING.

Fig. 48.

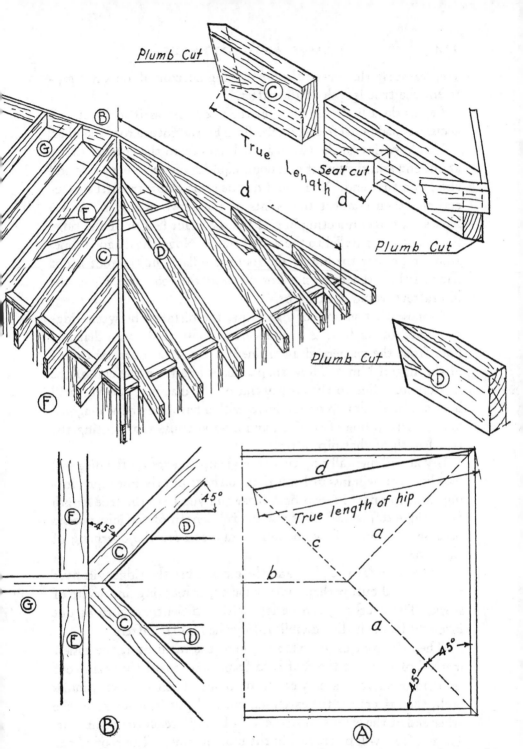

Fig. 49. Laying out a hip roof: (A) layout for length, (B) plan at peak, (C) hip rafter, (D) jack rafter, (E) common rafter, (F) framing of hip, (G) ridge board.

(representing the line of the hip), being horizontal, does not represent the true length of the rafter.

Let us do a little drawing on the floor just as if a direct and accurate shadow were cast on the floor by the future roof member.

You have drawn the two diagonal lines from the corners (*a, a*) at one end and they meet at a point equidistant from each side and also from that end. You could do the same thing from the other end and then connect the points of these two triangles. As we have said, this connecting line (*b*) is the exact length of the ridge line, since it is parallel to the actual ridge. Now, the diagonal lines would represent the hips if the roof were flat, but the roof is not flat and the steeper the slope or pitch of the roof, the longer the hip rafters would actually be.

Suppose that your roof has a rise, the distance between ridge and plate, of six feet. At the meeting point of the two diagonal lines from the corners, draw a line six feet long square with one of the diagonal lines. Now, snap a chalk line from the end of the six-feet-long line to the corner end of the diagonal and you will have a triangle drawn on the floor, with a base line of the diagonal line, a vertical line of six feet, and a hypotenuse representing the true length of that hip rafter.

If you will mentally tip that triangle up on edge on the diagonal base line, you will instantly see that you have put the line representing that hip rafter in its proper place and you have the true length from ridge to plate. This is not the full length of the joist needed because you must allow enough extra stock for the overhang of the eaves.

The seat cut at the plate and the cut against the ridge will have to be worked out, perhaps with some experimenting and waste of stock. The overhang can be left with sufficient stock to be cut properly from the line established by the regular rafters.

When the roof of an extension joins the main roof, the easiest method of framing the roof is to frame and board the main roof as if no other roof area were to be built. Then the extension is built, the rafters for the extension cut and put in place from the other end of the extension to the line of the plate on the main unit. These rafters will be framed in the usual manner. The roof of the extension will then be framed on the slope of the main roof, each pair of rafters being shorter than the preceding ones due to the slope of the main roof—and will be nailed directly on the main roofing.

If you will fold a piece of stiff paper in the middle and place it on the table before you like an "A" tent, it will represent the roof over an oblong building with no extensions or ells. Now fold a smaller piece of paper in like manner and place it against and at right angles to the first piece (Fig. 50).

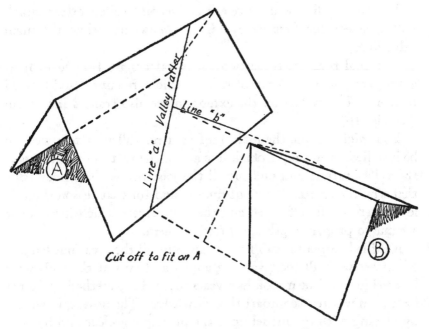

Fig. 50. Paper model of hips and valleys.

You will see at once that it is necessary to cut the sides of the second piece of paper on an angle before it can be fitted snugly against the slope of the first piece and leave no opening. You will have then an exact model showing the intersection of one roof with another roof surface. In fact, the simple model will illustrate more than we can describe.

The folded edges of the pieces represent the ridges of the two roof surfaces. The diagonal joints where the roof of the extension meets the roof surface of the main roof are called valleys.

Now, with your pencil, run a line up in the valley on the main roof paper and continue the line to meet the main roof ridges. Remove the smaller piece of paper and, on the main roof model, the line which you have drawn will represent the actual valley rafter that must be framed in if you are to have roof rafters exposed on the inside.

Replace the small roof model in position and draw a pencil line on the main roof in the other valley to intersect with the line first drawn. You will note that the ridge line of the small roof intersects the same point.

This second line will represent the second valley rafter which will intersect the first valley rafter somewhere below the main ridge line.

In actual practice those two valley rafters are framed in first, as they support the main roof rafters which are cut off and framed to them. The rafters on the extension are also framed into them (see Fig. 10).

You might frame the main roof as if no valley rafters were to be installed, then snap a chalk line across the rafters on the line of the valley rafters and cut out all the joist below these lines. But that would be a great waste of lumber and for that reason the valley rafters are first framed and then all rafters which intersect it are cut to proper length and fitted to them.

A skilled carpenter can lay out and cut all these various lengths of rafters with all their varying angles and cuts at the ends with his steel square, but it took him years to learn the method. Volumes have been written to impart the knowledge. The novice, however, by playing with the model until the principle is clear and by trial and error can learn enough to enable him to do the work. Some lumber may be spoiled while solving the problem, but that is part of the fun. When you have succeeded, as succeed you will, an inward glow will repay you for all the effort and lumber used.

It will be seen that both on hip roofs and where one roof meets another, different length rafters will be required at various places. These can all be figured out with a steel square if you care to learn the mysteries of that useful tool. Probably the better way is just to measure for each one, use your adjustable bevel to mark the cuts and learn by doing.

CHAPTER 8

Exterior Construction and Trim

Boarding and Sheathing

If the wall covering is to be vertical boarding with batten strips over the joints, start by putting on the boards at *each corner*, well nailed to the frame and to each other at the corner. Attach a board at each side of all openings and then fill in the spaces between these points. If the boarding is started at a corner and put on in continuous progress, much cutting and fitting will have to be done at the openings. Also, the panel effect formed by the battens will not be satisfactory. If the boarding is to be exposed on the interior, select the best face of the boards for the inside. The batten strips can be omitted until the roofing is completed. Once the walls are boarded and the roof is weather-tight, inside work can be progressing when the weather is unsuitable for outside work.

If boarding is to be put on horizontally, you will begin at the bottom of the wall. If matched sheathing is to be used, the tongue should always be up. Whichever type of sheathing is used, do not be sparing with nails. Use plenty of them, well set home and when in doubt, put in some extra ones.

The much-discussed question of diagonal versus horizontal boarding need not bother you at all. The diagonal type has its advocates but actual results do not prove its increased value nor make up' for the cutting waste of this method. If the horizontal or vertical boarding is set up tight and well nailed it becomes as strong as necessary. If you can spare the time and a little waste of lumber when laying under floors, the diagonal method has a real reason for its use as compared with the straight method. No real advantage, however, is gained by the diagonal method of boarding walls, with all due respect to the opinions of others and the many arguments advanced in its favor.

Roof Boarding

If the under side of the roof is to be exposed, on the interior of the camp, select the better face of the boards for the under surface and set all joints up tight. Nail all boards securely to the rafters, using three nails at each bearing except for boards of six inches or less in width. Lay the first board at the eaves with the edge pro-

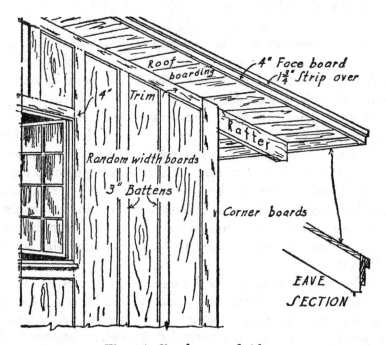

Fig. 51. Simple eaves finish.

jecting about one inch beyond the ends of the rafters or any finish strip and let the end extend well out beyond the wall, at least fifteen inches, for a good overhang at the gables. At this point, remember what we said about the advisability of prestaining the underside of the roof boards if they are to be exposed inside.

The ends of the roof boards can be cut square and laid to a line of projection at the gable ends, or they can extend beyond this line until one side of the roof is completed. Then a chalk line is snapped on the roof from roof ridge to eaves and the ends of these boards cut off with a continuous saw cut. On these cut ends, nail an edge strip at least two inches wide, the top flush with the surface of the roof. This serves as a finish for the gable. This same type of strip should be nailed across the ends of the rafters at the eaves (Fig. 51).

Cut any openings required for chimney or stove pipes. If stove pipes are to project through the roof, the opening in roof boarding should be at least twice as large as the pipe. The stove pipe fitting at the roof line should be made on a sheet metal plate, large enough to cover the opening with a good lap at the sides and to run under roofing above the pipe and lay over the roofing below the pipe (see Fig. 84). Rafters or woodwork should not be near a stove pipe and if not over six inches away should be protected by metal or asbestos board.

Wall Covering

Once the roof is weathertight, all effort should be made to utilize every day of good weather to complete the exterior. If it is a batten job, cut and apply the battens, nailed securely at each bearing with nails well set. Additional clinch nails should be driven through batten and board between regular bearings with one person holding a piece of iron against them on the inside while another drives them home from the outside. Two-inch nails should be used for the regular ⅞″ lumber and, if well clinched, will draw the batten to a snug fit against the board.

If matched siding is to be used, it will be applied horizontally with tongue up. This treatment is sufficient only for a camp built for summer use and is not entirely satisfactory for that purpose. For better construction and the added warmth and protection from bugs, the frame should first be sheathed with matched boards over which the siding, shingles or other outside covering is applied.

Before the outside covering is applied, the boarding should be covered with sheathing paper, carefully applied, well lapped at all seams, wrapped around all corners and run under all trim. Every effort should be made to cover the entire wall surface with an unbroken layer of building paper. In fact, this covering should be of such quality and so carefully laid and secured that it would serve as a weatherproof covering in itself for at least one season.

Trim

If shingles, clapboards or the various forms of siding are used for exterior covering, it will be necessary to put on the outside trim before laying the covering material. This exterior trim may consist of a finish board just under the roof line, corner boards, window and door trim and even a water table. But, if you are going to use clapboards for final covering, see the discussion on page 133 regarding placing of the door and window frames for even spacing of the clapboards.

Trim serves several purposes: to improve the appearance of the building, to furnish a stop against which the surface material can finish neatly, and to seal any crevices which might exist were it not for the covering made by the trim.

There are two methods of setting frames and their trim. The better practice is to set the trim directly on the studding flush with the boarding. A plain or molded member is then planted on the face of the trim, back from the outside edge, leaving a space over which the surface material is continued. This method is the more weatherproof. The other method is to set the frame with the trim lapping over the boarding and the surface material butting against the frame (see Fig. 54).

All door and window trim, finish boards and corner boards must have sufficient projection beyond the rough boarding to cover the ends of the clapboards and siding and the courses of shingles or other wall covering. Either the trim must have sufficient thickness of itself or the regular finish stock of nominal thickness ($1\frac{3}{16}''$) must be "furred out" (Fig. 52).

By that expression we mean that the actual thickness is augmented by other pieces of wood under the exposed finish. For example, if a finish board is used, as it customarily is, at the top of the wall surface, and the wall is to be shingled, the finish board must have a total projection of $1\frac{3}{8}''$ beyond the rough boarding. This is done by using $1\frac{3}{16}''$-thick finish boards over concealed strips, which make the full projection required. The upper courses of shingles are pushed up under the finish board. The top course of shingles will show an actual exposure of $4\frac{1}{2}''$ or whatever the coursing is, but the remainder of the shingle is behind the finish board.

Let us say this. Corner boards and any wall trim should have their surfaces flush so that the corner boards will be flush with wall finish boards under the eaves. So, first plan the projection of corner boards to receive properly the courses of siding and furr out all the finish boards including the finish board under the eaves the same distance.

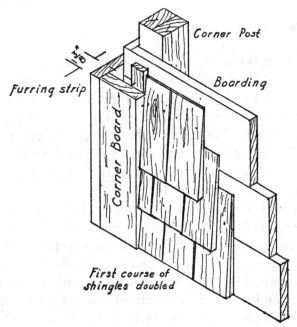

Fig. 52. Corner boards furred out for shingles.

Flitch-sawed boards and log siding will require a full two inches for this purpose. For these materials the trim should be solid stock and not furred.

Beveled siding is more often lapped at the corners and the resulting appearance is better than when corner boards are used. The use of corner boards or a special corner bead makes the work a little easier.

Shingles require at least 1⅜" projection of the finish boards; white clapboards only require a ⅞" projection.

Window and door trim is usually only ¹³⁄₁₆" thick, and the stop for the shingles or siding is made by applying a molding of sufficient thickness on the outside casing.

All exterior trim should be selected material as free from knots and defects as possible; all joints should be made up with white lead; and a coat of white lead primer should at once be applied unless you propose to use a stained treatment. The different types of trim are shown, and that type should be used which is in keeping with the effect to be obtained (Fig. 53).

Door Frames

The frames for all outside doors should be made of plank not less than 1¾″ thick, rabbeted on the inner edge for the door. If screen doors are to be installed, the outer edge should be rabbeted for the screen door, provided the depth of the frame is sufficient to allow for the projection of the hardware. The outer casing can be set back ⅜″ from the inner face of the jamb to form a rabbet for the screen door, if the depth of the frame is not sufficient otherwise for the hardware (Fig. 54).

Frames made by nailing a door stop on ⅞″ stock should never be used for outside doors because it is impossible to prevent a separation between the stop and the jamb on which it is planted. As there are only a few frames needed and they can be bought knocked-down at low cost, it is much more satisfactory to use the 1¾″ solid plank stock with the rabbet cut out for the door.

The type of outside and inside trim and the thickness of the wall construction should be carefully considered before ordering the stock for the frames. Sufficient width of material in the frame should be used to allow for the total thickness of the wall and trim. The frames should be erected with a clearance of at least ½″ between frame and rough stud to allow sufficient space to set the frame plumb and square by using pieces of shingles as wedges to line up the members of the frames perfectly plumb.

Thresholds for outside doors should be made of oak or hard pine 1¾″ thick with inner edge beveled and top surface sloped to the outside. The top of the threshold, under the door, should be about ¾″ above the finished floor to permit the door to swing over rugs.

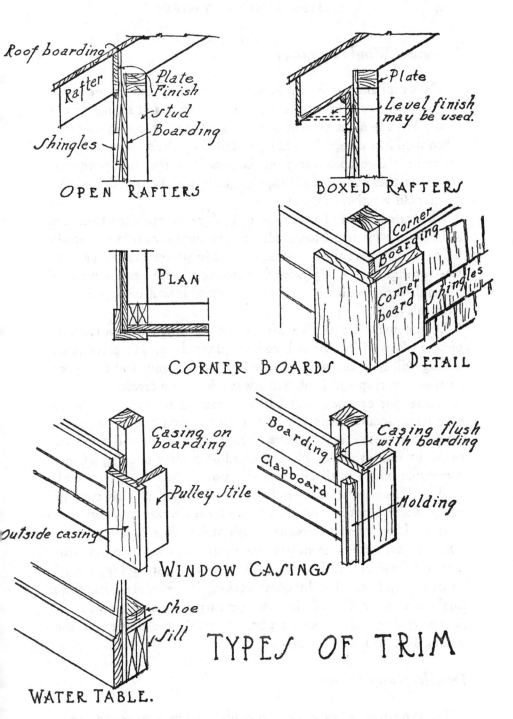

Roof boarding

Rafter

Plate
Finish

Stud

Shingles

Boarding

OPEN RAFTERS

Plate

Level finish
may be used.

BOXED RAFTERS

PLAN

Corner
Boarding

Corner
board

Shingles

CORNER BOARDS

DETAIL

Casing on
boarding

Pulley Stile

Outside casing

Boarding

Clapboard

Casing flush
with boarding

Molding

WINDOW CASINGS

Shoe

Sill

TYPES OF TRIM

WATER TABLE.

Fig. 53.

Casement Window Frames

The simplest type of window frame is the plank frame made for casement sash in which the sash is hinged and swings like a door. The casement type of window has many things in its favor when used in a camp. It is easily installed by the amateur carpenter and is the cheapest. It gives the benefit of the full opening in warm weather and can be made airtight by sash fasts with no leakage in cold weather (Fig. 55).

The frames should be made from 1¾" plank rabbeted from the solid wood with provision made for swinging screens and outside shutters. The sash should swing inward in preference to the outward swinging type. If properly fitted to the frames and secured by jamb-action sash fasts, no weather trouble will be experienced with this type.

Do not make the frames from stock ¾" thick with a stop, or piece against which the sash strikes, planted on. No amount of nailing will hold this strip tightly against the jamb and the space between the stop and jamb will always show as a crack.

Frames for casement sash can be arranged for sash in pairs or even triple arrangement, but it is better to put a mullion, or separating bar, between the sashes. There are commercial types of casement sash available which will allow a clear opening of any reasonable width with all the sash pushed back to one or both jambs. These are special—outside the demands of this type of camp, and are not within the scope of the average amateur carpenter. There are also casement sash and frames on the market which are an improvement over the simple type that we have discussed. These are made with built-in weather stripping, special hardware and are of light construction. These special windows might tax the ability of the amateur carpenter and we will endeavor to keep all of our suggestions within the powers of the willing but unskilled workman.

Double-Hung Frames

The type of window most commonly used in cottages and residences is the double-hung sash and frame, consisting of an upper

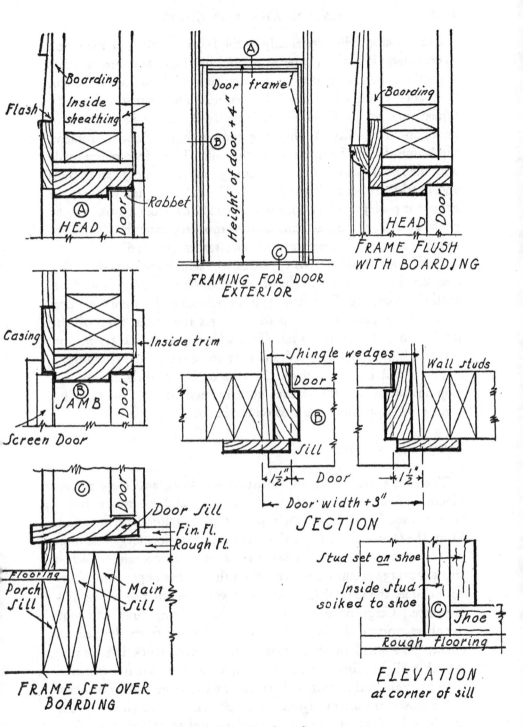

Boarding

Inside sheathing

Flash

Rabbet

(A) HEAD · Door

Door frame

(A)

(B) Height of door + 4"

(C)

FRAMING FOR DOOR
EXTERIOR

Boarding

HEAD · Door

FRAME FLUSH
WITH BOARDING

Casing

Inside trim

(B) JAMB · Door

Screen Door

Shingle wedges

Door

(B) Sill

1½" · Door

Wall studs

1½"

Door width + 3"

SECTION

(C) · Door

Door Sill

Fin. Fl.
Rough Fl.

Flooring
Porch
Sill

Main
Sill

FRAME SET OVER
BOARDING

Stud set on shoe

Inside stud
spiked to shoe

(C) Shoe

Rough flooring

ELEVATION
at corner of sill

Fig. 54. Exterior-door frame.

125

and lower sash sliding vertically in the frame. This type has much to commend it both in appearance and in practical usage. It costs more than the casement type, requires more skill to install and can be opened to only half the full opening. The frames can be obtained in most localities all made up ready to set in place or in knockdown bundles. If shipping and carting are not a problem, the frames should be made up at the mill. These frames are made with side and head jambs of yellow pine, preferably, and stools and outside casings of white pine. The side, or pulley stiles, are fitted for pulleys and a removable piece allows access to the weight pockets. A hard pine parting strip is rabbeted into the side jambs to make a separation between the two sashes (Fig. 56).

Frames are made in two types: one in which the outside casing is set on the boarding and the other in which the casing is set flush with the boarding. The first type is preferable. In some localities, an extra member is introduced between the outer edge of the jambs and the outside casing. This adds depth to the frame and acts as a blind stop. If the frames are to be set on the studding, a molding will be required on the face of the outside casing as a stop against which the surface covering will stop. This molding can be mill-applied or planted on at the job.

Design of Frames

The size, style and arrangement of windows, and their proper placing, affect the appearance of the camp and too much attention cannot be given to their proper proportions and location. From the standpoint of the view from the interior, large openings with undivided lights of glass may seem of importance. When this advantage is compared with the value of the appearance from the outside, the idea of large sheets of glass becomes of minor importance. Large openings, without the dividing lines of wood members, appear like black cavities and detract from the general effect. The small lights of glass require extra work in cleaning but that slight disadvantage is completely lost when compared with the ugly and out-of-scale results of the larger sheets of glass.

Windows are always specified or shown on drawings by the width and height of the glass and the number of lights of glass. Thus, twelve light 12″ x 14″ means twelve lights or panes of glass, twelve inches wide and fourteen inches high. Width is always

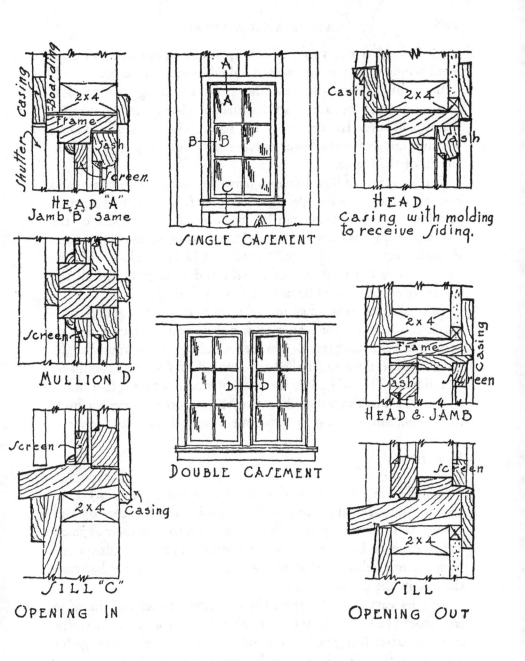

CASEMENT WINDOWS.

Fig. 55.

given first. A window may have a single sash as in a cellar or casement window, or two sashes as in a double-hung window.

In framing for windows, the studs enclosing the window on the sides and top, are set so that the outside edge of the exterior frame will meet the center of the stud. The piece of studding which is cut in for the lower portion of the opening is set to hold the sill of the frame.

Catalogues of sash and frames show the many sizes of sash, and over-all dimensions and details of frames from which the rough opening for the window can be obtained. After the size of the rough opening has been figured and the location of the sill has been determined, a piece of 1" x 2" stuff should be marked with the height above the floor line of the sill and head joist and all the similar openings should be laid off from this stick.

One point to remember in laying out window openings is to check carefully on the height of windows under which a sink or cook board is to be placed. For such windows, a minimum height from finished floor to finished window sill of four feet should be established. This will allow the back of the sink or a splash board to be set against the wall and not create a pocket between the back of the sink and window as is the case when sill is set too low.

Shingles

Shingles are always started at the lowest point and worked to the top. Beveled siding and clapboards are started at the *top* and worked to the lowest point. Shingles are laid so that their exposed ends form even horizontal rows with joints in each row alternated with the one below so that each shingle covers the joint between the two in the course below.

Shingles vary in width from three to eight inches and the wide ones should be split before laying. Shingles over 8 inches in width may split after being nailed in position as a result of shrinkage by drying. If they do, the split will come invariably just above the joint between the two shingles below. When you split the shingle, you can arrange the break in joints. When shingles are very dry they should not be laid tightly but should have at least ⅛" between them at the butts. Joints in a course should always occur over the middle of a shingle in the course below and the different widths should be tried to make this possible.

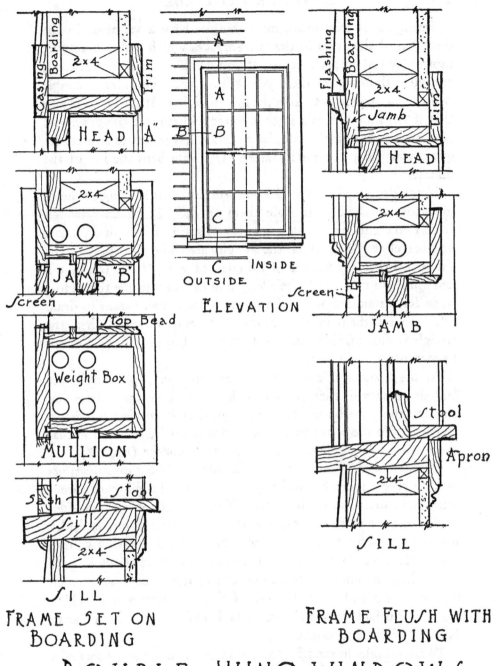

HEAD "A"

Casing · Boarding · 2×4 · Trim

Flashing · Boarding · 2×4 · Jamb · Trim

HEAD

JAMB "B"

Screen

2×4

JAMB

Screen

Stop Bead

Weight Box

MULLION

Sash · Stool

Sill

2×4

SILL

Stool

Apron

2×4

SILL

A

A

B · B

C

C · INSIDE

OUTSIDE

ELEVATION

FRAME SET ON BOARDING

FRAME FLUSH WITH BOARDING

DOUBLE HUNG WINDOWS.

Fig. 56.

129

Strange as it may seem, most shingles have a variation in the direction of the grain in the two surfaces which makes it important to lay the proper face up. If you will look at them or, better, run your thumb over them you will see that the average shingle will have a surface grain like the hair on a dog. It stands to reason that if the shingle is laid so that water will run off the grain and not into it, the shingle will absorb much less moisture and consequently will dry out much faster. This lengthens the life of the shingle.

If you desire stained shingles you will find that although a messy job, it is not difficult to stain them on the job. Make a trough from two eight- or ten-inch boards and support it to drain into a half barrel or tub in which the shingles are to be dipped. Cut the bands securing the bundle of shingles, take a part of the bunch and dip them two-thirds their length in the stain in the tub. Hold them for a moment above the tub to allow surplus stain to drain off, then set them in the trough, butt ends down. When the trough is full of shingles, the first ones dipped can be thrown loosely into a pile to dry.

At the corners, if corner boards are not used, the shingles are laid alternately so that one course is laid to take the corner and the first shingle around the corner laps over it and is trimmed to its bevel. On the next course, the two shingles are reversed so that every other shingle shows a cut edge at the corner (Fig. 57).

Corner boards, against which the shingles butt, are sometimes used to give a more finished appearance, but the shingled corner seems to be more in keeping with a shingled wall. Shingles on side-walls can have more area exposed than on roofs and can be laid 5 inches to 6 inches to the weather. The lower, or starting course, should always be laid double and the outer layer set about $\frac{1}{4}$ inch lower than the under course in order to form a drip. A $\frac{3}{4}$ inch strip can be nailed at the bottom of the wall surface over which the course is laid, forming a water table and causing the water to fall free of the foundations.

To lay shingles in straight, evenly-spaced courses, some sort of a straight edge should be used. It can be done by snapping a chalk line, but this is clumsy and each shingle must be held in place by one hand while, by sleight of hand the other manages to get a nail and drive it home.

To lay shingles easily it will be necessary to use a board equal in

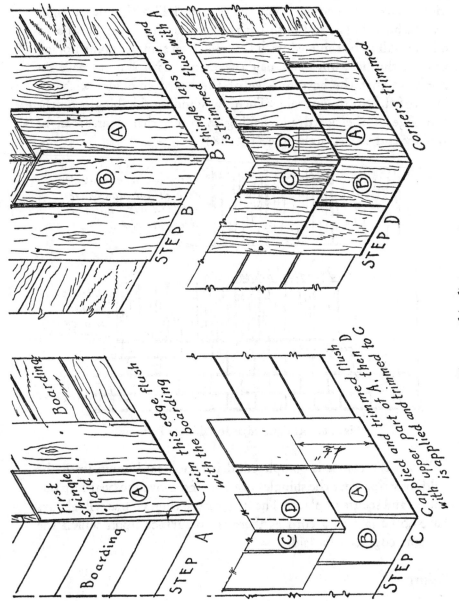

Fig. 57. Shingling a corner.

Within the figure (labels):

STEP A
Boarding
First shingle laid
(A)
Trim this edge flush with the boarding

STEP B
(B) (A)
B shingle laps over and is trimmed flush with A

STEP C
(C) (D)
(B) (A)
C applied upper part and trimmed flush, then D with is applied and trimmed to C

STEP D
(D)
(C) (A)
(B)
Corners trimmed

width to the desired exposure of the shingles and long enough to reach across the space to be shingled. At each end and in one or more places, depending upon the length, nail a shingle at right angles, butt down, and flush with the lower edge. Lay this board on the wall to be shingled with the nailed-on shingles point up and against the boarding, and nail the points with shingle nails set home, so that the bottom edge of the board coincides with the butts of the course just laid. Then, by standing the shingles on the top edge of the board and nailing in place, that course can be rapidly laid to a straight line (Fig. 58).

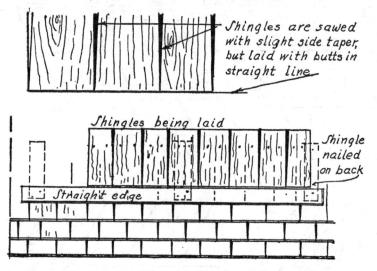

Shingles are sawed with slight side taper, but laid with butts in straight line

Shingles being laid

Shingle nailed on back

Straight edge

Fig. 58. Straight edge for shingle laying.

When the course is completed, drive the board down until the holding strips clear the shingles just laid and move the board up one course and secure in place. The first, or starting, course will always have to be laid to a cord as there is no surface upon which the straight edge can be laid.

Siding

Beveled siding or clapboards are laid by starting at the top of the wall, usually sliding the top edge of the clapboard under the finish board, adjusting the lower edge to a chalk line and nailing through the finish board to hold the top edge of the clapboard. The next line of siding is slid up under the first course where the spring of the first course will hold it in place until adjusted to the chalk line and will be secured when the nails are driven near the lower edge of the upper course (Fig. 59). All butt joints and the ends of each clapboard against corner boards or window and door trim should be cut to a close joint, well driven together and, if the surface is to be painted, the end joints should be brushed with paint or white lead and be driven tightly together.

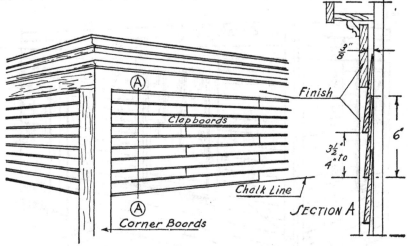

Fig. 59. Laying clapboards.

Spacing of Courses

Siding, clapboards or shingles should be spaced so that the horizontal lines of the butts will coincide with the tops and bottoms of window trim and the top of door trim. Make a stick the full height of the wall on which to lay out the spacing of the clapboards and the trim. All this layout on the stick must be well worked out in advance of setting window and door frames. Use one side of the stick to lay off the window frames; on the opposite side lay off the door frames; then on the side between these two faces space off the siding. If errors are made, plane off the side that is in error and try again. It may and probably will require a little juggling of window heights and side spacing, but it must be done if the work is to look right. If all this planning is done before the window framing is actually set, a slight movement of the frame up or down will permit proper spacing of siding. This is one of the reasons for thoroughly checking the framing before the boarding is applied. From the marked stick, the corners of the building are divided into the proper spacing and a chalk line, tightly stretched on nails from corner to corner and snapped against the building will furnish a guide for each course (Fig. 60).

Because the amount of exposure to the weather, or the width of each course, can be varied with all clapboards, beveled siding and shingles, the spacing required to line with the tops of doors and windows and the sill line of windows can be varied without

Fig. 60. Spacing siding.

cutting into the siding. This cannot be done readily with novelty siding or any form of tongue and groove or rabbeted edge siding because their width cannot be adjusted. If these forms of siding are used, you should plan the size of the openings to correspond with the units of the width of the siding so that no ugly cutting into the line of siding will be necessary.

Log Siding

Log siding is applied in the same manner as any matched siding starting at the bottom of the wall surface. Each successive course is lapped over the one below with the joint milled on the edge. As

the siding will be oiled, stained or left in the raw, the nails should
be galvanized or otherwise treated and be well set in to prevent
rust streaks from staining the wood. The heads of the nails should
be covered with putty colored to match the proposed treatment.

The ends of the siding can be mitered together at corners, but,
as these corners will tend to open as the material dries out, it is
much better to form the corners with 2-inch corner boards against
which the siding should be closely fitted. The same type of trim

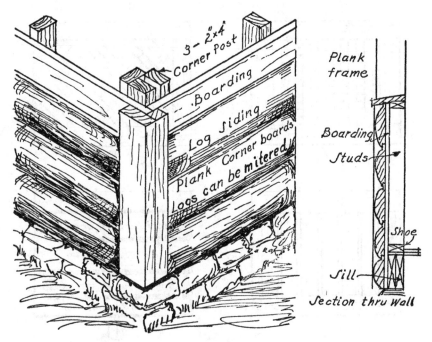

Fig. 61. Log siding.

should be used at all openings to prevent the cut ends of the log
siding from showing. To prevent the monotony of repeated
equal-sized units, random widths of log siding should be used and
the effect of real log construction will be more nearly accomplished than by using uniform widths for each course (Fig. 61).

Lattice Work

The sides and front of porches below the floor and perhaps the
space between sills and ground on the camp can be finished with

wide casings and lattice work in the panels. Strips of lattice stock, 1⅛″ x ¼″, are nailed over each other either in diamond or square pattern. The vertical strips in the square pattern are always on the outside and the openings are equal in size to the width of the strips. The strips are nailed to the rough work of the porch and the finishing casings are nailed on over these strips. Access panels or doors are made by using a frame of casing stock and nailing the lattice strips on the back of the frame (Fig. 62).

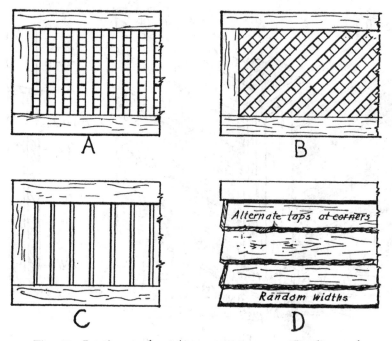

Fig. 62. Lattice work: (A) square pattern, (B) diagonal pattern, (C) ¾″ x 4″ boards, (D) flitch-sawed boards.

Three- to four-inch boards set vertically about one inch apart make a very simple but pleasing form with which to finish the space between sills and grade. They are made up with casings as described for lattice work.

Before laying the porch floor, you should select the form of lattice and make a detail to show the relation of the lattice and the finish trim to the sill in order that the porch flooring may project sufficiently over the finish (Fig. 63).

Whatever type of lattice is used, it may not be sufficient to keep out unwelcome nocturnal visitors. If there is a possibility of such unwelcome roomers under the camp, the lattice work should be backed up with half-inch mesh, galvanized wire extending about six inches into the ground.

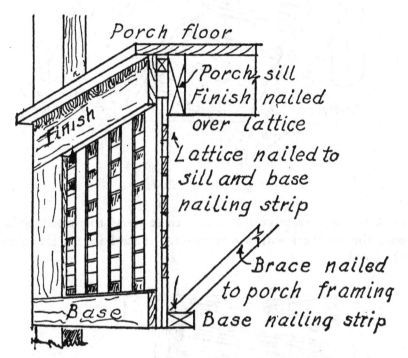

Fig. 63. Lattice framing detail.

Steps and Stairs

Steps will be needed at entrances and for porches. The simplest type and one that will serve in some cases is the ship's ladder, made by nailing plank steps between side planks. It is usual to gain or dado the ends of the steps into the side planks. If of any real length, cross bracing should be nailed on the back (Fig. 64).

A better type should be built on stringers, usually three. The two outer stringers are sawed from plank and the center one made by spiking the waste pieces cut out from the side stringers onto a 2″ x 4″ joist. If steps are more than three feet wide, two of these intermediate stringers should be used. The steps are made from plank and the risers are dressed boards. At "Dunwurken" we

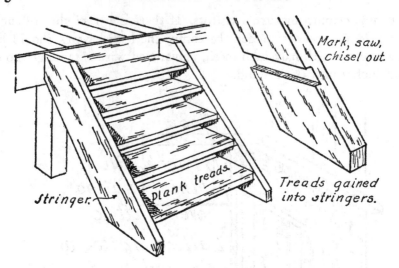

Fig. 64. Ship's ladder.

made the steps from two-by-fours, three pieces to a tread, spiked onto the stringers with a quarter-inch space between the pieces (Fig. 65).

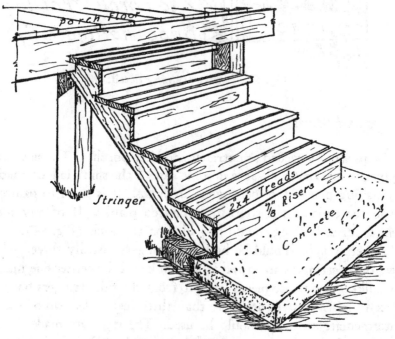

Fig. 65. Plank steps.

The more finished type of steps can be made with stringers cut as above and covered with finish lumber. The side pieces have their vertical edges cut to miter with the risers and the back edges of treads are dadoed into the lower part of the risers. The treads extend out over the side finish and are completed by a piece miter-cut into the end of the tread and returned against the side finish. A small molding is mitered at the angle under the front and ends

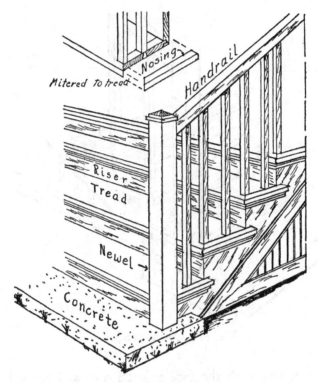

Fig. 66. Finished steps.

of the tread and is coped at the back edge. This treatment is shown in the drawings (Fig. 66).

One type which is easy to build and is used on many cottages is made by covering the rough outside stringer with a finish board cut to the same profile. The risers are then nailed in place and are cut off flush with the outside face of the board. Then the treads are put on with projection at front and ends of about three quarters of an inch. No attempt is made to cover the end grain of the risers (Fig. 67).

Railings are simple and easy to make. The posts are plain four-by-four stock with top rail made from $1\frac{1}{2}''$ x 3″ or heavier stock. Balusters of square $1\frac{1}{4}''$ stock are bevel cut to fit under the slope of the top rail to which they are securely fastened with nails. At the bottom they are toenailed to the tread, set into holes bored in the tread, or cut with a dovetail at the foot which is driven into a cut in the end of the tread. One baluster

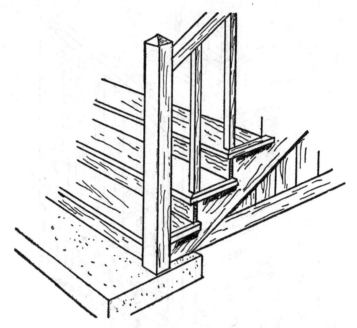

Fig. 67. Cottage steps.

should always line with the face of each riser and the others are spaced equally between risers. A top and lower rail can be used without balusters or intermediate posts where flights of steps are not too long.

A concrete platform, as the lowest step, is ideal for it keeps the woodwork above the ground and prevents decay. The bottom cut ends of all stringers resting on concrete or stone should be heavily coated with paint before erection as they can not be reached for treatment. This prevents absorption of moisture and conse-quent decay of the wood.

Laying out Stairs

The method of laying out steps and stairs is very simple once it is understood, and is the same whether the flight of stairs consists of only three steps to a platform or a full flight from one floor to another. The total height is called the "rise" and the total horizontal space occupied by the stairs is called the "run."

We first figure the total rise. If from one floor to a floor above, this is easy, because it is only a matter of measuring the distance between finished floors. If it is from a porch to the ground, it is not quite so easy, but is not at all difficult. In this case, by running a straight edge board exactly level from the porch floor to a distance beyond the point where the steps are to start, and then measuring from the underside of the board to the grade line or top of a stone or concrete platform on which the steps are to rest, the exact rise can be established.

We now have to figure the rise and run of each step. One rule easy to remember for this purpose is that *the product of the rise and run should be approximately seventy-five.* For example, if we wish to have a twelve inch tread, which is a nice width for outside steps, the rise should be six and one quarter inches; i.e., 6¼ x 12 = 75.

You should now cut a stick which is the exact length of the total rise from the foot of the steps to the porch floor and with dividers or a rule, proceed by trial to space the stick into exactly equal spaces as near 6¼ inches each as possible. A little variation from this dimension will not be important but the final spacing must be exactly equal. We now have the exact measurement for each rise and we have already established twelve inches as the dimension for each tread. We then take a piece of ten-inch board, one edge of which is perfectly straight, and with our steel square will perform a bit of magic (Fig. 68).

Near one end, but not at the very end, lay your steel square on the board with the two blades projecting over the edge which is straight and with the dimension of six and one quarter inches on one blade directly over the edge and the figure twelve on the other blade over the same edge, holding the square without slipping, mark with the pencil along both blades of the square to the angle.

You now have the exact lines on which to saw out the triangular piece which will make the seat for one tread and riser. Actually you do no sawing until the entire pattern for the stringer has been layed out. You can see now why we told you to use a piece of board instead of a good plank which you probably would wreck on the first attempt (Fig. 68).

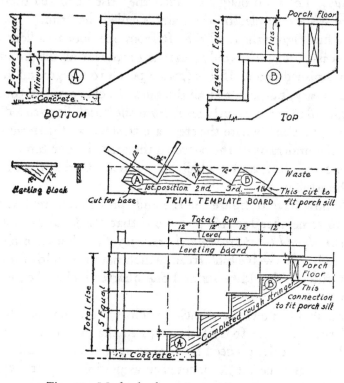

Fig. 68. Method of cutting stair stringers.

Having marked this first triangular piece, you slide the square along the board until the twelve-inch mark on the blade is at the exact spot that the six and one quarter mark was before and draw that triangle. That's all there is to it. Continue to repeat this action until you have laid out all the steps required.

Now let's go back to that end which we left at first. This is to be the end which will rest on the bottom support and will need special treatment. First, let us remember that it is the surface of the finished tread that is the controlling factor and that it is the even spacing of the finished treads which must be maintained. We are cutting the rough stringer on which the finished tread will be placed and the thickness of that tread has an important bearing on this first riser. Because the riser rests upon a platform or other support and because the dimension from the platform to the top of the *finished tread* must be exactly 6¼ inches, the first riser cut must be made so that the face of the cut will be 6¼ inches *minus* the thickness of the finished tread. We mark off that dimension downward from the corner of that first riser already drawn on the board and mark a line at that point parallel with the line of the first tread. That will make the seat cut or surface which will rest upon the platform or support and will thus complete the lower end of the pattern.

We now proceed to finish the upper end in a manner somewhat similar. The difference is in the fact that if the material of the top finished tread is thicker than the porch floor, it must be considered when the final cut is made. The dimension from the porch floor down to the cut for the top tread must be 6¼ inches *plus* the thickness of the finished tread. Please note that *plus*.

One other important point is the method by which the top of the stringer will be secured to the porch frame. If you will look at the drawing (Fig. 68) this will be better understood than from any description, and the method of making the cut can be clearly seen.

You now have a board which represents the plank stringers which are to be cut for the stairs. Place it in position, lower end resting on the platform or bearing and the upper end adjusted to the porch; test it with a level on the treads and make any changes at foot or top to make the treads level or with a very slight pitch outward. From this board pattern you proceed to lay out accurately the actual stringer on a 2-inch plank. Use your try square on the edge to mark the saw cut and then cut out the V-shaped pieces and make the cuts at the ends of the stringer. Keep the cuts exactly square with the surfaces of the stringer and carefully save the pieces cut out. These pieces, nailed on a two by four will make the center stringer and only two plank stringers will be required.

The stringers are now put in place, spaced at the proper distance, held in parallel position by light, temporary braces and the upper ends securely spiked to the frame of the porch. You can then put on the finished treads and risers, posts and rails.

We have gone into this matter at some length and we trust that, together with the drawings, the method is explained to your satisfaction. You may not have any stairs in the camp, but if you need them, the method is the same whether for three, five or seven steps, or a full flight from one floor to another. We know from observation that the planning and building of even the simplest porch steps is one of the most difficult details for the amateur carpenter. Here we have attempted to make it a simple operation.

We might add that a marking block can be made by sawing a piece to represent the saw cuts for the tread and nailing a projecting piece on the long edge. This marking board is moved along the stringer instead of the square as a template for marking all the steps (Fig. 68).

CHAPTER 9

Doors and Windows, Shutters and Screens

Exterior Doors

The exterior doors for the camp should be constructed with two factors in mind: protection for the camp, and an appearance in keeping with the general style of the exterior (Fig. 69).

The "batten" door, made from one thickness of matched boards with battens or cross pieces screwed on the inside, is the simplest type and is easy to build. This type is not suitable as a permanent exterior door but may do very nicely as a temporary closure until a better door can be constructed. There should be at least two battens, one six inches below the top of the door and one ten inches above the bottom with a diagonal piece extending from one batten to the other to prevent sagging of the door. The introduction of a middle batten and cross bracing between middle and lower batten, adds to the appearance.

A very rugged door, easy to build and in keeping with a camp, can be made of two thicknesses of matched boards, the outer layer laid vertically, the inner horizontally. This type of door needs no battens but should be well screwed together and not fastened by nailing (Fig. 69[a]).

Lay the outer layer across two horses with the matched boards forced tightly together by clamps or wedging. Then lay the cross layer and hold in position temporarily with a few nails, not driven home. Snap chalk lines as guides and set home the screws, a vertical row about two inches in from the outer edges with two intermediate rows. If the door is made of pine, the screws can be driven with a hammer about halfway in and then sent home with a bitstock and screw-driver bit. The exterior appearance will be improved if the edges of the boards on the exterior are beveled with a plane before they are put together. Do not use beaded sheathing and expect to obtain the same appearance.

a   SHEATHING DOORS   b   FRAMED

DUTCH DOOR   PANEL DOORS

SECTIONS

EXTERIOR DOORS

Fig. 69.

For an Early American effect, build the door in the same manner but run the boards at an angle of forty-five degrees on both sides (Fig. 69[b]). Such a door was in use in the early days in this country and was ornamented by large-headed nails driven in a diamond pattern. With the chalk line, lay out a cross pattern with lines ten to twelve inches apart. Complete the pattern work by driving clout nails at four- to six-inch intervals on the outer face of the door. The inner face should be fastened with screws for the nails are not used for actual fastening.

All doors made with two thicknesses of boards will show end grain on one half of the thickness. To cover this exposed end grain, strips ¾″ thick and of a width to match the thickness of the door should be carefully fitted to the vertical edges of the door. The edges of the door should be planed to allow a close fit and the strip applied with glue and secured with screws. The screws should be countersunk so that the heads are well below the surface.

Panel Doors

Paneled doors of various types are carried in stock by most dealers and can be purchased at low cost. The selection of such doors is dependent upon the type of exterior finish and the general style of the camp. Paneled doors for exterior openings should not be less than one and three-quarters inches thick (Fig. 69[c]).

Dutch Door

The "Dutch" door which is cut into an upper and lower portion is picturesque and practicable. Derived from the necessity of keeping live stock out and children in while allowing the entrance of air and sunshine, it has outlived its origin. We built one at "Dunwurken" under protest, but it has established its value, not only by its peculiar charm but because it allows fresh air and sunshine to enter without the attendant floor draft (Fig. 69[d]).

The "Dutch" door can be built easily of two thicknesses of vertical boards with all joints broken. Use top, bottom and two intermediate cross battens and cross battens between the lower middle and bottom batten. But do not attempt to make the upper and lower halves separately, hang them, and expect cabinet maker's results. Take this hint from us. Make up the face boards with the full length. Make the inner layer of boards with a close joint at the line of permanent separation. Complete the door, fit and hang it on the four hinges. Then, and then only, take the door down, put on a temporary straight edge as a guide and run your finest tooth saw along the straight edge to complete the separation of the two portions. Then put the two halves back on the hinges and the door will swing properly and the two halves, with a connecting latch, will swing as smoothly as a solid door.

Perhaps the drawings will show you more clearly just how this work is done. You will note that the two saw cuts are about ½" apart. This is done to make a double weather lap when the two halves are fastened together. It also does away with a through joint which would allow weather to penetrate. A half-round molding at this point is also a help. The two halves of a Dutch door are held together by a long wood turn-button, secured by a heavy lag screw. If the camp is shingled or finished with beveled siding, the Dutch door should be paneled, and will undoubtedly need to be the product of a mill.

Sash

There are two types of windows which are commonly in use: the casement sash and the double-hung sash. These have been partially described under "Window Frames." Common sash are made from clear white pine, are 1⅜" thick and are glazed with single-strength glass. The double-hung sash are made with weather-lipped meeting rails where the upper and lower sash meet when both sash are in the closed position (Fig. 70).

Each sash may have one light or pane of glass or may be divided by wood muntins into several smaller panes. The full lights of glass are easier to keep clean but the smaller lights are more attractive and add much to the appearance of the camp. A satisfactory compromise is made by the use of six or eight panes in the upper and a single pane in the lower sash.

Fitting Double-Hung Sash

Plane the top and side edges of the top sash (which is called jointing), and lightly bevel the edges. The projection of the meet-

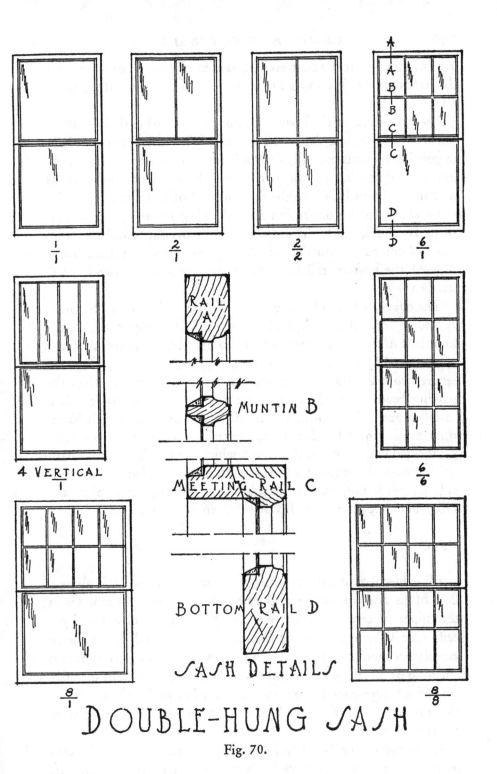

$\frac{1}{1}$

$\frac{2}{1}$

$\frac{2}{2}$

$\frac{6}{1}$

RAIL A

MUNTIN B

MEETING RAIL C

4 VERTICAL
$\frac{1}{1}$

$\frac{6}{6}$

BOTTOM RAIL D

SASH DETAILS

$\frac{8}{1}$

$\frac{8}{8}$

DOUBLE-HUNG SASH

Fig. 70.

149

ing rail member at the bottom will have to be cut out to fit around the parting strip, leaving a little play to allow for painting (Fig. 70).

Now the edges of the lower sash must be jointed and the bottom rail will have the surplus wood cut off. With the upper sash held in position by nails partially driven into the jambs under the meeting rail, set the lower sash in position. It will be found that its meeting rail will be above the meeting rail of the upper sash. Set the dividers to this dimension and, allowing for the proper bevel to fit the stool, mark the amount of this overlap on the bottom rail and cut off the surplus wood. Slightly round the inner lower edge of the bottom rail to allow it to slip easily by the finished stool cap.

The edges of the sash are grooved for the sash cord at the mill. A knot is formed in a piece of sash cord of the proper length, the knot laid in the enlargement of the groove already prepared for it and secured by a nail, the cord is then passed over the pulley and secured to the weight. The upper sash is first installed, then the parting beads are set home in their grooves and the lower sash is installed and held in place by the stop bead or band which forms the retaining member for the lower sash. All this work is readily performed before the inside casing, which covers the weight channel between the jamb and rough stud, is put in place. A removable pocket is mill-cut in the side jambs for easy removal if any subsequent repairs are needed or replacement of sash cords.

Ventilators

All gables should have a means of ventilation which will allow a flow of air and the escape of the heated air which accumulates in the upper space of a room. Whether this space is closed in by a ceiling or is the upper part of the rooms, either windows or louvre ventilators should be built in. This is especially true if the space is closed in by a ceiling of rooms below. Without a constant circulation of air, this space becomes unbearably hot under the effects of the sun, and will reflect the heat into the rooms below long after the sun has set.

If the space is enclosed and is readily accessible, small windows in the gable ends will serve both for light and ventilation. If, however, the gables are not easily accessible, the louvre type of ventilator is much better. These ventilators are made with a frame in which slanting horizontal members, gained into the side jambs, prevent the entrance of rain or snow but allow the free circulation of air. The opening should be screened and should have hinged shutters, swinging in, to be closed in cold weather. The construction and installation of these ventilators is shown clearly by the drawings (Fig. 71).

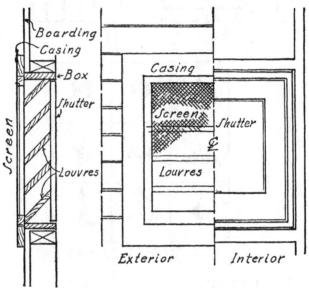

Fig. 71. Ventilator.

Shutters

Camps should be provided with sturdy wood shutters over all windows and glazed doors as a protection against storms and intruders. They also make a decorative feature when open and add much to the appearance. If the camp is to be occupied at intervals and for short periods, the shutters should be hinged to swing back against the outside wall when open. When closed they should be fastened by heavy screw eyes and hooks. With shutters hinged in this fashion, it is the work of only a few minutes to open or close for the season (Fig. 72).

If shutters are used to close a camp for the season and are not to be frequently opened, the hinges may be omitted and the shutters

SHEATHING   NARROW BOARDS

PANEL   CUTOUT DESIGNS   PANEL & SLATS

NARROW & WIDE BOARDS   PANEL

SHUTTERS.

Fig. 72.

can be secured from the inside by hooks and eyes. The shutters should be marked with a Roman numeral which can be stamped with a $\frac{1}{4}''$ chisel and a corresponding numeral placed on the window jamb. This will eliminate guess work when shutters are to be put on at the end of the season.

Shutters should be substantially constructed with cleats screwed to the inside and hung flush with the outside wall surface so that, when closed, no leverage can be gained to force them open. Hinges should be of the butt type which cannot be removed when the shutter is closed. If shutters are to swing back against the wall, some kind of hold-back must be installed if you wish to sleep when the wind is blowing. These can be a simple spring catch which does not show when shutter is against the wall but is not very secure. The regular hold-back used for blinds is excellent. For real swank, use the wrought iron elongated S holdback that adds real charm to the picture.

If glazed sash are used in outside doors, they should be made to swing in. A panel of No. 22 gauge galvanized iron, painted to match the exterior of the door, can be placed between the sash and its stops to provide protection when the camp is closed.

If the camp is designed for summer use, make a large opening on one wall of each bedroom and close that opening with a shutter hinged at the top. During warm weather, this shutter held open on braces, acts as an awning and makes a sleeping porch of the room. In cold weather, it can be closed tightly by sash fasts and become as weather-tight as the solid wall. The opening, of course, is covered with an inward swinging screen.

If the camp is built with vertical boarding battens, these large shutters are made to match the wall covering and when closed, only a saw cut at top and bottom shows that they are not an actual part of the wall.

Shutters can vary in design from those made with boards and cleats, to the paneled shutters with the ornamental cut-outs which can represent some fad of the owner. The style of shutter is dependent upon the type of construction and should be in keeping with the general scheme.

If the camp is built with plain boards and battens, the shutters should be made with boards not over six inches wide with cleats on the inside. Shutters made of four-inch boards with $\frac{1}{4}''$ separation look well with log siding or shingles or even with siding or clapboards. However, with siding or clapboards, if the camp is really dressed up, paneled shutters will be necessary to obtain the best appearance. Some artistic cut-out can be used as a decoration or an ornament, cut from plywood and painted a contrasting color can be applied to the panel.

Shutters made from boards and cleats should be built with screws rather than nails because the screws will hold through shrinking and swelling better than nails. If shutters are very wide, a diagonal brace should also be cut in between the upper and lower cleats to prevent sagging of the shutter. With paneled or slatted shutters, regular hardware used for blinds should be used rather than the butts described for the batten shutters.

Screens

It would hardly seem necessary to dwell on the subject of screens were it not for the fact that second only to a leaky roof as a cause of discomfort, come poor screens—or no screens at all. The difference is that pans can be placed under leaks but what can you do against the influx of flies? Not only should all openings be properly screened but, if the porch is to be used with any degree of comfort, it, too, should be screened.

For the doors, it will be much easier and just as cheap to plan door openings of stock sizes and buy the screen doors. For windows and porches, the screens may be purchased ready made or they can be made on the job. Screen doors will invariably sag after a time and to prevent this, a diagonal brace made of two heavy wires with a turn-buckle connecting them, should be applied from a point near the top on the hinge side to a point near the bottom of the door on the other side. By tightening the brace with the turn-buckle, the swinging edge of the door can be prevented from dragging on the threshold.

Screen doors are usually hung on surface spring hinges and are fastened by a surface catch with small knob on both sides. If small children or pets are a part of the family, the lower panel in the screen door should be protected by a large mesh wire screen applied on the outside to prevent damage to the screen cloth.

Screen cloth or woven wire is made in three distinct grades.

The black wire is the cheapest, has the coarsest mesh and must be painted frequently. It is entirely impracticable for use at the seashore. The next grade, called pearl wire, is galvanized, has a finer mesh and does not require painting, at least for a long time. Most expensive in first cost, but really cheapest in the end, is the standard 16 mesh to the inch bronze wire. This wire is the only type that should be used near salt water. It never requires painting and should last for the life of the camp. These several grades of screen cloth are made in a variety of widths and the available supply and

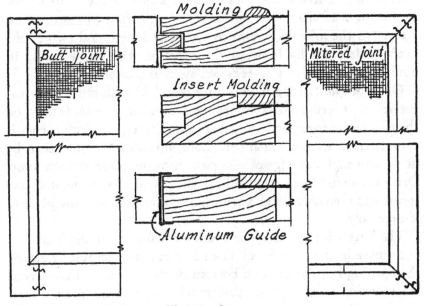

Fig. 73. Screens.

your dimensions will indicate the width which can be used with the least waste.

The construction of the frames is not difficult and the application of the wire, approached properly, is within the ability of the amateur carpenter. Window screens are made half or full length for double-hung sash. The full length screen allows the upper sash to be dropped for ventilation and is advisable for kitchen windows at least. Screens for casement sash usually swing from the side, as determined by the swing of the sash themselves and the need to get at the shutters from the inside.

Screen stock is carried almost everywhere and it is only a matter of estimating the total length needed. The simplest form is made from plain strips and half-round or flat moldings to cover the edges of the wire and the tacks which fasten it. The other kind has a rabbet into which the screen cloth is fitted and the piece removed in forming the rabbet is nailed back in place so that the face of the frame is flush. One can also buy screen stock in a bundle, the complete material for making one screen being included in the package (Fig. 73).

Screen frames are put together either with mitered corners or butt joints. There is not much choice either in the labor or the appearance. If the miter joint is to be used, four pieces of stock are cut in the miter box, two to the exact length and two to the exact width, usually between the edges of the outside casing in double-hung windows or between stops for casement sash.

One side and the top member are then laid with miter joint together and corrugated fasteners are driven into the surface to tie the two pieces together. Second ones are driven in. Each corner is completed in the same manner. Long finish nails should then be driven through the edge of one piece into the other at each joint. Drive the nails where they will not hit one of the corrugated fasteners and then set nails and crimps below surface to allow planing if necessary.

The butt joints are made in a similar manner but the joints are cut square in the miter box. The side pieces are the full length of the opening but the top and bottom pieces are cut to fit between the two side pieces and are that much shorter than the required width. All full-length screens should have a middle bar cut in at the height of the meeting rails of the sash.

Screen frames should be made from stock material which is ¾" thick. If frames are mitered at corners, the stock is 1¾" wide. If frames are made with butt joints, the top and side members are 1¾" wide and the bottom rail is 2¾" wide. The butt joint frames have one advantage over the mitered joint in that the extra width of the bottom member allows a certain amount of cutting to fit a stool which may not be level.

The moldings which are used to cover the edges of the screen cloth are ⁵⁄₁₆" x ⅝" and are put on with ¾" brads. The cloth is fastened with ⅜" screen wire tacks spaced not over two inches apart. If screens are to slide on splines at the sides, the material for the side rails should be the grooved type which is carried in stock and the spline material which will fit the groove should be obtained at the same time.

Here is the way to stretch screen wire tightly. Place two frames end to end with the outer ends raised on blocks A length of screen wire is then tacked first to one outer end and then to the other, pulled as tightly as possible. When these ends are securely tacked, take out the blocks and force both frames flat to the floor. This stretches the wire taut, without bulges. Then tack the inner edges and cut the two screens apart. It is then a simple matter to tack the wire to the other edges and cover the edges with the molding.

The method used to hang the screens will depend entirely upon the type of window to be screened. If hinged sash and hinged shutters are used, the screens will have to be hinged to swing in and be set between the shutter and sash. A spring plunger in the screen frame on the side opposite the hinges is set in a socket in the window frame and holds the screen in place when closed.

Where half-screens are used on double-hung sash, the usual method is to groove the edges of the screen to slide on a spline which is nailed to the edge of the casings between which the screen can slide. Another method for sliding screens is to nail to the casing an aluminum guide in which the sides of the screen slide. The screens have only to be raised until they are above the spline to be removed and are replaced as easily. Full-length screens can be hung at the top with special fittings which permit easy installation and removal and are fitted at the bottom with special fasteners.

Porches are screened by making frames of the height of the opening and about three to four feet wide. If the screens extend to the floor, a middle rail should be used to stiffen the frames. In locating this middle rail, be sure that it is below the eye level when one is sitting in a chair. Quarter-round moldings should be nailed around sides, top and bottom of the opening to be enclosed, against which the screens are set from the outside and held in place with hooks or the metal fasteners which are available at any hardware store. If two or more frames are required in each opening, they can be held tightly together by light metal plates made for that purpose. The quarter-round strip is also a protection to the screen frame when piazza floor is washed or swept.

CHAPTER 10

Roofing, Gutters, and Downspouts

Your camp now has a semblance of form: Walls framed and boarded, roof rafters in place and boarded, eave and rake finish in place and porch framed. The roofing material can now be applied. Every effort should be made to complete this part of the work as soon as possible. Once it is done, you are independent of weather conditions and can continue the inside work when outside work is impossible. Under the subject of "Materials" we have discussed briefly the different types of roofing which can be used and the final choice is to be governed by the appearance desired and the comparative cost.

Roll Roofing

This material will make a roof which will last for several years, is easy to apply and, if one of the slate-coated types is used, will not be out of place in any surroundings. After it has outlived its usefulness and is no longer weather-tight, it will serve as a most practical insulating material over which asphalt or asbestos shingles may be applied. Wood shingles should not be applied over this type of roofing because they will not dry out readily after a rain and will soon show signs of decay. Shakes, on the other hand, could be laid directly over the old roofing, because they should have a weather-proof material under them.

The better types of roll roofing are slate-chip-covered except for a narrow strip at each edge which is left to be cemented to the next strip. If this jointing is carefully done, no sign of roofing cement is seen, and the roof presents an unbroken surface. When received, the roofing is tightly rolled and should be unrolled, cut in the required lengths and be allowed to flatten out and expand in the sun. Unless this expansion is allowed to take place before the roofing is nailed in position, bulging of the material and unsightly wrinkles will be the result of haste.

Use care in cementing the joints, nail closely with the nails and tins which come with each roll and a very satisfactory roof surface will reward the effort. Use plenty of roofing cement at points where the roofing meets other materials, especially at vertical surfaces, chimneys and dormers. All vertical surfaces will have counter flashings turned down over the roofing which is well mopped into the angle and extended up under the counter flashing.

At the eaves and the projection at gables, the roofing can be bent down and tacked in place if utility is the only controlling factor. Much the nicer method is to use the special galvanized edging which is made for that purpose. This edging forms a neat finish and the roofing material is mopped into the space provided for that use.

Asphalt Shingles

Probably the most universally-used roofing material for new work and for replacing defective material is the asphalt shingle, slate-coated, either single or in strip form. They are made in a variety of grades, colors and weights and the variation in price is a safe index of the difference in quality.

The better qualities are spark-resisting, will not curl and make a pleasing appearance for they blend nicely with most surroundings. Do not, however, use the variegated shapes or the hideous color combinations that are seen on every hand, absolutely ruining any possibility of a charming composition which might otherwise have been obtained. Stick to the square corner, straight-course shingle; avoid diagonal coursing; and, if you must use variegated colors, get the soft shades which will blend into a harmonious combination.

This type of shingle is applied by the same method used for wood shingles, using special bung head nails. Flashings are to be carefully laid at junctions with vertical surfaces. At the eaves, one course of wood shingles should be laid, over which the starting course of asphalt shingles is applied. This prevents breakage at the edge. Better still, use the metal strip at eaves as described for roll roofing. Hips and ridges are formed by laying one course of over-lapping shingles bent over the ridge.

Wood Shingles

Wood shingles are used more than any other type of roof cover-ing due to their low cost and ease of installation. They should be laid with an exposure to the weather varying from four to five inches and should be fastened with coated nails.

When shingling a roof, the proper spacing for the courses is laid off with allowance for the coverage at the ridge by the saddle

Fig. 74. Shingling a hip.

boards. Shingles can be laid to a chalk line or by the better method of a straight edge board, held in place by shingles nailed at the butt on the underside of the board and nails through the tips into the roof. When a course has been completed, the straight edge is driven down and freed from the nails now covered by shingles and moved to the next position (see Fig. 58).

If you want stained shingles the method of staining them on the job is described under shingling of side walls. Or, of course, you can buy them already stained. This stain will add five years to the life of roof shingles and much to the appearance of the roof.

Hips are formed by shingling up the ridge over the other shingles with shingle edges lapping over every other course. One course is laid right over the angle and then trimmed flush and the shingle in the corresponding course is laid out over that and trimmed to its contour. In this way each course is alternated in the lap at the angle. Ridges are capped with saddle boards as described under Outside Trim (Fig. 74).

Flashings

Wherever roof surfaces adjoin a vertical surface such as on chimneys, dormers or walls, it is necessary to flash or make weather-tight the junction by working zinc, tin or copper sheets

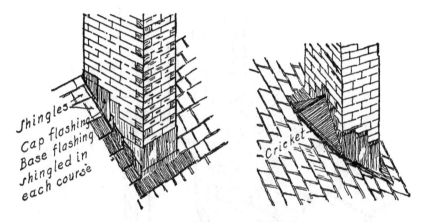

Fig. 75. Ghimney flashing.

into the angle so that one half of the sheet can be laid on top of a course of shingles and the other half can be bent to turn up against the vertical surface.

The turned-up part of the flashing is covered by counter flashing which is worked into the vertical surface and bent down over the flashing. Wherever chimneys adjoin roofing material, counter or cap flashing of three pound sheet lead should be built into the masonry joints at least six inches above the roof surface and, after the flashing is installed, is bent down over the flashing. Roll roofing will not need this separate flashing because the roofing material itself can be turned up against the vertical surface. In this case, a beveled strip of wood should be installed in the angle over which the roofing is laid. This will prevent breaking of the roof-

ing material at the angle. The turned-up roofing is covered by
the counter flashing (Fig. 75).

Wherever a chimney comes in the slope of the roof, a cricket or
small gable should be built on the roof above and back of the
chimney and be covered with metal or roll roofing. This will
divert water and snow and prevent leaks at this point (Fig. 75).

Dormers

If dormers are built on the roof, particular care must be used
to flash with copper or zinc sheets under the window sill in order

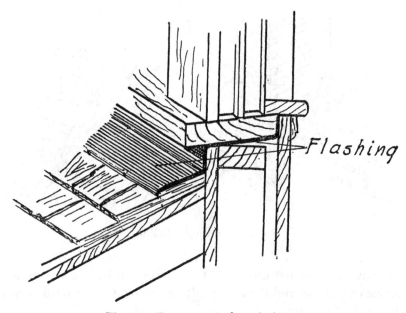

Fig. 76. Dormer window flashing.

to prevent water from being driven under the sill. This is one of
the weakest spots in the defense of a house against rain and snow.
The flashing is made with a sheet of metal, the full length of the
sill, extending under the sill out over the roofing and turned up
and nailed to the back of the sill. The sill should never be so set
that it can rest on the roofing but should be raised sufficiently to
have at least two inches between the underside of the sill and the
roofing. This space is filled with a piece of finish over which the
flashing is formed (Fig. 76).

Where dormer walls join the main roof line, each course of shingles should have a sheet of flashing shingled in and turned up at least six inches against the sides of the dormer. The dormer wall covering extends down over this flashing and is cut off parallel to and about three inches above the roof material.

Gutters

It may not be considered necessary to install gutters on a camp but they will be a necessity over exterior doors and especially on porches to prevent the drip from the eaves being blown into the porch or dropping down the neck of some unsuspecting visitor.

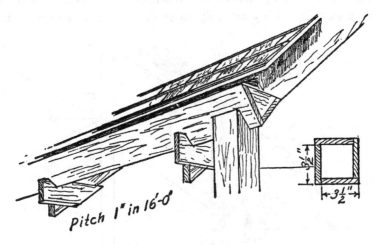

Fig. 77. Board gutter.

The simplest form of gutter is made by securely nailing together two pieces of three-inch stock to form a V-shaped trough. The pieces should be lightly nailed with the joint slightly open, roofing compound run in the angle until it has penetrated the joint and then the sides thoroughly nailed. This will squeeze the compound to a watertight fit. If the joint is made up dry, the natural shrinkage will allow it to leak a stream (Fig. 77).

The gutters should have a uniform pitch throughout their length and care be taken that no sags are allowed in which water can stand. A cord stretched tightly from end to end of the gutter will check this. The gutters can be supported on wood strips, in the top of which a V-cut is made to fit the gutter, nailed to the ends of the rafters.

Appropriate downspouts for this type of gutter can be made by nailing four three-inch strips into a square section with joints well leaded and securely nailed. A V-section is cut in the top of the downspout into which the bottom of the gutter will fit closely. A two-inch hole, bored in the bottom of the gutter into which a short, flanged, lead tube is fitted, leads the water into the downspout.

Molded Gutters

Standard pattern gutters worked out of solid wood are available in most sections. They are easy to erect by nailing to the ends of

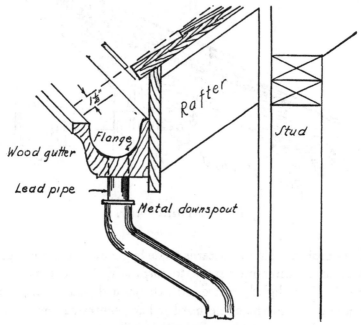

Fig. 78. Molded gutter.

the rafters or to the finish. Pine and fir are the most common woods although cypress or redwood are sometimes available and are much better for their long life properties (Fig. 78).

As these stock gutters are never over sixteen feet in length, it may be necessary to splice to make the required length. The splice

is made by a diagonal cut and not a butt joint and the joint must
have, on the inside surface, a piece of sheet lead lapping the joint,
cut into the wood and bedded in white lead, so that the surface is
flush with the waterway of the gutter. Use copper nails to secure
the lead because the creeping, peculiar to lead, will pull tacks out
of the wood (Fig. 79).

It is customary to use corrugated metal downspouts with these
molded gutters (see Fig. 78). Wood downspouts of circular section are sometimes used into which the wood gutter discharges by

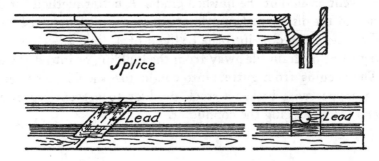

Fig. 79. Splicing wood gutter.

means of a lead pipe goose-neck flanged over on the inside of the
wood gutter and bent in a reverse curve to allow the downspout
to be close to the wall.

Metal Gutters

Metal gutters with special slip-joint fitting requiring no solder,
together with closed ends, goose-neck fittings and downspouts are
listed in mail order catalogues and can be procured direct in some
localities. All joints should be made up in white lead and be installed so that the water will run over and not into the joint.

Metal gutters are made of galvanized steel and must be kept
painted if they are to last any length of time. The most common
type of conductor is the round corrugated and can be had in 2",
2½" and 3" sizes with elbows and fittings to match. An oblong
corrugated section is also available in 2" x 3" and 2½" x 4" sizes
with stock fittings to match.

Metal gutters are suspended from the roof by special stock
metal fittings which should be spaced to give ample support and

prevent sagging between supports. Conductors should be securely fastened to the walls with metal fittings, usually from four to five feet apart and should be wired to the fittings. Conductors are connected to the outlets in the gutters by goose-neck fittings or by a combination of elbow fittings.

If conductors are to discharge directly on the ground, they should be fitted at the foot with an elbow to discharge the water horizontally. The wash from the gutter should be prevented by a special splash board of stone or concrete or a bed of coarse gravel to prevent erosion of the finished grade. A better method for disposing of the discharge from the conductor is to cement the lower end of the conductor into the bell end of a drain tile elbow and carry a line of drain tile away from the building or into dry wells.

The opening from gutters into conductors should be protected by a copper wire basket a stock product to prevent leaves and debris from clogging the conductor.

CHAPTER 11

Fireplaces and Chimneys

A camp and a fireplace are inseparable. The mere mention of either of them brings visions of the charm and delight of the open fire. They are cheerful on rainy days or in frosty weather, but it is in the evening after the appetites are satisfied with camp cooked food and the devotees of Madame Nicotine have commenced their evening rites that the real appeal of the camp hearth is apparent.

The wind may howl like a Banshee around the shack or the rain may beat on roof and windows but snug and sheltered, drowsy and tranquil, the weary mind loses itself in dreamy study of the pictures in the leaping flames and the hypnotic crackle of the glowing coals.

If a fireplace is a part of your building plan for the future but cannot be included at the early stages of the construction, remember what we have already said—do all framing for the proposed construction and fill in the opening with temporary framing and flooring. It may also be advisable to install the rough foundations up to the underside of the floor joists.

First of all a fireplace must be efficient. It must have a good draft and not smoke, it must be safe and not be a fire hazard and it should be attractive and in keeping with its surroundings. In no case, however, should the attempt to gain an artistic effect be accomplished at the expense of efficiency and safety. There are definite rules that establish all dimensions and details of the construction but in addition, there is craftsmanship in the handling of the materials that is difficult for the beginner (Fig. 80).

The first requisite for a good chimney or fireplace is an adequate foundation. This means that the excavation must be carried down to a good bearing soil below any possible frost line. The excavation should be filled with rocks as large as can be handled, laid close and well bedded. The use of cement mortar to slush into all joints and crevices is recommended. At or near the grade line, at least one foot in thickness should be stone and cement to form a firm slab on which brick or stone laid in cement and lime mortar can be carried up to the point where the support of the hearth is to start.

The hearth, which is level with the floor, is supported on masonry if not too high above grade. It can also be carried on a brick arch turned on a wood form from the face of the chimney to a joist header framed in the floor construction. If the brick arch is used, a filling of concrete is put in to a level for the finished hearth material.

The efficiency of a fireplace depends entirely upon three things;

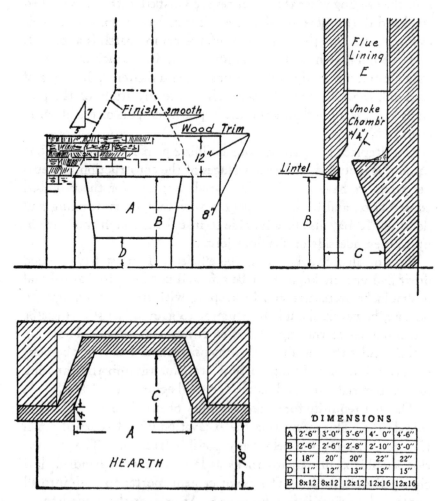

DIMENSIONS

A	2'-6"	3'-0"	3'-6"	4'-0"	4'-6"
B	2'-6"	2'-6"	2'-8"	2'-10"	3'-0"
C	18"	20"	20"	22"	22"
D	11"	12"	13"	15"	15"
E	8x12	8x12	12x12	12x16	12x16

Fig. 80. Fireplace construction.

the fireplace itself, the smoke chamber which is never seen but is more important than the fireplace, and the chimney flue.

We will start with the fireplace itself which is the one part that is seen but depends for its real efficiency on its silent and invisible partner, the smoke chamber (Fig. 80). The width of the fireplace opening should be determined by the size of the room and we start with that dimension because all other dimensions are based upon it. In other words, the width of the opening should be in proportion to the length of the wall in which it is built. Roughly speaking, the opening should be one-sixth of the total length of the wall space of which it is a part. Two feet six inches is the smallest opening that should be used and this looks well on a wall of twelve to fourteen feet in length. This width increases with the size of the room in due proportion. One other controlling factor is the size of wood that is to be burned in the fireplace. Cordwood is cut in lengths of four feet. As few camp dwellers would care to burn four foot lengths, it is sawed into two or three lengths. Sawed once it can be burned in a fireplace three feet wide; sawed twice, in a two-foot-six opening.

The height of the opening should not be over two-thirds of the width but not less than thirty inches. The depth should be not less than eighteen inches. Twenty inches is better and twenty-four inches should be the maximum for the largest sizes.

If the fireplace itself is to throw out the maximum of heat, the sides should splay or slant towards the back and the back should slope forward from a point one-third the height from the floor to form the throat, which is four inches wide and should extend the full width of the fireplace opening. The throat should be set from four to eight inches above the lintel which forms the top of the fireplace opening. The finished front of the fireplace should be designed both for safety and appearance. The side jambs should be at least twelve inches wide and, for large openings, even wider to maintain due proportion between the fireplace and the room itself.

Proper throat construction is vital for an efficient fireplace and this point must be carefully watched. The slope of the back will allow the construction of a smoke shelf which should also be the full length of the opening and be leveled off at a point above the fireplace opening.

At this point let us urge you to spend a little money. A cast iron combination throat and damper, properly made of heavy material, will insure that this most vital point is correctly made. The use of the damper allows an economical use of firewood. A roaring fire may require a full opening but slow burning logs will need only a small opening, preventing loss of heat up the chimney. The damper should be hinged at the back of the frame and, when open,

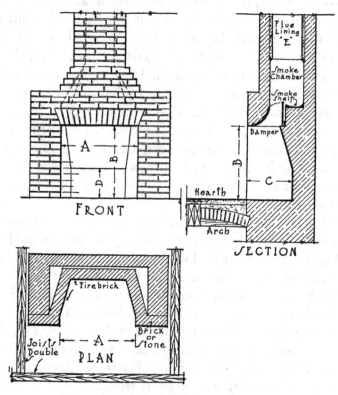

Fig. 81. Fireplace with iron damper.

will tend to prevent smoke being driven into the room by down drafts. When the fireplace is not in use, the damper can be entirely closed, keeping bugs out and warm air in. The combination has the further advantage in that it furnishes the support for the fireplace opening except in the extreme sizes where additional bars or angles may be needed (Fig. 81).

We now have the smoke shelf built and the damper set. The next step is the construction of the smoke chamber, that impor-

tant, unseen partner. The smoke chamber is the space from the
top of the throat to the flue itself. The side walls start at the top
of the smoke shelf and are drawn in gradually to the size of the
chimney flue. This angle should never be more than at the ratio
of one foot for each eighteen inches of rise and should be made into
a smooth surface with cement mortar not less than one half inch
thick. You now have a large and commodious smoke chamber
with a gradual and smoothly finished slope to the top which is
reduced to the actual size of the flue or chimney.

The flue, or chimney, is the third partner in the efficient fireplace and on its height, size and lining much depends. For its size
we again go back to that controlling width of the fireplace. The
total area of the fireplace opening, width multiplied by height,
determines the minimum size of the flue, which should never be
less than one-twelfth of the fireplace opening area. The smallest
flue should be eight by twelve inches and that may not be sufficient
unless all other conditions are perfect. The efficiency of the chimney increases with the height. Terra cotta flue linings should
always be used, starting on top of the smoke chamber and carried

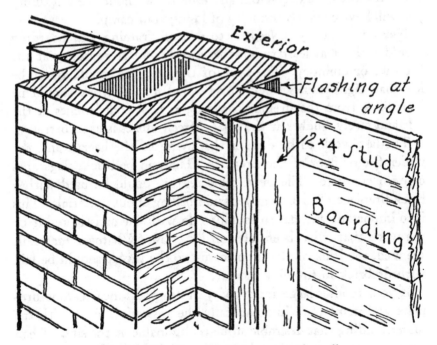

Fig. 82. Bonding chimney to outside wall.

to a point just above the top of the chimney. All joints should be well bedded in mortar, joints wiped clean on the inside and, the the space between lining and brick, well slushed with mortar. The chimney should be carried well above any roof surface or ridges, never less than four feet.

Remember that a chimney on the outside will never work as well as one inside the walls. It will work but not as well. If the fireplace and chimney are built partly in and out on a wooden wall, a four-inch projection should be built as a part of the chimney construction against which the wall studding is placed. Then the outside sheathing can lap over the projection against the chimney. Needless to say, careful attention should be given to metal flashing at this point as well as at roof surfaces which the chimney may penetrate (Fig. 82).

We have not said anything about an ashpit under the fireplace and its cleanout door with the ash dump in the hearth. We say this for these things in a camp fireplace. NO. There are plenty of uses about a camp for wood ashes. Therefore, clean out the fireplace when needed, always leaving a good bed because the fire will burn better and give out more heat. Without the ash dump you will have one less possibility of losing your camp.

Now as to safety. Needless to say, all framing and boarding should be kept at least two inches away from all masonry at the fireplace or chimney. The back of the fireplace should never be less than eight inches thick. Any wood mantel work should be kept back from the fireplace opening at least eight inches at the side and twelve inches at the top—fifteen inches is even better.

The last work to be done is the laying of the hearth and the under-fire or floor of the fireplace. This can be brick, flagstones or even concrete. Tile of suitable texture could be used with a brick fireplace. We have as yet said nothing about materials. This is so important and has so much to do with the artistic result of the work that it has been left until the last. Whatever materials are used, the back of the fireplace up to the throat should be laid with firebrick in fire clay mortar.

If your room is large and woodsy in its appearance, a stone fireplace and mantel are just naturally the answer. This is with the understanding that desirable stone is obtainable at the site. When we say stone, do not misunderstand us and think of using paving

BRICK

BRICK

STONE

STONE WITH WOOD MANTEL

WOOD MANTEL

TRIM FOR PINE PANELWORK

Fig. 83. Mantel designs.

stone. Nothing could be in poorer taste than the monotonous regularity and chilling greyness of that combination. But if you can get stone with variegated surfaces, especially seam-faced, with life and color you are truly fortunate (Fig. 83).

Brick in endless variety is always practicable and in good taste, but beware the mason who likes to crochet with brick. The more simple the pattern, the less detriment to the room. A stone fireplace and chimney breast need no trimming other than a mantel if you must have one. This can be made of cement or with rock and cement but beware the dovecots and catch-alls with which some chimney breasts have been punctured with the mistaken idea that they are cute.

If the room should be finished in knotty pine or similar material, nothing could be more artistic and restful than a plain brick facing around which the paneling is cut. A wide-molded frame, mitered at the corners, around the top and sides of the opening requires no mantel which, after all, is a catch-all, and adds nothing to the appearance.

In connction with the construction of the fireplace, an economical source of hot water is obtained by the installation of a trombone coil of ¾″ brass pipe of three lengths which is exposed on the fireplace back at a point well above the fuel line. This coil is connected to a hot water tank in the kitchen and an ample supply of hot water is always available during such periods as the fireplace is in use. Even a little waste material on chilly mornings will provide an astonishing amount of hot water.

Fireplace Heating Unit

In the larger type of camp you might be interested in the possibility of a metal heating assembly built into the fireplace construction and forming a heating chamber between the fireplace and the masonry. Grilles in the side of the chimney breast open into this chamber and flues and discharge heat either into the upper part of the room or into an adjacent room. It allows a circulation of air which is heated from the fireplace, utilizing heat which would otherwise be lost. In effect, this unit converts a fireplace into a hot air heater, without in any way detracting from the appearance or appeal of the fireplace. It's great advantage is that the room is heated by a circulation of air and is uniformly warm instead of by direct heat with its attendant cold corners. These units are manufactured by several firms and full directions for installation are furnished with the units.

Brick Chimneys

While we have discussed the construction of chimneys in connection with fireplaces, a few suggestions are included here for the construction of chimneys used for stoves or heating units. Chimneys may be built without flue lining in order to save money, but in the long run the added expense will be justified. This is true not only from the standpoint of durability but that of safety. How often in your travels do you see a chimney standing stark and alone, surrounded by the few charred remains of a camp! The chimney survived the fire but was also the cause.

Most chimneys are built with walls only one brick thick and the best of masons cannot entirely fill the end joints between bricks with mortar. A few years use, mortar drying out, joints opening—a hot ember sneaks out of the flue where it belongs and all that are left are the stack and charred ruins.

Above all things, if you do not use the flue lining, do not allow the parging or plastering with mortar on the inside of the chimney. This looks practicable but the mortar dries out, in time falls off and in so doing, pulls some of the mortar out of the joints. Be careful of the openings into the chimney. Use a piece of terra cotta tile to form the opening for the smoke pipe into the chimney. Keep all woodwork away from the chimney especially at the point where the stove pipe enters.

All brick chimneys should be capped out with concrete or the top courses of brick will soon become loosened. Do not make the top flat but rather on a slope. The wind, blowing across the top and deflected by the slant, tends to increase the draft.

Metal Smoke Stacks

In small camps, and even as a temporary substitute for a chimney in large camps, a metal smoke pipe can be installed for stoves which will be satisfactory and safe, if properly installed. Where the pipe pierces the roof, it should be fitted with a metal collar plate to eliminate any possibility of overheating woodwork or roofing. This collar should be located as near the ridge line as possible and the top of the chimney should reach well above the ridge line. The pipe above the roof should be made of galvanized iron, fitted with a shanty cap and securely guyed with galvanized iron or copper wire. The pipe should be painted frequently with aluminum paint. The pipe inside the building should be black iron and can be painted with special stove pipe enamel (Fig. 84).

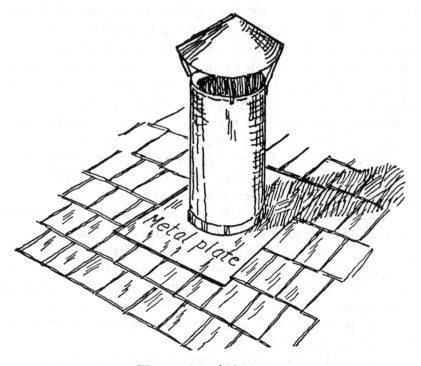

Fig. 84. Metal chimney.

All pipe should be well made with locked seams and made so that each length will fit tightly into the next section. Do not attempt to use the flat material which is made into pipe on the job. If a stove is set near a wall and the smoke pipe is set vertically to the underside of the roof, follows the slope of the roof and then pierces the roof, the maximum benefit of the heat in the pipe will be utilized.

Tile Chimney

Even better than the metal smoke pipe and yet low in cost, is an outside chimney made of terra cotta drain tile. This is usually supported on a timber bracket just below the entrance of the stove pipe. The lower, or first, section is a T section with the lower end filled with cement and an extension from the T is carried inside the wall where the hub end receives the stove pipe. The sections of the drain tile should be set with the hubs up and the joints well filled with cement mortar (Fig. 85).

Stoves

There is a wide range of stoves available to meet the needs of utility and the budget, either as a cooking or heating medium or a

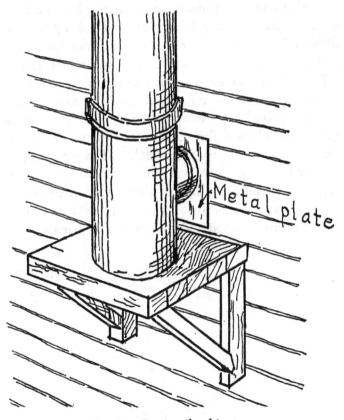

Fig. 85. Drain-tile chimney.

combination of the two. The simplest and most practicable unit in a small camp, or in the kitchen of a large one, is a laundry type cast iron stove. This has a square top with four holes and a round body burning wood or coal. A stove pipe oven, available through the mail order houses, set just above the stove will bake and roast to perfection and uses only waste heat.

A brass coil of one turn around the inside of the firebox and connected to an open metal tank, set above the level of the stove, will provide ample hot water. Here in this one unit is ample heating for a single room camp, complete cooking equipment and hot water supply.

Kitchen ranges with ovens of sizes from small to large are next in order for the culinary needs. If your camp is used in the summer, and you object to the heat from a wood or coal stove, there are excellent oil stoves now on the market. There is now available at a reasonable cost, compressed gas in tanks which makes possible the use of gas stoves, gas refrigerators and gas lights. The tanks are furnished in pairs which are housed in a metal cabinet outside the building. One container is used at a time, the other kept for a spare. You will find a company dealing in this gas near your camp.

For heating the living room and adjacent rooms, one of the newer types of sheet iron, airtight stoves will heat to an astonishing degree and hold fire almost like a coal stove. These are desirable where wood is the only fuel available. The next type of heater is the old-fashioned parlor stove which will burn either wood or coal. You can find any number of them at a low price in second-hand stove stores. We prefer coal as fuel for it does not require as much attention as wood and the fire can be banked at night.

CHAPTER 12

Interior Woodwork

Finished Floors

The first work to be done on the inside of the camp will be the laying of the finished floors. In a residence this is usually one of the last things for obvious reasons. In a camp which will have few if any partitions, the finished floor can be laid over the entire floor area and the partitions erected later. This procedure has one great advantage in that changes in partition layout can be made at any time without change or patching of flooring.

Floors are subject to more wear and require more care than any other portion of the camp. It is therefore true economy to use the best of materials for this purpose. A single floor of matched boards might be sufficient for the summer camp, but only as a temporary makeshift should it be considered.

The finished floor should be laid with dressed and matched material, thoroughly dry, and securely nailed and driven tightly together. Square edge boards nailed through the surface may look well for a time, but invariably the boards will shrink and leave cracks the full thickness of the flooring. These cracks will always be spewing out the dirt which necessarily collects in every crevice. In some localities, there is a type of soft wood flooring with a ship lap joint. This type makes a close joint like a tongued edge but requires surface nailing. It may add to the atmosphere of some types of camps.

The first point to be decided is whether the floor is to be painted, covered with linoleum, or finished natural. Spruce, fir or pine if properly laid and kept painted will make a satisfactory floor material. If natural finish floors are desired, hard pine, birch, maple and oak in standard flooring material are satisfactory. Hard pine or fir should be rift-sawed to prevent splintering. If you will look at Fig. 86, you will see why this is so. Rift-sawing (*c*), or quarter sawing as it is more often called, produces boards in which the grain is perpendicular to the surface; slash sawing (*a*), on the other hand, produces boards which in a majority of cases have the grain running at an angle with the surface and the thin edges of these layers splinter off very easily. If linoleum is to be used, a finished floor of narrow, tongued and grooved material that will not buckle must be laid. All joints or rough edges must be smoothed

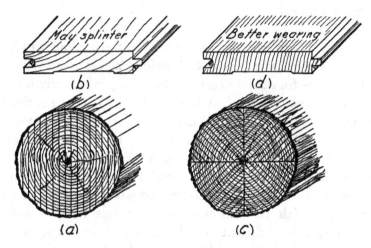

Fig. 86. Slash sawing and quarter sawing: (*a*) slash sawing, (*b*) slash-sawed flooring, (*c*) rift or quarter sawing, (*d*) rift-sawed flooring.

because the linoleum will show every one of them after a little time. For toilet rooms and kitchen floors, even in a rough camp, you cannot beat linoleum, properly laid, for ease of care and long life.

All finished floor should be laid over a layer of building paper on the rough floor, with joints well lapped and edges butting the shoe at the exterior wall framing line. At least use a waterproof paper and, if the camp is to be used in cold weather, put down heavy roll roofing. It will repay its cost for at no point of the camp is it more important to have sufficient insulation than at the floor. In the average camp no point is more neglected. We repeat —don't spare the insulating material at this point. One can always sheath walls if necessary but to replace the lack of insulation at the floor is another matter.

If possible, a finished floor should be laid at right angles to the under floor. If the upper floor is laid in the same direction as the under floor, any shrinkage or movement of the under flooring will affect the finished floor. For this reason, we have recommended that the under floor be laid diagonally. While this will result in some waste when cutting boards it does not involve much added labor.

Finished flooring should be laid with the first board fitted to the baseboard or at the shoe which forms the base of the exterior wall. If there is any possibility that this wall edge is not perfectly straight, a chalk line should be snapped parallel to and at a distance of a little less than the width of the first strip of flooring. The first board is then so fitted to the wall line that the inner edge of the strip coincides with the chalk line. This procedure will start the flooring with straight joints. The tongue edge of the board is the outer edge and the next strip is driven onto it after it has been toenailed to the underfloor. The wall edge of the first strip of flooring will have to be secured by driving the nails through the board and setting the nails with a nail set (Fig. 87).

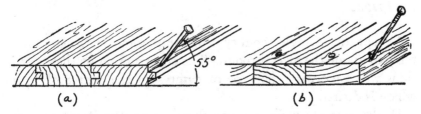

Fig. 87. Toenailing: (*a*) matched flooring, (*b*) square-edged flooring.

Each strip is then driven on to the tongue of the preceding strip and toenailed through the tongue. As butt joints will have to occur in each line of flooring, the joints should be arranged to stagger at least two feet to prevent a line of joints being conspicuous. To assist in driving each board into position, a short piece of flooring should be used with the groove edge placed over the tongue of the strip to be driven home. This will avoid battering and damaging the tongue.

To lay the last two strips with tight joints, the wall edge of the last strip should be fitted to the wall and the width of the last strip should be such that the two strips, placed in position, will hump up at the joint. Driving this hump down will force the two strips into close fit with each other and the wall.

Each piece of flooring should be nailed every eighteen inches with the nails well set. Even when well set, they should not show when the next piece of flooring is put in position. With hardwood flooring, it is advisable to dip the nail in soap or wax and, if the flooring is especially hard, it may be necessary to drill for the nails. Flooring is usually nailed with 8-penny cut nails or with flooring brads made for the purpose. For soft woods, an 8-penny coated nail will give better holding strength.

Soft wood floors may have to be smoothed at the joints but will not require any scraping. Hardwood floors, on the other hand, will require scraping and sanding. The scraping is hard work if it is to be done by hand. If a power sanding machine can be used, the work can be quickly and easily done as the only hand work will be in corners and against walls. If you must have nice hardwood floors, it will pay to import the necessary skill and experience to finish them properly.

Partitions

Except in the single-room type of camp, some partitions will be built to divide the several rooms. The construction of these partitions will vary with the type of camp and the degree of finish which is desired.

If the exterior walls are not sheathed on the inside and the framing is exposed, the easiest type to build and the one which costs the least, is made of dressed and matched boards set vertically. We are talking of the wide boards of pine or spruce and not the narrow width so commonly used. For this type of partition, special molded members can be obtained both for base and cap. Another member with side rails and head members forms a door frame with rabbet for 1⅜" door (Fig. 88).

The floor and cap treatment can be accomplished with ⅞" quarter-round molding nailed to floor and ceiling if there is one, against which the boards are nailed. The partition is finished by nailing another quarter-round molding against the boards at the floor and top on the opposite side. Unless a heavy weight, like a lavatory, is to be supported, no studding is required.

If the inner face of the exterior wall is to be sheathed or covered with a finish material, the partitions can be built with studding set vertically on a floor shoe. The studs should be spaced on twenty-four-inch centers which will allow the use of standard four-foot wide material without wasteful cutting. If vertical sheathing is to be used on the partition, an extra horizontal nailing piece should be cut in between the studs and halfway between top and shoe.

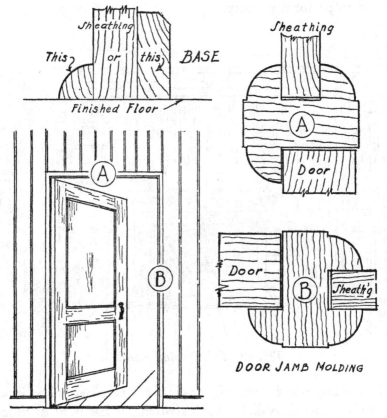

Fig. 88. Door-jamb moldings for sheathing partitions.

At the present time, knotty pine sheathing with beveled and molded edges is much in vogue and has much to commend it where a finished and artistic treatment is desired. A variety of patterns are on the market and the material is easy to install and finish. Window and door trim should be in harmony with the period which it represents. This type of molded edge sheathing should not extend to and rest on the floor because the numerous recesses invite dirt and are impossible to clean. A base board, at least four inches high with a slight bevel on top, should first be installed. This base board should be set forward from the wall so that the face projects beyond the face of the sheathing. Then the sheathing is bevel-cut at the bottom to make a close joint on top of the base board. The addition of a quarter-round molding around the walls at the floor line protects the walls and allows a broom to perform its duty.

Fig. 89. Knotty-pine interior.

Like many other materials, originally a necessity when it was the only material available for partitions, it has been developed with very pleasing results when properly used. It is absurd to use it as a wall lining and then apply *over* it the same type of finish around door and window openings as would ordinarily be used with modern plaster work.

Window and door openings are finished by using a square edge of the sheathing as if it were a casing on the sides of the frames but flush with and tongued to the sheathing, not planted *over* the sheathing (Figs. 89 and 90[B, D]). At the head a piece of the

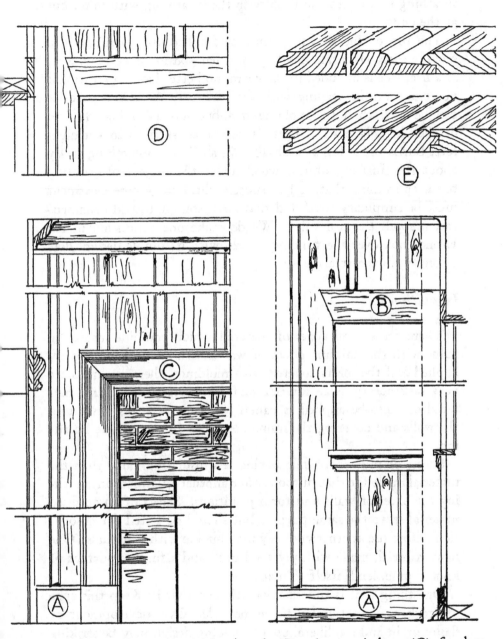

Fig. 90. Knotty-pine trim: (A) baseboard, (B) trim at window, (C) fireplace rim, (D) trim at door, (E) typical types.

sheathing is cut into and flush with the sheathing, with miter cut at the ends.

The top of the sheathing may be finished with a simple cap mold, a more elaborate molding, or a half-beam effect (Fig. 89). If a fireplace is included in the room, no better looking treatment nor one more in keeping with the real early American practice can be used than the molding member shown in Fig. 89 and detailed in (Fig. 90C). There is no mantel shelf to collect cigarette burns and act as a catch-all. We shall have something to say about the finishing of this wood under the subject of painting but keep in mind that, to be a success, this knotty pine treatment must be simplicity itself and that any attempt to add ornamentation spoils the real value. We do make one concession in the valence box over the window which, with its simple design, does belong with the treatment.

Insulation

There are several types of material which combine insulating value with the finishing effect of wall sheathing. When properly applied and the joints covered with moldings, these materials are very satisfactory as an interior surface covering. The same material can also be applied as panels between the studs, insulating the walls and covering the numerous joints in the outside boarding.

Sheets of plywood, while having less insulating value than the material made for that purpose, offer another treatment in sheathing the exterior walls and form partitions. Sheets of compressed material serve the same purpose but should be tested for absorption before use as otherwise they may buckle with dampness. One new material, made with plywood back and a finished surface of knotty pine, lends itself to many uses.

One thing that is almost axiomatic and that is: Keep this type of work as simple and plain as possible. Over-development of flashy grain and too liberal use of molding design may be striking at first but soon becomes glaring and obnoxious. Soft, even tones and absence of gingerbread moldings will always be restful and harmonious.

Whatever type of partitions are to be built, one point must be emphatically impressed on your mind. Any partitions enclosing a toilet, if you are fortunate enough to have one, should be of soundproof construction. So also should any partitions separating bedrooms. This sound deadening can be accomplished in several ways and at very little cost during construction. With the several forms of sound-deadening material in common use, it is a very simple matter to build partitions that are soundproof. A partition in the average summer camp is sadly lacking in qualities which are conducive to privacy and retirement.

Kitchen

Probably the completion of the kitchen and its facilities will be the first in order. The installation of the sink and drainboards, the cook's work counter with cupboards and drawers, and numerous shelves will complete this unit and allow the cook to reign undisturbed in his or her own domain (Fig. 91).

Sink

The sink need not necessarily be large, but should be set under a window and at a height that will permit work without backache. If you have followed our advice, the window is already set at a height from the floor which will allow the sink and its back to be set under the stool and not across the window itself.

The sink should be from thirty-four to thirty-six inches above the floor and never less than thirty-two inches. For a small kitchen a thirty-inch sink will suffice, although a thirty-six inch length is better. If the sink is installed in a one room cabin with room at a premium, the twenty-four inch size will work out. Preferably, the sink should be enameled iron with a one-piece back. If the costs are to be kept to a minimum, a wood back either painted or covered with zinc will do nicely. At least get an enameled sink and not the plain cast-iron affairs so often seen.

The sink will probably be installed in connection with drainboards and a work shelf. If not of the self-supporting type, the sink will have to be supported on a framework of four- or five-inch stuff which is made a part of the assembly. Cover the drain boards or work shelves with good, sound, matched boards running

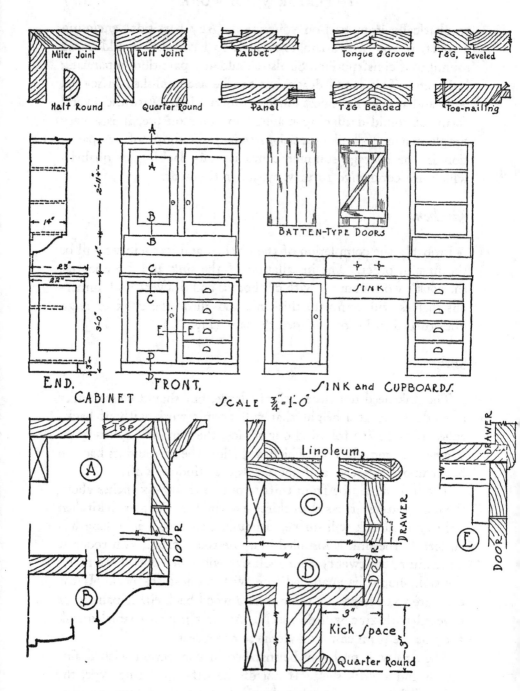

Fig. 91. Kitchen details.

188

lengthwise and, where not resting on cupboards or drawer cases, support the frame with diagonal braces to the wall.

The work shelf and drainboards should then be covered with linoleum. Remnants suitable for this purpose can be purchased at surprisingly low cost. Run a piece of hardwood half-round molding, or even aluminum molding, around the exposed edges with molding flush with the top of the linoleum. See that all nails are well set and all joints are smooth. The top of the drainboards or shelves should be well cleated with screws from the bottom. Be sure to lay the linoleum over a layer of felt, the whole cemented down with plenty of linoleum cement. Rub linoleum down and put weights over padding to hold down until dry. This working surface has no superior except tile and that, certainly, one would not expect in a camp. Complete all counter tops by fitting the useful quarter-round molding at the angle between the top and the walls.

Cupboards and Drawers

On one side of the sink, the counter can be supported on a set of drawers. These cases of drawers can be purchased complete, ready to case in and cover, at a price almost less than the cost of materials were you to build them yourself. It is not practicable nor good economy to attempt to make them unless you are a cabinet maker and have access to power tools. We advise leaving open the space under the sink.

Above counters with about fourteen inches between counter top and cupboard, numerous cupboards with either open shelves or doors can be constructed. These are easy to build and a liberal and frequent use of the level and plumb will assure the proper swing of the doors. It is usually better to stop the top of the cupboards at a point seven feet above the floor than it is to run them to the ceiling (Fig. 91).

Making Cupboards and Drawers

For the benefit of those who might like to make their own drawer cases and drawers, we shall explain some of the essentials of this type of work.

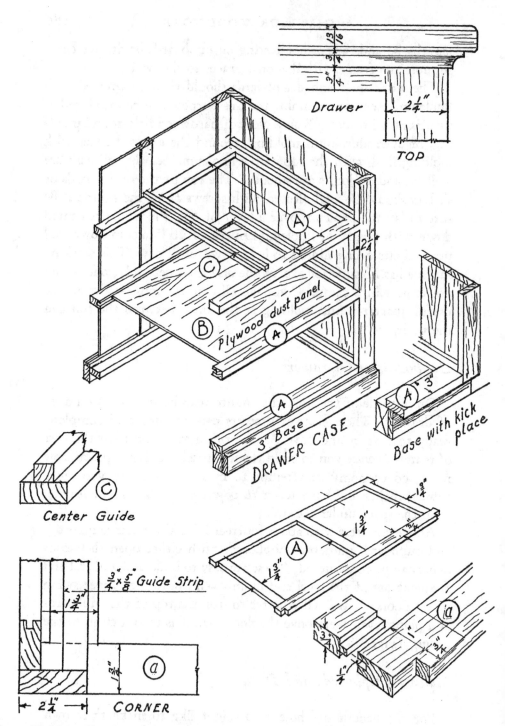

Fig. 92. Drawer-case construction: (A) drawer slide, (B) dust panel, (C) center guide.

In the first place, a drawer case is a framework in which the drawers may run easily (Fig. 92). The sides and back may be paneled, sheathed, or left uncovered; but the framework is the same in any case. The most important feature is the drawer slide, on which the drawer does slide. This may be just a stick fastened to the side of the case, but the best and the fundamental construction is shown at (A) in Fig. 92. If dust-proof drawers are desired, a plywood panel is framed in as shown at (B). The front corners are notched (a) to make front edge of frame flush with the side casing. Instructions for notching, mortising, and gaining are given on page 209.

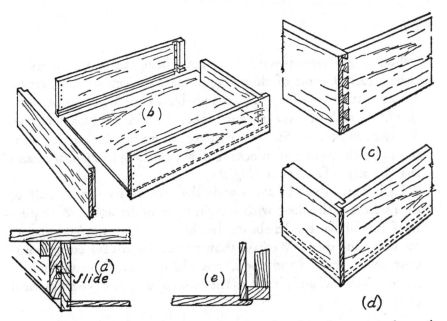

Fig. 93. Drawer construction: (a) slide, (b) plain front, (c) dovetail, (d) ploughed, (e) lip front.

A long drawer needs a center guide to ensure easy operation without jambing at one end. This construction is shown at (C). Blocks glued on the bottom of the drawer on each side of the guide strip hold the drawer in correct alignment.

A drawer in its simplest form is a box, made to slide. In fact, a good strong box can be made into a drawer by nailing a strip on each side which will run in guides secured under a table or bench top (Fig. 93 [a]). The sides of a drawer are rabbeted into the front and nailed to the front as shown (*b*). This prevents the front being pulled *off* the drawer, which would happen if the nailing were through the front into the ends of the sides. At (*c*) is shown a dovetailed corner and at (*d*) is shown a special machine-cut corner.

All four sides of the drawer are rabbeted to receive the bottom, usually of plywood. If plain lumber is used for the bottom, the back piece should not be rabbeted at the bottom (*b*) but should be cut to allow the bottom to slide in the grooves of the side pieces. Expansion will take place *under* the back piece and not push it out of position.

Closets

Full-length closets—and there never seem to be too many of them—can be built of sheathing or partition material wherever convenient or possible. Closets in which clothing is to be hung should be at least twenty-four inches deep in order that clothes hangers can be used. St. Peter's ledger has more debit entries occasioned by the results of knocking down clothing in shallow closets than by any other reason (Fig. 94).

Each closet should have a wide shelf about five and a half to six feet from the floor with hanging rod underneath. A sloping shelf just above the baseboard height is a much needed support for boots and shoes. We have shown some designs for corner cupboards with molded and sawed tops which are easy to construct in place. They will add charm to the room as well as serve a practical purpose.

Interior Door Frames

We have already spoken of stock moldings from which door frames, in sheathing partitions can be made. In other types of partitions, the frames will be made preferably from rabbeted stock to fit the thickness of the partition. Simple and narrow casings will cover the joint between frame and wall construction.

When erecting frames, be sure that the jambs are perfectly plumb, parallel and without wind or twist if the doors are to swing properly. This means constant use of the level. No thresh-

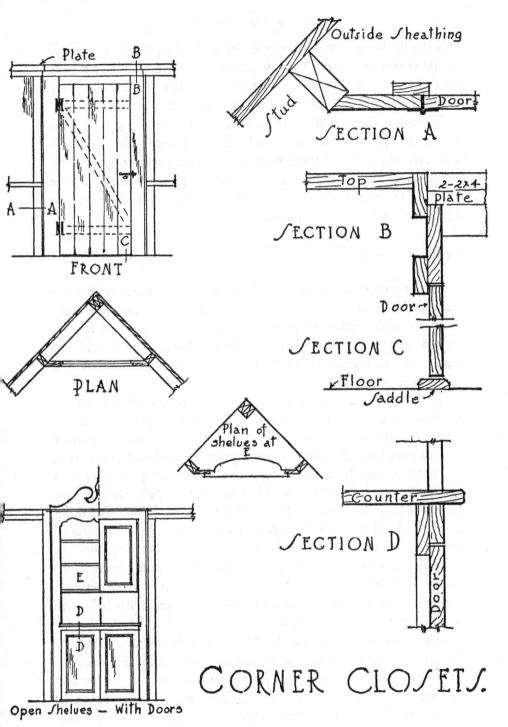

Plate

B
B

Stud

Outside Sheathing

Door

SECTION A

A — A

FRONT

PLAN

Top

2-2×4
plate

SECTION B

Door →

SECTION C

Floor
Saddle

Plan of
shelves at
E

Counter

SECTION D

Door

E

D

D

Open Shelves — With Doors

CORNER CLOSETS.

Fig. 94.

193

olds should be used for interior doors with the possible exception of bathroom openings. We say rabbeted frames because we have never had any success with nailed-on stops. Nail as you will, they will still roll off and show daylight between stop and jamb.

Sheathing doors which are to be hung in sheathing partitions can be hung in an opening cut in the partition material, and a stop can be provided by screwing a two- or three-inch piece with miter joints at the top to make a finish against which the door closes. This is easy and cheap but shows end grain in the partition boards at the top of the opening.

Interior Doors

The construction of interior doors follows to some extent the same details as described for exterior doors. The types will vary from the plain batten door to the ready-made paneled doors purchased from a manufacturer. Cupboard doors should be of the same type as the room doors with the same details of construction (Fig. 95).

The simplest door is made from stock sheathing with two cross battens and a diagonal batten serving as a brace to prevent sagging. Sheathing should be matched but avoid the use of the narrow beaded patterns. The plain sheathing with edges beveled almost to the tongue, has character and is in keeping with your camp. If doors are made of square-edge boards, and they have their merits, the cracks should be covered with half-round molding. The doors on the bedrooms at "Dunwurken" were constructed from dressed hemlock boards, a wide one in the center and narrower ones at the sides. On the entrance side, the edges of the joints have a deep bevel. On the room side, three battens and cross bracing between the middle and lower battens and joints covered with half-inch molding make a pleasing design.

In a pine-sheathed room, the doors are in harmony if made of the same material or they can be copies of early paneled doors.

In addition to the types of door construction included under room doors, a very neat and easily-made cupboard door can be fabricated from screen frame stock or any narrow wood stock. Miter the frame stock and on the frame thus made, apply a piece of plywood, leaving a border of one inch between the edge of the

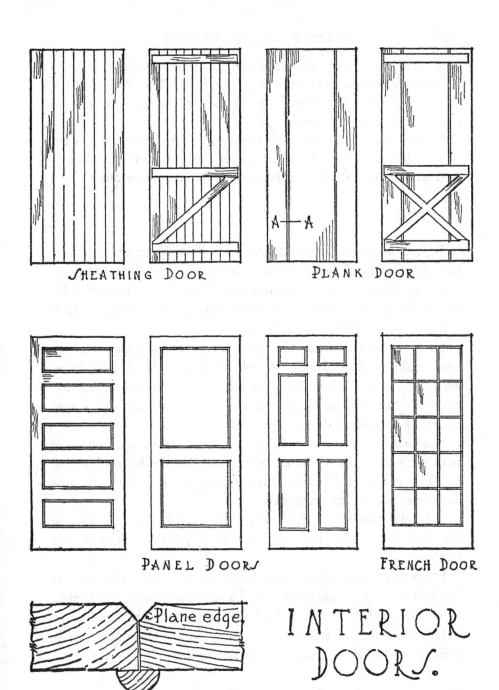

SHEATHING DOOR   PLANK DOOR

A — A

PANEL DOORS   FRENCH DOOR

Plane edge

SECTION "A-A"

INTERIOR
DOORS.

Fig. 95.

195

panel and outer edges of the frame. Another method uses rabbeted stock in which the plywood panel is set. The corners of the
frame can either be mitered or the top and bottom rail can be
butt-jointed between the side pieces.

If available, cupboard doors can be cut from five-ply veneer,
⅝″ thick and will need no battens to prevent curling. The appearance of these doors is in keeping with the surroundings.

To Hang a Door

If your door is a framed door,.you will find projecting lugs at
top and bottom. Saw off the lugs. Plane the hinge edge of door,
then the lock edge, to fit the opening, allowing ⅟₁₆″ on each edge
for clearance. The lock edge should have a slight bevel to allow
the door to swing into the rabbet.

Plane the door to fit at the top, then scribe and plane the bottom, making allowance for threshold if any. If there is none,
allow at least ½″ at bottom to clear rugs. Set the door in position
and by wood wedges place it in the rabbet to show the proper
clearance on sides and top.

Mark the location of the butts or hinges, remove the door, and
with try square and marking gauge mark for the hinges both on
the door and on the jamb. With a sharp chisel outline the cuts
and chisel out for the butt seat.

Take the pins out of the butts, screw each half in its place on
the door and on the jamb, set the door in position, and put pins
in place.

If the door shows too much space at the hinge side, the cuts for
the butts must be made deeper; if the door binds at the hinge side,
a piece of cardboard under the hinge will relieve the trouble.

It is somewhat of a trick to properly hang a door but a little
patience and study will accomplish all things!

Combination Dish Closet and Table

When space is at a premium, especially in a one-room camp,
a dish closet and table can be combined. The dish closet is built
as usual with the bottom shelf thirty inches from the floor. The

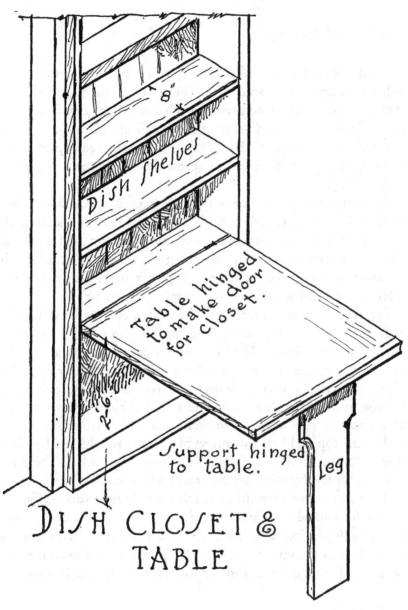

Fig. 96.

door of the closet is hinged at the bottom to drop down on a supporting leg to form a table. At meal time a convenient table for four people is available and at other times the closet takes up only twelve inches of the floor space (Fig. 96).

Tables and Benches

Once the roof is on and the camp closed in, some sort of table will be needed for general use. The simplest table, and yet one that is sturdy, can be constructed with four legs cut from your 2″ x 4″ stock, with a 4″-wide skirt board at the top and a top made of wide boards. Nail a ¾″ x 4″ piece across each pair of legs and a similar ¾″ x 4″ stretcher across the top of these two pieces (Fig. 97[a]).

At "Dunwurken" we made two tables with sawbuck-type legs of 2″ x 4″ halved together, with two stretchers connecting the two sets of legs. The maple tops were glued up for us at a near-by shop. One table was used in the living room and the other on the screened porch. When a large group was to be seated the two tables end to end would seat ten people (Fig. 97[b]).

For the ambitious carpenter, the real trestle table is detailed (Fig. 97[c]). The legs are halved together (d) and a mortise is cut through the joint. The two sets are connected by a stretcher (e) with a tongue fitting into the mortise and tightly locked in place by a wedge driven down in a narrow mortise cut in the tongue of the stretcher. The completed table is shown at (f). One point to remember when making a table with sawbuck legs is that the top and bottom spread of the legs should not be equal. The width across the top should be several inches (2″ in this case) less than at the bottom. If the cross legs were made with the top and bottom the same width, the table would *look* top heavy.

Benches can be made of 2″ plank 11″ wide and the same length as the table, on legs cut from the same size plank, with saw cut at the foot as shown (g). The plank is well spiked onto the supports and braces are fitted under the top to make the legs rigid.

Gadgets

The spaces between studding, whether sheathed on the inside or not, offer intriguing possibilities for all sorts of practical uses.

Book shelves can be made from 7″ to 10″ stock as shelves cut in between side pieces nailed inside the studs (Fig. 98[a]). Newspaper and magazine racks are made by using side pieces, 4″ wide at

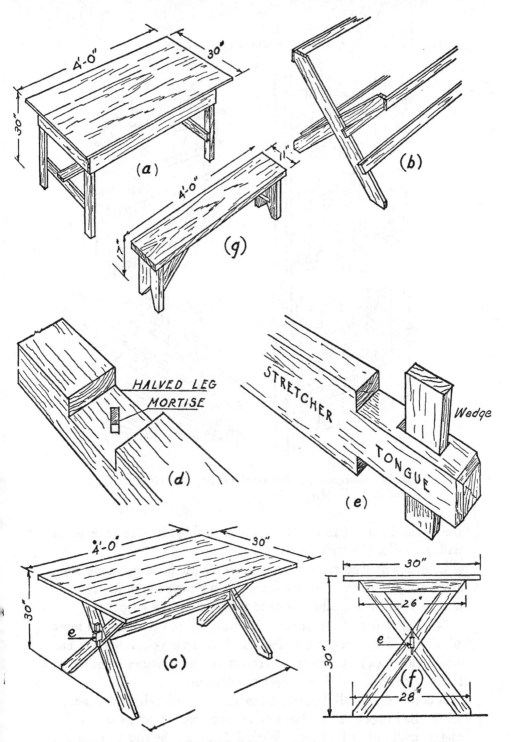

Fig. 97. Tables and benches: (*a*) plain table, (*b*) sawbuck table, (*c*) mortised
stretcher type, (*d*) halving legs, (*e*) stretcher, (*f*) end view of (*c*), (*g*) bench.

Fig. 98. Gadgets: (*a*) bookshelves, (*b*) magazine rack, (*c*) shoe shelves, (*d*) plain shelf.

the bottom and 5″ to 6″ at the top, across which are screwed or nailed 1½″ x ½″ strips (*b*).

Convenient shoe racks to keep shoes off the floor are made from any available stock. The back strip is set far enough in front of outside boarding to allow heels to drop below the strip (*c*).

Wide shelves in bedrooms with a hanging rod underneath serve admirably for closets when lack of floor space prevents the enclosed closet (*d*). Curtains of attractive material can be hung on the outside of this shelf to cover the contents.

A convenient wall desk can be made of boards with cleats across the ends, hinged at the bottom and supported when in use by metal braces or sash chains. With a catch at the top to hold the lid when it is folded up against the casing, you have a disappearing desk (Fig. 99).

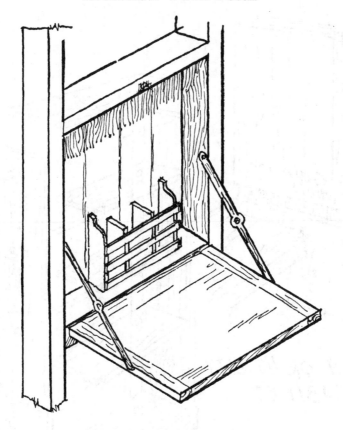

WALL DE/K

Fig. 99.

Narrow, horizontal spaces above window heads need only a board hinged at the top and a catch at the bottom to become convenient storage spaces for medicines, toilet articles, and supplies.

A free-standing bookcase or dish or utility cabinet is shown in Fig. 100.

Seats

Built-in seats will sprout almost of their own accord. It may be a long, cushioned lounging place under a window with storage space for bedding underneath or it may be part of a corner to make a dining nook in combination with a table (Fig. 101). It

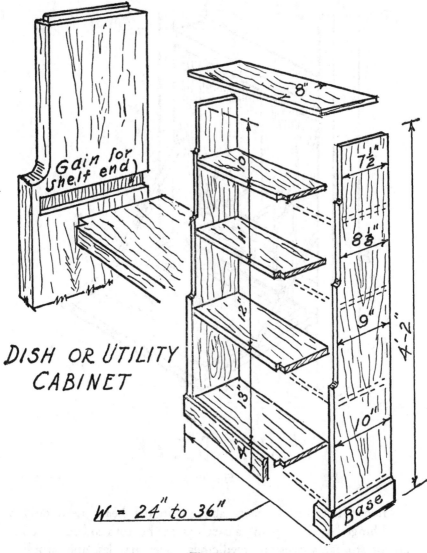

Gain for shelf end

DISH OR UTILITY CABINET

8"

7½"

8⅛"

9"

10"

4'-2"

Base

W = 24" to 36"

Fig. 100.

may be in the warm corner behind the living-room stove or beside the fireplace. Of the delights of the latter, we talk with enthusiasm from long experience. Our favorite is fitted with a hinged seat which covers a storage space for kindling and fire wood and is fitted with high-shaped ends against which the head naturally slumps. What a place on a cold morning in which to bask in the heat of the stove while dressing, or the last thing at night with

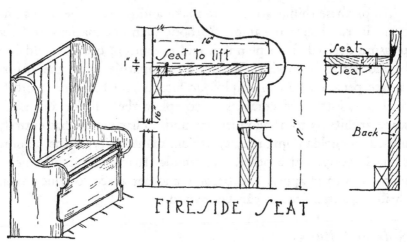

FIRE/IDE /EAT

Fig. 101.

slippered feet on the rail of the stove with the smoke curling up from the briar to grin at the less lucky ones in the chairs!

One very practical combination seat end table, sometimes called a "Dutch" seat, fits perfectly into a camp and serves as a table with the back let down and a fine wall bench with the top tipped back (Fig. 102). Even drawer space, always useful, can be included.

Fig. 102. Dutch seat.

All of these things are easy to make and occupy the hands and mind in the hours at camp. Without such occupations and the pleasure derived from planning and execution, camp would just be another place to visit. We deeply sympathize with the unfortunate person who can employ architects and builders to create his lodge, interior decorators to complete the interior and landscape architects to develop the grounds. That person has entirely missed the golden opportunity which, of necessity, is the blessing of his less oppulent brother. No wonder that such establishments soon loose their appeal and become another place to which their thrill-saturated friends can be invited.

Beds and Bunks

One-third of our lives is, or should be, spent in bed. It is nature's own method of recuperation and has no substitute. Why leave a comfortable bed at home with the mistaken idea that, truly to rough it and show a real pioneer spirit, one must toss and turn and probably curse on a bed not fit for human occupancy. It may have been grandfather's, or you or your friends may have figured that it was too good a mattress or spring to throw away, but it is the greatest mistake in the world to retain any such abomination or to subject your helpless friends to such punishment.

Perhaps it was just such experiences over many years in different cottages that led us to the solemn oath that, so help us, no piece of discarded bedroom furniture would ever be carted to any camp of ours. We had seen too many camps used as a city dump. Whenever any relative or friend was ready to throw something out, he immediately thought of us and wondered if we couldn't use it at camp. To some we said "no," to others, too sweet to hurt, we said "yes," and then pitched the stuff off at the first dump. So it was that when we came to plan our sleeping quarters and equipment, we shipped the best of new springs and mattresses to camp. The roof may leak, the fires may go out, but always one retires expecting to find a night's rest such as nature intends a human being shall have.

What type of support those springs may have, be it rough poles or ornate examples of the Grand Rapids fraternity, the real essence is there and the results have long since justified the cost.

Types of Beds

The type of support and frame for springs and mattresses will depend entirely upon the physical arrangement of the space. The material for those frames will depend upon good taste and the budget.

If the camp is in its infancy and limited to one room or one room and a kitchen, the most practicable arrangement is to use two double bunks of single width. This arrangement will accommodate four people, the least that any camp should expect. Sooner or later you will use all four spaces. The single-width bunks occupy the minimum of floor space and the upper bunks are easy on the bed-maker. There is one other advantage in the fact that you will have single beds. The double-width bunks are less elastic in the possible assignments and the upper bunk is a nuisance to the one who must make the beds.

If separate bedrooms are a part of the plan, small bedrooms will have more usable floor space if the double, single-width bunk is used. In this arrangement you will find all the advantages of twin beds.

If the bedroom will allow the use of a full-width (four and a half feet) bunk with ample floor space, we highly recommend the built-in bed which we developed at "Dunwurken" (Fig. 103). Leaving sufficient space between one wall and the bed for access, we constructed a bin on the floor with the head against the wall. The sides were made of sixteen-inch boards, on the upper edge of which we fastened a half-round molding, slightly wider than the thickness of the boards. The projecting edge was on the inside face and we neglected to plane it off. Lo and behold, we found that the little edge was worthy of a patent for it held the tucked-in bed clothes in place and made a veritable sleeping bag of the bedding. Small moldings made a panel effect on each side and end and a quarter-round molding at the angle between floor and frame made sweeping easy. These beds are similar to the lower bed on Fig 103 but set out from the wall.

Inside this bin affair, blocks supported the spring at the right height and our beds were complete. Perfect? Yes. No cold air circulating under the mattress and no floor space under the beds to be swept and painted. We have discovered one flaw to be corrected next time. With the side pieces straight up and down, there is no space for toes when making the bed. The next ones will have a three-inch cut under three inches high in the same manner that we build all kitchen cabinets to prevent continual and disfiguring kicking of baseboards. This improvement is shown in the drawings and it is offered for the benefit of mankind.

Occasional photographs are seen of built-in bunks charmingly represented as nautical in effect. These are more interesting in a picture than on a hot night when very little air is stirring. It is bad enough to build bunks into the corner of a room from necessity without closing in the foot and perhaps having a wooden valance across the side. One can always keep warm in cold weather with sufficient bedding, but only an electric fan will provide a circulation of air in some of the totally-enclosed bunks represented as cute ideas.

On the market there is a double-deck bunk, made of wood and inexpensively priced, which can be used as a double-deck bunk or separated into two single beds. It has much to commend it. Metal double-deck bunks are also available but, while extremely practical, somehow seem out of place in the camp.

Bunks can be constructed very easily from plain boards in the simplest manner or can be framed with mortise and tenon joints, either free standing or attached to the wall at head and one side. The upper bunk should have a face board wide enough for part of its length to prevent the restless sleeper from falling out of bed. We would recommend that the lower bunk be built in without any space under and that the upper bunk have a bottom of plywood. It is also important to keep the top of the face boards in the right relation to the mattress. If too high, difficulty will be found when getting out of bed if the mattress under a person's weight is below the edge of the facing board.

An additional bed at night and a comfortable couch for the daytime can be constructed in a corner of the Living Room by building a frame to enclose a standard single spring. The ends and sides of the frame can be closed in with sheathing or panels. If two large drawers, possible in the six and one half length, are included underneath, they will provide handy storage space.

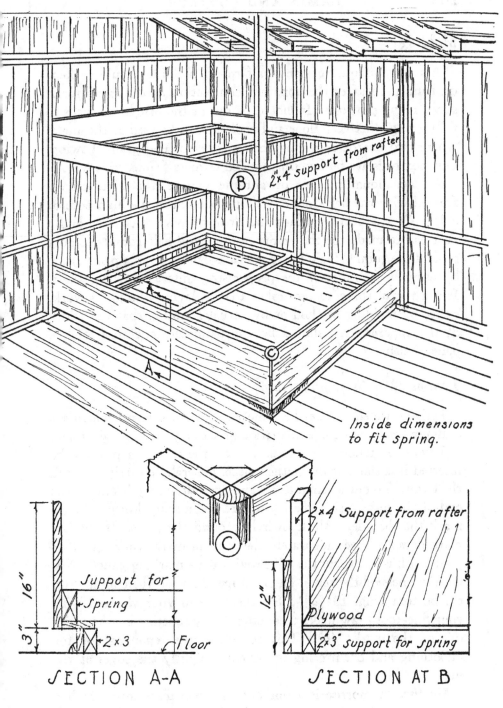

Inside dimensions
to fit spring.

2"x4" support from rafter

SECTION A-A

16"
3"
Support for
Spring
2×3
Floor

SECTION AT B

12"
2×4 Support from rafter
Plywood
2×3" support for spring

Fig. 103. Built-in beds.

Molding

A supply of quarter- and half-round molding should be kept
on hand even after the apparent completion of the camp for it
serves many purposes. It should be put at the base of all walls to
fill the angle between floor and wall. It can be used at the angles
where two boards come together to prevent end grain showing.
Our box beds are built with rounded corners framed this way.

An occasional picture or antique map can be attractively
framed with the half-round molding painted in the high note of
color. Cracks between studs and door frames are covered and a
neat casing made for the frame by mitering half-round molding
around the frame. Plain board surfaces can be given a panel effect
by using half-round, of the proper size, mitered at the corners.
It is a useful thing to remember that in laying out panel work,
either by molding method or by actual framing, that the width
of the apparent rail should be approximately one sixth of the
panel width.

Tenons, Mortises, and Gains

Perhaps we should at this time explain these terms which we
shall use freely, with an explanation of the easy way to make them.

Tenon. A tenon is a tongue cut on the end of a piece to be
inserted in a slot cut in another piece, generally entirely through
the latter. To cut a tenon easily and accurately, lay it out on the
end of the piece, using the try square and a sharp knife point to
mark the shoulder. Mark entirely around the piece. If the last
mark does not meet accurately the starting mark, your square or
your work is not accurate. Then with your marking gauge mark
the thickness of the tenon on the upper face, on the end, and on
the bottom (Fig. 104[a]). Set the piece in your vise and with
your fine-tooth saw make these cuts, always cutting on the *waste
side* of the marks (b). This completes the tenon except for
smoothing and chamfering or beveling slightly the edges at the
end.

Mortise. A mortise is a slot cut into one piece into which a
tenon is to be fitted; a mortise which is not cut entirely through
the piece is a *blind* mortise. To cut a mortise, with your try square

and a sharp knife point mark across the stock to show the length and exact location of the mortise (Fig 104[c]). Carry the cross marks entirely around the piece to insure accurracy, but do not make deep marks which would be difficult to remove. With the marking gauge mark, from each side of the stock, the sides of the

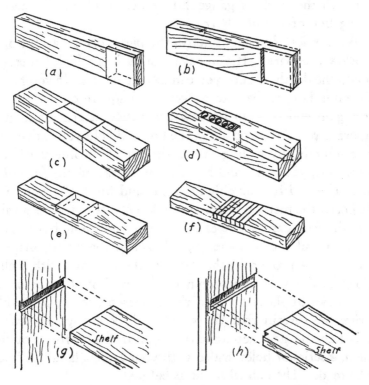

Fig. 104. Tenons, mortises, and gains: (a) marking tenon, (b) sawing tenon, (c) marking a mortise, (d) cutting a mortise, (e) marking a gain, (f) cutting a gain, (g) gain for shelving, (h) blind gain.

mortise. These marks made with the marking gauge should be made as deeply as possible to give a clean-cut edge to the mortise. We always keep a sharp point on our marking gauge to serve as a knife point when there is need for a deep cut.

Now with an auger bit, a trifle smaller than the width of the mortise, bore a series of holes *within* the mortise marks (d). Remember what we said about not boring entirely through from one side, and reverse the stick when the screw point of the bit penetrates the underside and complete the hole from that side. With a sharp chisel and a mallet (not a hammer) proceed to cut out and finish the mortise, working from both sides again.

To make a *gain* that is continuous across a piece, with your try square mark the size and location of the gain across the grain. Then with the marking gauge draw on each side of the piece the limiting line of the depth (*e*).

Make a series of saw cuts across the piece, being careful not to cut below the marks. If you have a miter box which has stops to regulate the depth of cuts, you can be sure of this. If you have no such miter box, to be sure of getting a square cut at the sides of the gain and to keep the saw accurately at the mark, nail a temporary piece of wood along the line and hold your saw against this as you cut. By nailing this on the side of the line that will be chiseled out, you can avoid leaving nail marks on the face of the wood. Then with your chisel cut out and finish the gain. On a wide board the method is not so simple (*f*). If you have a rabbet plane, the gain can be cut easily. If not, you should lay out the cuts, then nail the temporary guide across the board, make the saw cut to the proper depth, and pare the gain out with a chisel.

To make the blind gain shown at (*h*), mark it off as before and bore a series of short holes to the proper depth, as for a blind mortise. Be certain that the wood is thick enough so that the point of the bit does not come through. If the board is not thick enough, a series of holes drilled with your largest hand drill point can be made. Then chisel it out as before.

CHAPTER 13

Paints and Painting

This is a subject which the writer approaches with care, not from lack of experience but rather as a result of long and varied experience. At one time we were asked if a good specification could be written for painting. The answer was that it could be but would not be worth the paper upon which it was written. The entire result of years of experience with paint and its application can be summed up in the advice to buy the best materials from reliable dealers. A gallon of paint covers a large surface and any misjudged saving in price per gallon is spread out so thin that it does not even show. Do not attempt to economize on the quality of either paints or brushes.

Brushes

Speaking of brushes again brings up the subject of false economy, and false it is if you or your friends are to do the painter's work on the camp. A cheap brush will spread the paint, it is true, but what a different action a real brush will have and how much easier it will do the work! Buy good brushes adapted to the purposed for which intended; use them for no other purpose and take care of them.

Brushes should never be allowed to stand on their bristles in a can, but should be supported free from the bottom. Bore holes through the handles and run a heavy wire through them to rest on the edge of the can in which they are suspended. When not in use and if they are to be used frequently, clean them out as much as possible by brushing out on an old board and suspend them in a mixture of oil and turpentine. If they are to be put away for some time, clean them out thoroughly in turpentine when the brushes have been used for paint, stain or enamel. Varnish brushes should be cleaned with benzine and shellac brushes with alcohol.

After they are cleaned out and are dry, wrap them in paper to preserve the shape of the bristles.

If you have a varnish brush, use it for nothing but varnish. Paint brushes can be used for most kinds of paints except lacquers. They are a different type of vehicle and can be only used with a new brush or one which has been used in lacquers only. They can only be cleaned with a lacquer solvent, and we have yet to clean one successfully for future use after it had once hardened.

Paints

Paints are divided into two general classes: those for exterior use and those suitable only for interior use. The less you know as to their real composition, the more confidence you will have in their value. There was a time when pure white lead and pure linseed oil were the *sine qua non* for all paints. Today paint is being manufactured for a wide range of uses and, when properly applied, for the purpose for which it was developed, far excels the former product.

On outside painting, a master painter will mix lead, oil and turpentine and other ingredients and will produce a paint of lasting quality. However, a master painter will probably not be a part of your camp building crew. You will have to depend upon the advice of the dealer, a thorough stirring and mixing of the contents of the can and your own ability to apply it for the results to be obtained.

All paints must be thoroughly stirred and we do not mean maybe. Not a stirring of the top liquid but the vigorous and continued stirring of the contents of the can until the entire mass is a uniform, creamy mixture. The upper part of the liquid content should be poured into a clean can, the paint left in the original can should then be completely broken down into proper condition and the liquid in the second can returned for continued stirring. If the paint has been used before and has been on the shelf for some time, it should be strained through several thicknesses of cheesecloth after the final stirring.

Make it a practice to save all friction or screw top cans. One can never have too many clean, dry cans. A word of caution: You will use many cloths in connection with your painting; burn rags immediately that have been used in painting or staining. If put away in other than metal containers, they become a fire hazard from the chance of spontaneous combustion.

Stains

For outside work there are two types of stains: those with an oil base and those with creosote base. The latter has a strong odor which disappears after a time. The advantage of the creosote stain is the preservative value of its use. Stains are suitable for the board-covered structures, flitch-sawed boards and cedar or redwood siding. One camp which is most attractive, was stained with crank case oil, from which the carbon had been strained and a little turpentine added. This, with the trim painted a deep red, made a cheap finish and one that was particularly pleasing in combination with the woodsy surroundings.

One value of outside stains is that the woodwork can dry out and season without damage to the coating. Later, if it is found desirable to paint the work, the stain has made an excellent priming coat. If log siding is used for outside surfacing, brushing out with hot linseed oil improves the appearance of the wood and adds a preservative. The first coat should be mixed with turpentine to increase its penetration. At least two coats should be applied, each coat being allowed to dry thoroughly before the next is applied. Do not add turpentine until the oil has been heated and has been removed from the source of heat.

Staining seems to be the general type of finish for the interior of a camp and there is every reason for this treatment. Oil stains are most commonly used as well as the ready-mixed stains which penetrate the wood and leave the surface with a velvety surface. If oil stains are used, they are wiped off almost as soon as applied to obtain the desired effect. They are not so pleasing in their final appearance as the thinner stains.

Inasmuch as these stains do not change their color after drying, one should experiment on pieces of the wood, always remembering that a large surface will appear darker than the small surface of the sample. The universal tendency is to stain too dark. If a light tone is applied first, a second coat can be applied. If the first coat is too dark, the damage is irreparable.

Light browns and light grays are the better choice of colors. These, with painted trim of deeper shade of the same color or a contrasting color, produce artistic and pleasing effects. Always keep a can of stain handy to stain new gadgets and equipment as soon as completed.

Trim

Whether shingles, siding or outside boarding is stained or painted, the outside trim, window and door frames, should be painted. Clapboards and beveled siding are always painted.

A priming coat, thinned with turpentine, should be well brushed into the woodwork, care being taken to fill every crevice and nail hole. When this coat is dry, all knots and pitchy places should be given a coat of shellac, all holes should be puttied and a second coat of paint, full body, should be applied. Let this suffice for the first season while the wood is seasoning and any movement is taking place. The next year the third coat can be applied and should be sufficient for several years. The inside of the gutters should be painted every year and this may be necessary for window stools.

At "Dunwurken" we used a trim and trellis enamel for trim. It has been on for three years and is as bright and fresh as when first applied.

Porch Floors

The wood floors of porches should have a priming coat and one coat of outside paint. When this is thoroughly hardened, give them a coat of Porch and Deck paint as a finished surface. This same treatment should be given to all outside steps and platforms.

Interior Floors

If the finished floors have been laid with soft wood and are to be painted, they should receive the same treatment as described for porches. Deck paint has been made to endure under hard usage and has varnish in its composition. Do not use any other than the best quality of paint for this purpose. When painting floors, do not brush the paint out too much. Too niggardly use of paint, spread by hard brushing, will prevent any possibility of a glossy, durable finish. A prodigal use of paint, well flowed on the surface and into every crevice will produce just the finish that you want. Allow ample time for the paint not only to dry but to harden thoroughly. Floor paint does not develop a real wear-resisting surface until it has had time to harden even after the surface appears firm and dry.

Color Schemes

It is a principle of interior decorating that the floors should carry the darkest tones, the walls should be a little lighter and the ceiling lighter in tone than the walls. Ceiling beams are often finished in a dark tone with the panels between the timbers finished in a lighter shade of the same color. This may be striking in effect but makes the ceiling appear much lower than it is. Another well-tried idea is that any room should present such a harmonious combination in color and detail that no one feature is too obvious. It is also of importance to remember that sunny and light spaces can be finished in grays and cool colors, while rooms darkened by overhanging growth or lack of windows need the buffs, yellows and other warm colors.

The easiest and, in many cases the most satisfactory, colors for unfinished cabins are produced by the brown stains, not too dark on the walls and almost colorless on the ceilings. Floors of brown or pumpkin yellow, if sunny effect is needed, over which a few colorful rugs are scattered will make a delightful and restful combination. Any strong note of color should be introduced by lamp shades, draperies or cushions.

At "Dunwurken" the living room, shaded as it is by the porch, was finished in shades of brown and the floor was painted with pumpkin yellow enamel. The sash and trim around the windows were painted an orange blending with the floor. Chairs were finished in orange and black and the center table to match the walls. We have lived with that color scheme for five years and it is still as charming and restful as when first completed.

Grays, if used in light shades on the warm side, are always in good taste, and the bright notes of color can be made with the trim if used sparingly. Any attempt to liven the room by bright colors on trimmings or by variegated panels makes a bedlam of color. Paints should be used with discretion and restraint.

The walls of the kitchen can be done in light brown stain with the sash in orange or the most pleasing of all combinations, ivory with green used sparingly as trim.

We have in mind a cottage whose kitchen, which was painted entirely in ivory, was liberally and injudiciously trimmed in filling-station red. Perhaps if the female decorator had used a little restraint the results would not have been so devastating. But, with an entire can of paint and a new brush, and their tantalizing temptations, much of the surface as well as cans and boxes were covered with the fire alarm specialty. Perhaps you are old enough to remember the period of the red dining rooms. That period holds the all-time record for divorces.

Bedrooms, finished in light grays, with moldings and dresser knobs making the color accent in rose or red and with slate-colored floors are cool- and airy-looking for summer camps.

Comparatively new in the markets are the paints for interior use made from casein. They come in paste or powder form and are prepared for use by mixing with hot water. They are extremely inexpensive, spread easily and have surprising covering ability. You will need no special skill in their application and they dry out to a flat, even surface, showing no brush marks or laps. This paint is available in a variety of colors, can be applied to almost any surface without preparation and dries within four hours. One coat is sufficient.

Keep all of your paint material and brushes in a special closet, handy at all times, and the many things around camp will receive their proper share of the paint. The pump and platform will look better with a fresh coat of green; the window boxes in a new coat of color each spring will make a pleasing contrast to the vari-colored flowers cascading over their edges. Even the shed floor will eventually have a painted surface, using odds and ends mixed together, with great ease in cleaning as the result.

At this point we repeat a bit of advice given heretofore. Paint the handles of all outdoor tools a bright orange or yellow which will be a contrast to the green of the grass or bushes where you are apt to lay them. If borrowed, they are easily identified.

Natural Finish

Certain types of wall treatment may be improved by a varnish or wax treatment either on the raw material or over stain. Most varnishes and all shellacs dry with a gloss of varying degrees. Flat varnish which is cut with wax or other materials, dries with a matt or flat finish. Waxes can be used for a dull gloss or almost a matt finish.

Natural finish which must withstand the effects of wear or dampness should be finished 'with spar varnish. Flat varnishes can stand neither wear nor dampness, but are more pleasing and artistic where the other requirements are not so important. Spar varnishes are advisable in kitchens or bathrooms where a natural wood finish is wanted. Flat varnish, over an underbody of regular varnish is better for all other types of work. Because very few camps would be finished with varnish, and because your dealer's advice is available at all times with complete samples and directions for the asking, we will not dwell on this subject further.

Knotty-Pine Finish

We are, like many others, a little prejudiced in favor of this old time method of finishing a room. It is a beautiful background for furnishings properly chosen and makes a cheerful and home-like room. It must be done in good taste with no attempt at bizarre effects. The wood should be selected with care and the boards should be of random widths, laid random, to avoid any appearance of uniformity or regular pattern.

The finish applied to the wood can complete its beauty or wreck its effect. The end in view is to produce a surface apparently mellowed with age and with a patina, or deep sheen, reflecting years of rubbing by immaculate housekeepers. This appearance can be obtained by the use of water stains or by a light fuming with diluted ammonia. The stains must be light in tone and the finished color should be the tone of warm honey.

Years ago when the demand for this type of finish was increasing, the writer did some research work in the matter of finishing this wood for the best effect. Various painters and cabinet-makers were inveigled into helpful suggestions with the following results.

Give the woodwork a light coat of white lead, linseed oil and turpentine primer in which just enough lamp black is introduced to give a light gray tone. Then proceed to take it all off with a paint removing compound. Silly? Not at all. Clean off all traces of the compound with benzine, sand lightly if required, and give a thin coat of wax. Your surface will appear hoary with age and will have a patina of corresponding depth.

To emphasize the value of this method, I should like to tell of an incident which happened years ago when the writer designed a private office which was to be finished in knotty pine. Lengthy and detailed instructions were given to the painter to be followed during my absence on a business trip. Upon returning, a visit was made at the first opportunity to see the results of the treatment. As if it had been transplanted out of the early homes of our ancestors was a room whose walls had the softly glowing texture and surface sheen that only time and loving hands can produce. Finally the truth came out. The painter had tried to get the effect with stain and only after the second attempt and the confession on his part that he had not followed the directions of the architect did the owner rise in his wrath and order him to take it all off and start right. The cheap, raw look was removed by the compound and when the wood had dried, there it stood, centuries old but alive and radiant. A light waxing completed the work to the satisfaction of the proud owner and the complete surprise of the painter who could not believe the results of his own work.

Hardwood Floors

Right at this point we pause and are tempted to stop. We know nothing about finishing hardwood floors. There was a time when we thought we did but that was years ago and we have both written specifications for and superintended the workmanship on acres of hardwood floors. We still say that we do not know.

Years ago, a master painter gave the writer the only perfect specification for producing a long-wearing hardwood floor. It was to finish the wood, use the best varnish or shellac, then lock the door and throw the key away.

Tell anyone, workman or amateur, that you would like to know how to finish a hardwood floor and the directions will fairly bubble out and will be as varied as the advise on bringing up babies.

Varnish has its devotees, shellac has its enthusiasts and wax its bigots, all right and some wrong. We can eliminate wax from kitchens and bathrooms.

If you should use oak for flooring, you will use a paste filler which is spread on the floor, rubbed well in and the surplus rubbed off. When dry, a coat of thin shellac will act as a binder. Birch, maple or yellow pine will not require a filler. We now come to the dividing ways and to more of a quandary than faced Hamlet. Wax can be used over the raw wood and is used over shellac. It is not suitable for the type of camp which interests you. We mention this fact just to show that we have not overlooked its possibility.

We now are narrowed down to the choice between varnish and shellac. Each has its vociferous advocates and each is equally popular. We have no deciding vote to cast. If it is to be varnish, the best of floor varnishes made for that special work should be used. If shellac, get pure gum shellac and good alcohol.

The number of coats to be applied will depend upon your wood, your pocketbook and your endurance. Do not put on thick coats, allow plenty of drying time between coats and sand each coat before applying the next. Several thin coats are better than fewer heavier coats. Varnish should be flowed on and not brushed out. Shellac sets almost immediately and laps will show if brush is worked over surfaces which are almost dry.

For a kitchen floor of birch, subject to much tracking and wear, an oil treatment is by all means the most satisfactory in every way. There are several floor oils on the market, excellent in quality, but I should like to call your attention to one treatment that can be relied upon and one which the writer has used for years. Copied from an author who learned its value abroad, it had to be literally forced down the throats of reluctant painters until the actual results were seen. Incidentally, as a base for wax floors except on open grain-like oak, it has no superior.

Flood the floor with a mixture of equal parts of linseed oil and turpentine to which enough japan drier has been added to assure an early set. Work the oil well into the wood with rags and allow to dry for twenty-four hours. Then rub off the surface residue with burlap and the resultant surface is ideal. An occasional light coat of the same oil mixture, rubbed down after twelve hours, will keep the floor surface in perfect condition.

CHAPTER 14

Water Supply and Utilities

The availability of an adequate supply of good water is important. It may be that the camp is to be built where there is an existing water system and it will only require piping from the mains to the camp. In most instances, however, the camp will have to depend upon natural resources, usually a spring or a well, either dug or driven, or even a brook or pond.

Regardless of the source of the water, it should be laboratory-tested before it is used. Water may be clear as crystal and yet be laden with germs. Take no chances with running brooks. A clear brook coming, apparently from a wilderness, may have dangerous contamination above your location. In most localities, either state or local organizations will do it for you at little or no expense. This is done so carefully that a sterilized container will be furnished in which to transport the sample of water.

If you are fortunate in having a spring with an ample supply of pure water, you should take every precaution to prevent any pollution. The spring should be lined and covered either by rocks and masonry or by planking. The larger sizes of tile pipe make excellent material with which to protect the spring and, with a removable concrete cover, are ideal. If the spring water is cold, the overflow can be utilized to provide a cold box or spring house in which milk and supplies may be kept. Perhaps the spring will be at a sufficient elevation to be piped right into the camp.

Wells are either dug, driven or drilled. The first two are the more common on the ordinary camp site. If the well is dug, the sides should be lined with large stones which are gradually arched over to form the top on which a plank frame or concrete cover is set. As a pitcher pump and the few feet of pipe required can be purchased for very little money, it is a much more practical combination, although not as picturesque, than an opening and a long pole on which a pail is hung whenever water is to be drawn. The use of a pump, moreover, avoids the need of an opening in the platform with the ever-present danger to children.

It may be possible to run the pipe from the well into the kitchen and have the pump at one end of the sink. In this case, be sure to bury the pipe below the frost line.

The base of the well lining and the entire enclosure may be constructed of rock. If so, the walls from a point three feet below the surface to the curb should be made watertight by cement mortar and the soil packed around this portion should preferably be of a clayey composition to prevent surface water or drainage from entering the well. The use of the large sizes of clay tile, with joints set in cement mortar for the upper portions of the well casing, are ideal. The bell ends should be up, as the bell end makes an excellent place to fit with a cover of either plank or concrete. If the curb cap on the well is of concrete and of sufficient size, the pump should be set at one side and a tight fitting manhole should be set in the center to give access for cleaning. Well curbs are frequently fitted with ventilators but most health authorities agree that air and light should not be allowed to enter the well as their presence encourages the formation and growth of fungus.

It is almost unnecessary to say that a well should never be located near any cesspool or other source of contamination, nor where there is any danger of underground seepage even if the source is not near. A strainer should always be installed at the lower end of the suction pipe and the pump should be of the type that will allow all the water in the pipe to drain back into the well when the handle is held up. This is imperative if you anticipate the use of your well in freezing weather.

A driven well is made by driving a pipe, the lower end of which is fitted with a steel well point. As the point is driven deeper, short sections of pipe are added. The well point is of steel, with a series of holes screened with copper wire. In addition to the short lengths of pipe and a well point, you will need a driving cap and a heavy sledge. If the soil is not too heavy and a vein of water is penetrated by the point, a driven well may give an abundance of water. In cases we know of, our friends have always found that if they struck a vein within a twenty feet depth, it was money saved in the long run to dig a well and not be annoyed by a clogging well point.

A drilled well involves specialized apparatus and power and is done by regular contractors who make this work their business. It is only in exceptional cases that this type of well would be necessary at the average camp.

If you have developed a good spring or well, it is possible to have the convenience of running water in your camp. If electric power is available or if not, by gasoline engines, it is perfectly simple to install one of the small, self-contained outfits which can be purchased at surprisingly low cost. They not only furnish home conveniences but afford a certain amount of fire protection.

These outfits consists of a tank into which the pump forces water against the pressure of the air in the tank until the desired pressure is reached. At this point, the power is automatically shut off. When a faucet is turned on or a closet is flushed, the air under pressure in the tank sends the water through the pipe. When the pressure drops below the determined point, the electric or gasoline pump will again automatically build up the pressure.

You may also have running water in camp by pumping water with a gas engine pump into a storage tank at a higher level than the camp. If a constant flow of water in ample quantity is available and a drop of sufficient amount can be made, you can install a hydraulic ram to pump water up into the storage tank. This flow of water can be either a stream or the overflow from a spring. The initial cost of the ram is low and the maintenance cost is nothing. These rams require a lot of water but with that and sufficient head, will force water to considerable height.

An artistic temperament may demand an old-fashioned waterwheel, either of overshot or undershot type as a source of power to deliver water into a storage tank. The writer must confess that he was never content without a waterwheel at "Dunwurken."

Toilets

This subject is of extreme importance. On the nature of the installation and the manner in which it is cared for, depend in a large measure the convenience and health of the occupants of the camp. If the camp is located within reasonable distance from a water main and a disposal system, the problem is only that of the usual town house. As the majority of camps are located far from

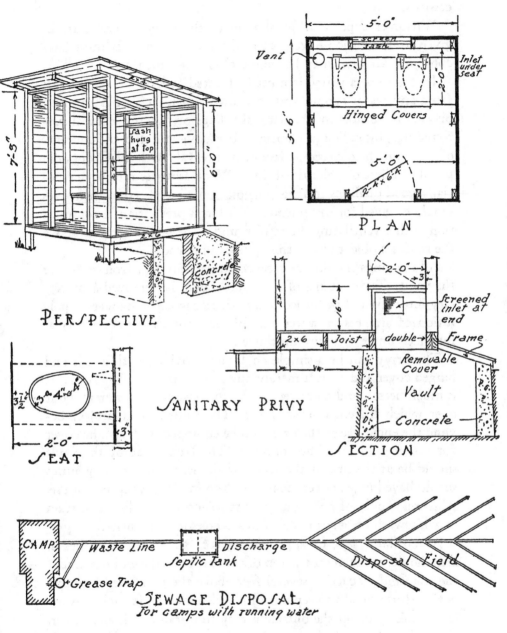

Fig. 105. Utilities.

any such conveniences, it becomes necessary to provide these necessities.

Whatever type of disposal is used, the utmost care must be given to its location in respect to the water supply. It must have constant care or it may become useless and a menace.

If it is to be a privy, it must be located at least a hundred feet from any water supply and at a lower level. It should be given privacy if possible by the natural foliage or, lacking natural surroundings, by judicious planting. It is advisable that the contents of the vault be covered at frequent intervals with ashes, dry soil, powdered lime or chloride of lime. Wood ashes seem to have especially good qualities for this purpose and all ashes from the stoves should be saved for this purpose. With this precaution in conjunction with a ventilating duct from under the seat to a point above the roof, no objections to this type can be made.

All openings should be screened to prevent flies from entering the vault. The contents of the vault should be removed at necessary intervals and be buried where there can be no danger of pollution of streams or water supply. Do not use the contents as fertilizer under any circumstances.

The privy can be a simple enclosure provided with a seat and hinged cover and a vault merely dug in the ground (Fig. 105). It is much better, and costs very little, to construct a concrete vault over which the enclosure is built. The vault should project beyond the enclosure at the back and be equipped with a tight cover for ease in removing the contents. The front edge of the vault should be at the line of the front of the seat. Any seat openings should have hinged covers that will drop in place when not in use. A liberal supply of paint on the seat structure and floor and stain or whitewash on walls makes for a wholesome condition.

A ventilator pipe of approximately 25 to 30 square inches in area should be taken off the top of the seat or at the end just under the seat, and be carried several feet above the roof line. Equip it with a storm hood to keep out rain and snow. A six inch galvanized smoke pipe on the outside is easy to install and is efficient in its results. A screened opening of the same area should be made from the outside at the opposite end of the seat and just under the seat. The ventilating duct can be made of wood if the joints can be made airtight.

Septic Tanks

If running water is available in the camp, the most satisfactory method of dealing with the problem is to conduct toilet and waste lines into a septic tank and disposal field, if the budget permits. This type of disposal uses an underground tank equipped with two chambers, in which the sewage remains for a time and a bacterial change takes place. Then the liquid automatically drains off through a line of pipe into a disposal field which consists of radial arms of drain tile buried in porous soil.

Septic tanks can be constructed of wood, masonry or tile on the site, or metal tanks, complete and ready to install can be purchased. Complete information on the different types of septic tanks and disposal fields is easily available from local health authorities, U.S. Public Health Service and similar agencies. Full information should be obtained and a thorough study of the subject made before any decision is reached. If you decide to purchase a septic tank, full instructions for its installation will be furnished with it.

If a suitable location is near the camp, a cesspool will serve for any camp unless the load on it is beyond its capacity. By suitable location we mean a spot in gravely or sandy soil, not clay or a clay loam, where there is no possible way by which its contents can leach into a water supply. The construction is the same as described for dry wells. Be sure to put a trap on any plumbing fixture discharging into a cesspool.

Dry Wells

Sink wastes can be easily and safely disposed of by dry wells. These are made by excavating a large hole to a depth of five to six feet, preferably in sandy or gravely soil, and filling the hole with rocks or very coarse gravel to within two or three feet of the surface.

If the dry well is to be used in freezing weather, the sink waste pipe must be kept below the frost line and this may increase the required depth of the hole. The dry well should be at some distance from the camp and, above all things, where it cannot be a source of danger to the water supply. It is advisable to install a good grease trap in the sink waste line to intercept the grease and fat before it can enter and fill the dry well.

Garbage and Waste

Take proper care of garbage and waste at the camp, for lack of care in this respect may cause you plenty of trouble. All rubbish should be burned and this should include tin cans, which after being burned out can be thrown in a suitable dumping place. Empty cans, if not burned out, will attract animals and rodents even if buried.

We learned this the hard way. We made a heavy frame, boarded over, with a tight fitting hinged cover and, after digging a neat hole, set the frame in place, intending to move the cover from time to time to a new hole and fill in the first one.

Nothing that we did could prevent our four-footed neighbors from excavating under that cover and dragging contents around. That fine scheme was abandoned and fire took care of garbage and tin cans.

Rubbish, and this includes most of the garbage, is best burned in one of the heavy wire or metal receptacles made for that purpose and at a safe distance from the buildings.

Lights and Lighting

If your camp is located within practical distance of a utility company's lines, lighting is not a problem. But most camps are not so blessed and it becomes a question as to what type of lights should be used. In a small cottage, especially one used mostly in the summer months when the days are long, a few kerosene lamps will serve every purpose. In a larger camp which may be used in the winter months we have a different problem. For bedrooms and kitchen, kerosene lamps will serve all needed purposes. Lamps with reflectors made to hang on the wall in the kitchen will give a most satisfactory light. In the living room, however, where reading and cards may require better light, a hanging lamp over the table will be most satisfactory. Round wick burners, which served us before the advent of the electric light, will give a soft, mellow reading light of ample capacity.

Next in value is the Aladdin type of lamp which combines the principle of the Welsbach Mantle and the round wick kerosene lamp. No reading light could be any better than this one. The lamp should be hung from a pulley over the table, by a chain carried to the side wall. In this way the lamp can be raised for general illumination or lowered for reading. Be sure to carry the chain through a pulley at the wall and knot the chain at a point that will allow the lamp to descend to the reading position. The knot will save your sweeping up the pieces of one lamp if the chain should slip in your fingers.

The gasoline lantern makes a brilliant illumination and is an ideal source of light.

Small and efficient self-contained electric lighting units, driven by gasoline motors, have recently been placed on the market. These vary from small units furnishing current for a few low-voltage lamps to larger units furnishing lighting current and current sufficient to run a pumping outfit. These compact units cost little to buy and little to run. One 800 watt outfit generates 110-volt AC current and is easily installed in a small space. It is fully automatic, and the turn of any switch starts it or stops it.

Wood Shed and Work Shop

This may be a part of the main structure, a separate building, or semi-detached with at least a connecting roof. The shed or work shop can be a rough structure or can be built to match the camp. The inside can be fitted with all kinds of conveniences, both for the housekeeper or the amateur craftsman. There should be a good work bench with racks or cabinets for tools, two full-length closets for paints, brushes and outdoor tools, bins for coal, kindling and wood. Overhead space can be used for storage.

Just as soon as possible in the progress of construction, erect a solid work bench equipped with a woodworking vise and a bench stop. The front plank on the bench should be $1\frac{1}{4}''$ thick of smooth, straight hardwood—the rest of the top can be $\frac{7}{8}''$ boards furred up to the level of the plank. This gives a solid bed on which you can pound to your heart's content and not dance everything

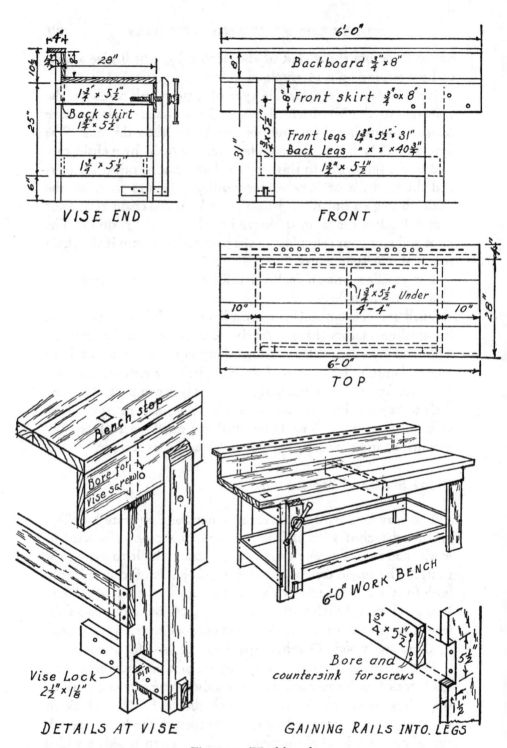

VISE END

FRONT

TOP

Bench step

Bore for vise screw

Vise Lock
$2\frac{1}{2}" \times 1\frac{1}{8}"$

DETAILS AT VISE

$6'-0"$ WORK BENCH

Bore and countersink for screws

$\frac{1\frac{3}{4}"}{4} \times 5\frac{1}{2}"$

GAINING RAILS INTO LEGS

Fig. 106. Workbench.

228

on the bench to the floor. You can install a cabinet-maker's vise, or make your own by installing a vise screw and handle attached to a 5″ piece of hardwood (Fig. 106). Keep handy a board two feet long and a foot wide, with a hole bored near one end by which it should be hung, upon which you can mix paints and save the surface of the bench.

Screws, nails, bolts and small fittings can be kept in empty jars with screw tops. Put two screws through the screw top of the jar from the underside into the underside of shelves and screw the jar, with its contents, into the cap. At a glance the needed item is seen —a twist of the wrist releases the jar, and it is replaced as easily.

CHAPTER 15

Costs, Assistance, and Contractors

Our real object at first was to tell our readers just how they could proceed to build a camp with their own hands. The thought then occurred that there were others who might wish to do a part of the work only, and still others who would have all the work done but would like to know what it was all about. Because most of us have to do a little planning for the things we desire, something about costs would also be expected.

Costs

It is inevitable that, when considering the possibility of building one's own camp, the first question is that of cost. Many fortunate ones are not hampered by this limitation. Perhaps the more blessed are those who must overcome this obstacle. Their enjoyment of the reality will be more keen because of the difficulties overcome.

An attempt to give accurate estimates of the cost of any given size or type of camp is not only misleading but useless in most cases. Location, local materials and prices, labor costs and other contributing elements affect the figures so much that an accurate estimate for any one locality would be entirely out of line in any other place. Then, too, it is almost never that anyone actually follows any published plan in its entirety or in the use of materials. Some departure is invariably made from the scheme as shown by a plan. At first consideration it may appear to be the ideal layout and perfect "except for." When that "except for" is translated into a final and approved plan, the camp may bear but slight resemblance to the original scheme upon which the published estimate was based.

Estimating can be an exact science and there need be but little guess work in it. To make an accurate estimate, carefully detailed plans, complete and comprehensive specifications and an exact knowledge of local labor and material costs are necessary. Most necessary of all is the knowledge of the local conditions and prices. In our particular case it is not possible to meet all of these necessary requirements, and therefore no definite set of costs can be included.

If it is a question of finding out how much the materials will cost, any local supply house or mill will gladly make an accurate estimate from your sketches, rough though they may be, and such description as you may make. The prices of both lumber and other materials used in the building will vary from season to season in the same locality.

"But," you may say, "give me some idea of what a camp can be built for under average conditions."

A camp consisting of a single room and a kitchen can be built at a cost of one hundred and fifty dollars for materials or for even less. This cost would increase in proportion to the demand for better materials or more elaborate equipment. This figure, of course, does not include any expenditures for labor.

As a rough rule-of-thumb method of estimating labor for installing material, double the cost of the material and you will have the cost of material and labor. It is not expected that you will enter the contracting business where you would use this method, but you will find it useful at times.

You might say, "How much will it cost to build my ideal camp with a living room, kitchen and two bedrooms, doing the work myself and using the plainest of materials?"

In answer to that question, we suggest that you try this method. Allow two hundred dollars per room counting the kitchen as a room. In our opinion you will not be far from a good estimate of the *actual cost of materials*. At least you will be no farther from the actual cost than you might be if you used a figure established as a close estimate for a camp built in some other section of the country.

The important thought upon which we have been dwelling is that for the best of reasons we have not pictured a camp that may appeal to you personally and then said that this camp could be built for the sum of $735.57. Perhaps it could be built for that exact amount but the important and everlasting fact is that you would not build it for that amount. You might build it at a total cost of $525 whereas the other fellow would expend $1100 on the identical plan.

This wide spread of costs can be more striking in a camp or small cottage than in a finished house because there are so few separate items that enter into the construction of a camp or cottage. An example of this variation in cost is in hardware. A perfectly practical thumb latch and handle can be purchased for a quarter; a better grade with somewhat the appearance of hand-wrought iron will cost thirty-five cents. Or you can pay $2.50 for a latch which will wear no longer nor serve its purpose any better. It is true that the latter type has a character and an appeal that justifies the increased expense if you can afford it. However, you have increased the cost on that one type of equipment tenfold.

We might go from item to item in the same manner and prove to your complete understanding how futile any statements as to approximate costs would be. This is a reason and not an excuse.

The central theme running throughout this book and the fundamental idea is to tell you how you could see the fulfillment of your desires at the minimum of expense. If what we have said is true, and we have reason to believe that it is, the cost of the materials alone would be about one-half of the cost if you contracted to have the entire work, materials and labor, completed by someone else. Then all that would remain for you would be the payment of the bills and the installation of the furnishings.

Perhaps by so doing you have failed to receive the biggest thrill of all—the creation with your own hands of something useful, enjoyable and of lasting value. That is the visible evidence of the results of your labor. What about the intangible results of honest labor in nature's sanitarium? Do dreamless nights of sound sleep and healthy appetites compensate in some measure for blistered hands and complaining muscles? These same muscles, however, soon adapt themselves to painless and tireless effort when given a reasonable chance.

Now some of our readers will say, "All that you have said is true and is appreciated at its true value. What can one do who has neither the time, the strength nor the ability to do all the work? We could do some of the work, the light carpenter work inside and we would love to paint."

Fortunately that question is easily answered. There is no abrupt demarcation between those things which you can do and those things which must be done by others. This dividing line can be determined by yourself and is dependent upon your time, your strength and your developed ability and to a large extent upon your own inclinations.

There will be plenty of rough and rugged work if you are to create a vacation home in some undeveloped location, but there is always available all the help you may need. Somewhere near at hand you will find it if you will investigate and make the right approach. "Dunwurken" had its "Jack" and in every locality will be found a "Jack" if you are fortunate.

The location selected for "Dunwurken" was ideal in many ways but presented many problems. A thick second growth of almost impassable density grew out of a terrain so thickly imbedded with rocks of all sizes that the land resembled a huge peanut bar. These rocks would later be used in retaining walls, flagstone walks and a dam, but days of labor would be required. Time could not be spent on this sort of work. Long weekends were the only available time for the owner to complete the actual construction of the camp and winter, with its deep snows, was not far away.

Then Jack appeared, coming through the woods from the mountain side where he lived a solitary life. He was unshaven, unkempt, but with a shrewd and kindly gleam in his deep set eyes; his speech revealed that here was no ignorant son of the soil.

What a day's work that man could do! Tireless, patient and kindly, day after day he did all the heavy and tedious tasks and his work is irremovably woven into the pattern of that camp like the bright threads in a Scotch plaid. When a well was needed, a forked twig became a thing of magic in his hands to locate the spot. We had heard of divining rods and didn't believe they worked. He didn't care whether we were believers or not—he would dig the well at that spot and if he didn't strike water in twelve feet he would fill in the hole and it would cost us nothing. His tireless energy dug the well and stoned its sides in Cyclopean masonry. At twelve feet the water drove him out—we paid and now believe. This well is unfailing in the dryest of seasons with icy cold water in the hottest weather.

When the digging was nearly completed, a gigantic stone apparently blocked any further progress. Did it stop Jack? Certainly not. With a small portion of dynamite judiciously placed, the hands of an invisible genie lifted that stone right out of the well and left it at one side without even jarring the sides of the excavation. If a dam was to be built, if a tangle of undesirable trees and shrubs was to be removed, or if new construction was to be painted during the week, Jack could do it—his own boss and time-keeper.

It was in his moments of relaxation during lunch hour or when rolling his occasional cigarette that the inner man was revealed. Well read, with a grasp of the past and a current knowledge, somewhat of a philosopher, his was a soul which could march side by side with broadcloth and linen.

May you find another "Jack" when you undertake to create a place for your enjoyment. May you receive as much in services rendered as we have.

But, to receive you must also give. Clothes are but civilization's method of combating nature's temperatures and complying with the requirements of modesty. They have nothing to do with the spirit that is perhaps concealed by those clothes. Jack would not work for everyone. He was their equal, in some cases their superior, in everything except exterior appearance. Nor was he dependent upon their patronage, and patronage is the proper word. If you wish to receive from the "Jacks" of your own environment, the real service which they can render, remember that they are the ones that can do you the favor.

It has been the writer's privilege, over a long period of years, to associate with workmen of many trades. Much has been learned from them because much can be learned by a receptive and appreciative mind. There is a certain inherent dignity in most men who do skilled work with their hands. A man who can make a fine joint in woodwork or wipe a joint in lead pipe will be found to have something substantial and dependable in his character.

Perhaps all of this moralizing is an untimely digression from the real purpose of this book. But, after all, we are trying to help you to build your camp. If you are to seek for and employ assistance, the way you use that assistance is certainly as important as the proper handling of the other tools.

In your particular case, it may be necessary to have all of the rough construction work done by others. If so, the services of local builders can be utilized to any extent desired. There are few locations today suitable for your purpose that do not have within their environments, the type of workmen that will be required. Few trades are required for the construction of a camp or cottage and no difficulty should be encountered in securing able assistance for the work.

The trade which you will probably need, even if you do the rest of the work yourself will be that of masonry, particularly if a fireplace or brick chimney is included in your plans. Many amateurs have performed splendid work in the carpenter's line but when it come to masonry, that is another matter. Men without any previous experience have constructed good and safe fireplaces but they are few and far between. Laying brick is a trade; building fireplaces is an art; and neither can be acquired by instinct.

There are two methods by which this extra labor is obtained. One is by direct contract and the other is by day labor. Under a contract, one party agrees to do certain work and furnish certain materials at a fixed price. Under the other method, the labor is paid for by the day and the materials are purchased either by yourself or by the contractor. The direct contract has the advantage of a fixed cost while the job done by day work may vary over the estimate given.

If the work is to be done by direct contract it is necessary that very definite details be incorporated in the agreement. The first requisite is a set of plans showing all details of size, arrangement, materials and equipment. Next, a comprehensive specification of the work to be done, the materials, quality, sizes, etc., to be furnished and installed and then a contract signed by both parties setting forth therein the conditions of the work, the terms of payment and the responsibilities of the contracting parties.

Get the best contractor within reach and pay a reasonable price and the results will be satisfactory. All the specifications ever written and all the "whereas" and "wherefore" clauses cannot make a poor workman do good work. The good workman needs no specification clauses to insure his craftsmanship. He must live with himself, and his monitor is his own pride—not a stereotyped clause in a contract.

If you are to work along with your assistants, craftsmen or

common laborers, there is a certain benefit in hiring the men by the day or week and working to the extent of your ability with them. Something goes into that camp or cottage that cannot be described. It can only be sensed during the time of construction and really appreciated after the work is completed.

Whatever form of labor you employ and under whatever conditions they become your employees, be certain before a stroke of work is done that you are protected against any action of law caused by injuries received on the work. Even if you have a contract for the construction, be absolutely certain that you, as the owner, are amply protected, because the Liability Insurance clause in the contract is not sufficient of itself for your protection. The laws on Liability and Compensation vary in different states to a large degree. Check each angle of this matter before assuming any risk.

Another very important point in any contract relations is the matter of fire insurance during the contruction period. If the camp or cottage is of any size at all, it is a desirable feature to see that insurance is carried on the building and on materials delivered. The cost of the insurance will always come out of your pocket although it may apparently seem to be carried by the contractor.

CHAPTER 16

The Guest House

Our first guest house, crude as it was, served as the summer home of the three growing boys, increasing their own pleasure and decreasing the wear and tear on the camp. It was only a 10′ x 10′ tent set upon a wood platform with a fly over the tent extending five feet beyond to serve as a porch. The fly assured a dry tent in continued downpours and a cool tent in hot weather.

Erected in the pines by the side of a small brook which ran into the large pool, it had an attractive location. At first the tent was supported by the poles which came with it. A later improvement included the substitution of a skeleton frame, doing away with the annoyance of the pole in the center of the entrance and preventing the sagging of the tent when wet.

We made a big mistake at the very first move. The tent was said to be a full 10′ x 10′ size. Anxious and overeager, we built the platform 10′ x 15′, the extra length to serve as a small porch. The platform was completed and nicely painted by the time the tent was received. It was only 9′ x 9′! So we erected it on the platform with six inches of the floor projecting *outside* the tent walls on each side. When the first rain came, we learned that the sides of the tent should extend down *over* the edges of the platform. So, get your tent before you build the floor.

That tent outfit served for seven summers, with seldom less than three occupants at any one time. Absence of one of the brothers meant a guest of one of the others. All their things were either hung or contained in foot lockers. A wash bowl on a stand in a corner of the porch and an endless supply of water from the brook was all that was needed, together with frequent use of the pool, for bathing. If they could not find "Where is my?" there was no one to blame but themselves, and their mother could have leisure hours as a result.

We have told you how this problem was solved in a simple and easy way, yet one that gave the keenest zest to the summer for the boys. Perhaps this simple form will be just the answer to your own desires. But it is not enough to build a platform and then set the tent with the regular poles and call it a day. We did that very thing and only by trial and error did we learn some of the details shown in four final results (Fig. 107).

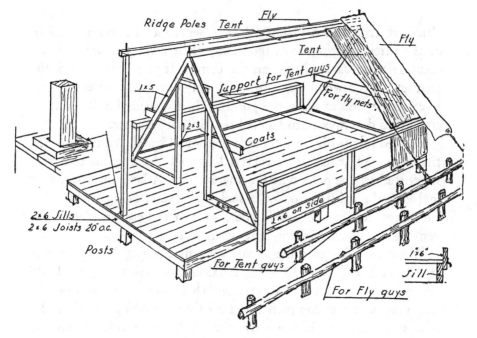

Fig. 107. The tent house.

First we built the frame for a doorway through which a man could walk without being reminded of the use of strong language before young children. You will also note a bar across the frame on both sides of the door, an answer to a request for some place to hang clothes.

Then the mosquitoes chipped in their little mite. It was not practical to screen the entire tent. Never let anyone sell you the idea that you can be comfortable in a tent with a netting *front* on a hot night. It may be hot with all the sides up, but it will be worse if you depend on a netting front only.

Fortunately we had three cot nets left from our own auto-camping days. But how best to hang them? The answer is in the other bar across the back supports which inevitably replaced the rear pole. An upright at the foot of each cot held the other end of the netting, and that problem was solved. In the daytime the occupants moved too fast for any mosquito and at night, with the netting tucked well in, the sides of the tent rolled up, what could be better?

If you have ever slept in a wall tent in a night rain and had the wet eaves sag on your sleepless body, you will at once see the reason for the bar supports on each side of the tent *over* which the tent guy ropes pass but to which they are not tied. They are carried to and secured on the innermost horizontal bar, or they can be secured by separate stakes which, however, the long bar makes unnecessary. We shall say more about this later.

On the two sides and on the back of the platform a 6-inch board is nailed to the sills to project 4 inches above the floor. This serves to keep out wind and rain and as a place for hooks over which the loops at the bottom edge of the tent can be secured.

The ridge pole supporting the tent fly has two holes which the pin in the rear support and the pin in the extreme front pole will fit. The pins must be of sufficient length to allow a spacer

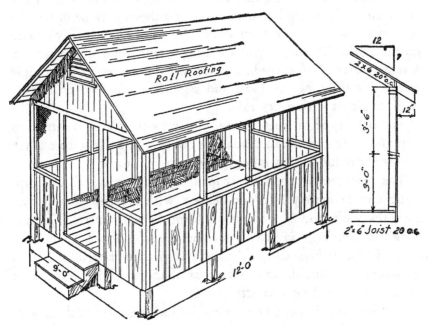

Fig. 108. The next step.

block 2 inches thick between the top of the tent and the fly. This will keep the fly, properly guyed, from resting on the tent.

Do not, as you value a night's sleep, let those two cloths touch during a rain. The pole at the front end of the fly ridge pole is kept in position by a block nailed to the floor in which the end is fitted.

You will notice that the only framework *within* the tent is the material that replaces the two poles. The baseboard is also inside the wall of the tent, or else. "Ah!" someone says, "why not make a sturdy frame, screen it, and then drop the tent down over the frame and not have all those guy ropes and bars?" There are several very good reasons for *not* doing so. The first reason is the comparative costs. If you are to do all that it would be much more practical to construct the little camp (see Fig. 108) which, simply constructed, would cost only little more than the tent over the frame.

The second reason is in the nature of the material of which the tent is made. It is almost unbelievable to anyone without the experience that there can be so much difference between a dry and a wet tent. You may retire for the night with all guys well slacked away and in the morning find the canvas tight as a drumhead and every guy will twang like a harp. A greenhorn may be lucky if a part of the tent has not torn away because of the excessive strain on the cloth. Oh! no, if you are using a tent, remember that it is a tent and treat it accordingly. If you put a tent over a rigid frame, it will either be loose and sagging when dry, or tearing itself to pieces with every rain.

The next type of guest house with respect to cost is shown in Fig. 108. We can assure that this type can be built with a small outlay for material if it is kept simple and plain.

The platform is no more than a tent platform; 2" x 4" uprights approximately 3 feet on centers, with shoe and double cap, form the walls; and 2" x 6" rafters form the roof frame. The rear is sheathed entirely and the front and the sides about 3 feet high only. This sheathing can be dressed and matched boards or batten construction; indeed, any treatment that would be given to a camp can be used on this little shack.

The open portion can be screened by tacking one width of wire screening right around the front and two sides and using a screen

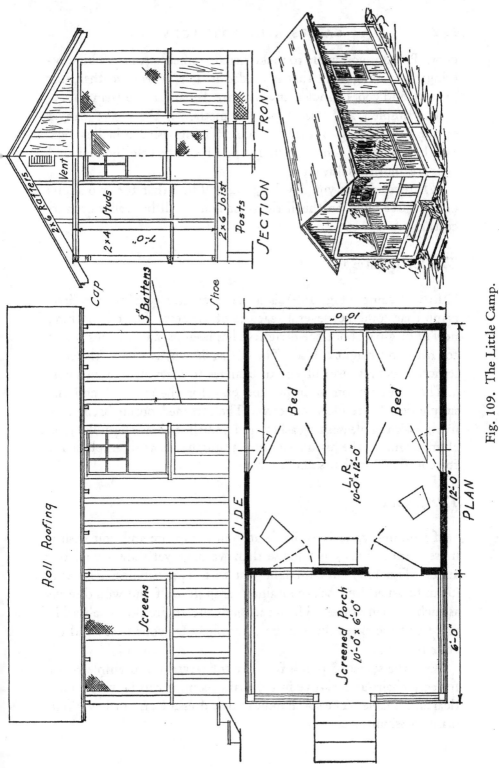

Fig. 109. The Little Camp.

Roll Roofing

3" Battens

Screens

SIDE

2x6 Rafters

Vent

Cap

2x4 Studs

7'-0"

2x6 Joist

Posts

Shoe

SECTION

FRONT

10'-0"

Bed

Bed

L. R.
10'-0" x 12'-0"

12'-0"

PLAN

Screened Porch
10'-0" x 6'-0"

6'-0"

241

door. Perhaps you want to make fitted framed screens. This covering of opening is all that is needed in fair, warm weather, but privacy and cool or inclement weather demand more than this.

The simplest and least expensive method is the use of canvas curtains that roll up or draw on rods. Sliding sash can be installed. Sash hinged at the top to swing in and up and be held by hook and eyes are another solution.

Whatever details you develop, you will find that for two adults or for three children this little guest house will be well worth its cost.

The Little Camp

In this camp (Fig. 109) is a compact and comfortable little camp that combines several features of interest. There is nothing new or original about the design; it has been used in various forms for many overnight cabins. The size as shown, as well as the construction details, are subject to changes to meet your own ideas.

The construction is simple and easy for the amateur and the simple details are clearly shown. The screened porch becomes a living room in pleasant weather, and a small stove with smoke pipe chimney makes the main room into a snug haven with ample space for comfortable chairs and a table.

The Annex

If running water is available at your camp site and you wish a more commodious guest house than we have yet shown you, the annex (Fig. 110) may intrigue you with its possibilities. Indeed, it can be an entirely self-contained camp in itself and would serve as such in many cases. The dimensions shown are not at all arbitrary and the exact size can be determined by your needs and by your budget.

With the screened porch for pleasant weather and ample room for easy chairs and a stove in the main room, it can be very practical and livable. The space indicated as dressing and utility offers many possibilities.

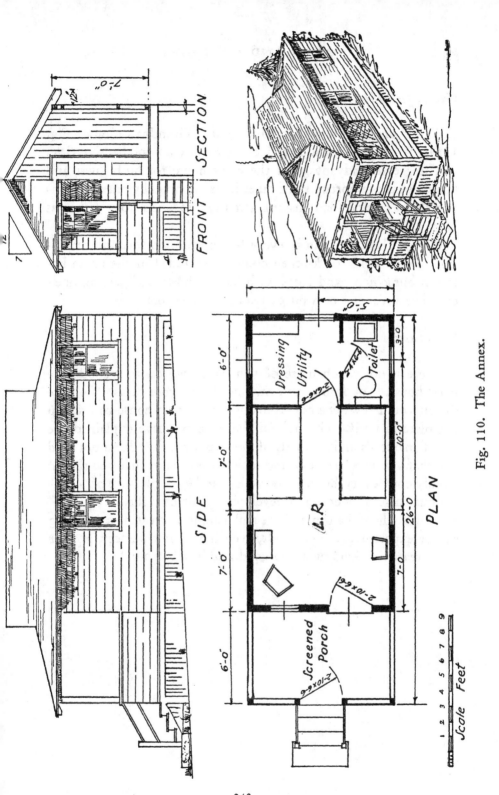

FRONT | SECTION

SIDE

PLAN

Dressing
Utility

Toilet

L.R.

Screened
Porch

1 2 3 4 5 6 7 8 9
Scale Feet

Fig. 110. The Annex.

243

Grandpa's House

As our final sketch we introduce you to Grandpa's House (Fig. 111). We use that name for lack of a more comprehensive title.

The greatest advantage of the guest house for both guest and hosts is in the opportunity of quiet hours at times by oneself without the necessity for constant attention to one's duty either as host or guest.

Here in this camp can be every feature for comfort and relaxation. Perhaps a little kitchen could be included in the angle between bunk nook and bath, with its possibilities of getting one's own late breakfast or a bit of tea of an afternoon.

Conclusion

There is not much more of value that we can say about the guest house. You know your own needs and your ideas. We have shown you a few schemes from the simple tent house to a camp complete in itself. Throughout the book we have explained the use of materials and methods of construction. We have not told you that you *must* use such and such materials nor that you should blindly copy everything. Now yours can be the pleasure of working out these problems and developing your own ideas.

That is where the fun and the real delight of creating something can be experienced. The result, even if it is not perfect, is your own creation. Good luck and good building be yours!

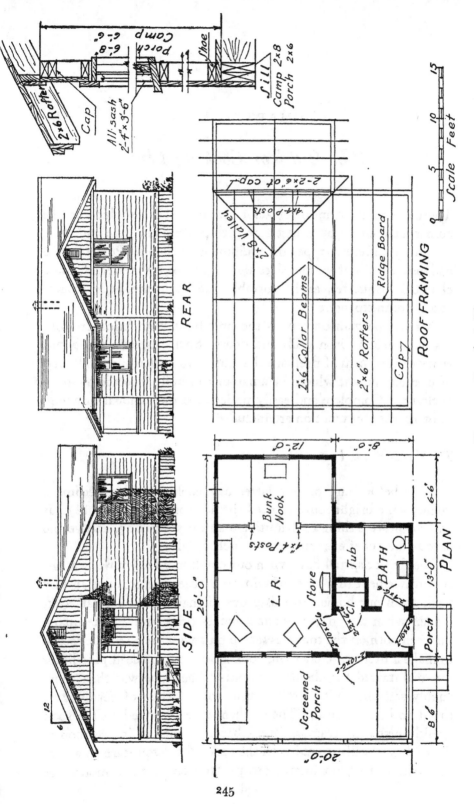

REAR

SIDE

28'-0"

12
6

ROOF FRAMING

2x6 Rafters
Cap

All sash 2'-4"x3'-6"
Porch Comp. 6'-8"
Comp. 6'-6"
Shoe
Sill
Camp 2x8
Porch 2x6
2x6 Rafters
Cap

2-2x6" of cap
4x4 Posts
2"x8" Valley
2"x6" Collar Beams
2"x6" Rafters
Ridge Board
Cap

PLAN

Bunk Nook
4x4 Posts
L.R.
Stove
2"x10"x2'-6"
2"x6"Cl.
Tub
BATH
2'-4"x6'-6"
2'-4"x6'-6"
Porch
2-10"x2'-4"
Screened Porch

12'-0"
8'-0"
6'-6"
13'-0"
20'-0"
8'-6"

0   5   10   15
Scale Feet

Fig. 111. Grandpa's House.

245

CHAPTER 17

The Outdoor Cooking Fire

There are many forms of outdoor cooking facilities which can be constructed either by yourself or with professional help and there are many different types of equipment available. Portable and collapsible grills of various sizes and degrees of elaborateness, using charcoal briquettes, easily portable and requiring little storage space, are inexpensive.

A more permanent type is the unit built with brick or stone masonry around iron grills and doors. Such has been the popularity of this form of fireplace that there are now available all sorts of iron equipment which the amateur can build into the masonry enclosure. Complete and easily understood dimensional drawings showing the construction are included.

The Flat-Rock Fry

Long before any of our latter-day cooking places became a vogue, some bright soul invented the flat-rock fry (Fig. 112). It was the nearest thing to primitive man's first cooking, and yet no *cordon bleu* chef ever turned out such delights.

The first crisp fall day, when our children were young, was the commencement of a series of trips to a large pine grove at an easy walk from our home. In this grove of majestic pine a flat rock, hidden when not in use, about 2 inches thick and 2 feet square, fairly smooth on the top, was set up on two walls of smaller stone to make a firebox. Under this rock a brisk fire of dead pine limbs was maintained for about two hours. The stone was then thoroughly scrubbed with a stiff brush, with no fear of germs after that two hours of heat. Then, when water dropped on the rock would burst into steam, on went bacon, plenty of it. As soon as the rock was well covered with the bacon fat—you learn to adjust the rock so that none runs away—on went a huge mound of onions, with the bacon pushed out to the sides to crisp. Frequent stirring and turning of the onions until they were a fragrant, honeylike mass not yet browned, was a pleasant anticipatory task. Then, with the onions carefully pushed away from the center of the stone, the *steak,* usually a sirloin, was gently and reverently laid on the hot rock. Turned several times until well seared and finally completely buried under a mound of the hot, steaming

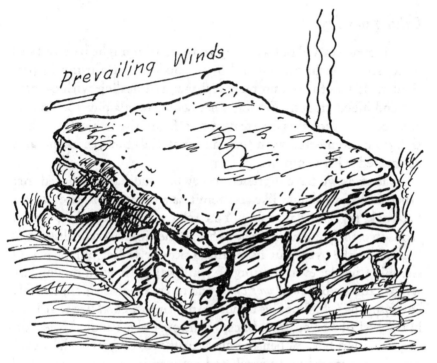

Fig. 112. Flat-rock fry.

onions, it was left slowly to bake to a medium stage. The fire, of course, was maintained all the time with wood that would burn without smoke.

Even all this was not sufficient but must be augmented by other varieties of food. On a companion fire near by, was hung in covered cook pots, "reading from left to right," as the papers say, green corn, string beans, potatoes, both white and sweet, and finally, an impressive pot of coffee.

About the time the steak was just right and the onions were a golden brown, the better half arrived at the scene with her contribution of the largest sized baking pan with piping hot cream of tartar biscuits. Raking the onions off the steak and applying quantities of butter to it, we served the feast. Needless to say, nothing was left but the rock. We have seen many outdoor cooking outfits and have eaten the results of them in all sorts of places, from a guide's brookside noon meal in Nova Scotia to a city banquet, but none of them even approached the flat-rock fry.

Baking in Clay

This book started out as a help to those who might be interested in construction in general and in the building of a camp in particular. It was to contain technical material dealing with carpentry and allied trades. We find that somewhere along the line we allowed our thoughts to stray away from the subject to those things not connected with tools and materials but yet inseparably connected with camp life.

As long as we have digressed somewhat and have detoured into other paths, we should like to submit as a companion piece to the flat-rock fry the clay bake. You take a nice fresh fish, say of from two to five pounds in weight, species immaterial; dress it as if to go in the oven, but never mind skin or scales; put plenty of seasoning inside, even dressing if you like; tie it with one or two wraps; and embed it in *wet clay*, one to two inches thick, entirely covering the fish. Put this bundle gently into a good fire that has a heavy bed of hot coals and heap coals over the bundle. Keep the fire brisk and hot. When the clay turns red, or gray—clays vary —and is commencing to crack and you can see that it is hard, roll out the bundle. After it has cooled so that you can handle it with holders, break off the baked clay, which will take with it all skin or scales of the fish, and serve. Remember it must be clay and not just any old *mud*.

Have you ever eaten a partridge cooked in this manner? Leave the feathers on, draw and clean the insides, season well, pack in wet clay, and put into the fire.

The Companion Fire

In connection with the flat-rock fry we referred to the companion fire. It is a companion fire in two senses. In the first place, it is a companion fire to the one under the flat rock; and, in the second place, that type of fire has always been a companion and as a companion it has no equal except for a friend and a dog. If you would understand this viewpoint, sit down with Henry Van Dyke's *Fisherman's Luck* and read there the chapter on "The Open Fire."

Properly made and properly maintained, this form of cooking fire will cook anything you may wish to cook. With a reflecting oven you can even bake bread, biscuits, or other baked foods. Lacking a reflecting oven you can make even a spider and a cover serve very well.

Lay two small logs, from 4 to 5 inches thick and around 4 feet long, about 6 to 8 inches apart at one end and not over 12 inches apart at the other end (Fig. 113). Remove any vegetation under or between the logs or, even better, scoop out the dirt between the logs to a depth of 2 or 3 inches. This is your range and, with two forked sticks at the ends and a stout pole resting in the forks, it is complete.

Fig. 113. The companion fire.

You have, of course, laid the logs in a direction which will allow the breeze to blow lengthwise of the logs, with the wider opening to windward. Now start a *small* fire near the *windward* end, using any light, dry material that will burn readily and with a hearty blaze until you have a fairly brisk, but not large, fire. Then commence to put on dry and sound wood or green wood, without which you cannot get a heavy bed of live coals. You will be working the fire, with the wind, toward the narrow end. After your good wood is burning well, with little or no smoke, you can start the kettles, which you hang on the pole over the fire. We used a variety of double-end hooks roughly bent from steel wire with which the height of a kettle above the fire could be adjusted. Remember that you do not need a bonfire to cook over.

All the time you are judiciously adding hardwood to the windward end of the fire, gradually working it toward the small end until at that end you have a deep bed of coals giving out strong heat but little flame. Over that portion of the fire your frying pan or spider can rest on the side logs. You see now why the space tapers between the two logs. Here you can fry your bacon and eggs, broil your steak, make the coffee, and perform all the operations possible on a range.

While the meal is being eaten, a pail of water is hung over the fire to heat for dishwater.

The last act and the most important one is to douse with water every vestige of fire until there is not the least spark alive in the fire, the logs, or the ground around the fireplace.

Outdoor Grill

We have quoted "Dunwurken" very freely throughout this book because the results of actual experience may carry more weight than mere ideas. We learned by trial and error and we made mistakes which we have honestly acknowledged. The main fact is that we did learn and we wish to save you from the same mistakes.

For seven summers the camp was occupied by the owner's sister and her family, which included four children whose appetites, normally excellent, were greatly increased by the active life in the woods. To avoid the heat of food preparation in the camp and to have the thrill of food cooked in the open, we built of common brick, one old iron grate, and one length of tile flue lining, a very simple unit, merely an enclosure 12 inches wide, 24 inches long, and 12 inches deep (Fig. 114). The 8″ x 8″ flue lining was the chimney bricked up for a part of its height. Over the grill a piece of sheet iron was used when we started the fire and cooked hamburgers and hot dogs.

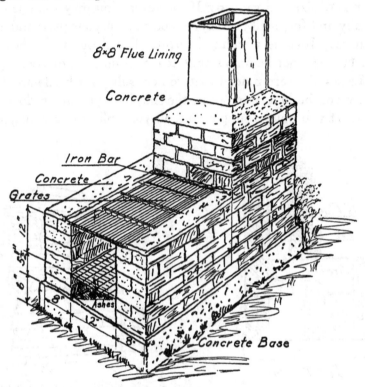

Fig. 114. A simple outdoor grill.

We learned two important factors for success. The length of the firebox was laid out parallel to the prevailing winds, with the chimney at the far end so that the natural draft was through the fire and up the chimney. The other important factor was in the height of the cooking surface. Taking advantage of a natural rock outcropping, we built the firebox at a height which would make it possible to work over the grill without getting down on one's knees or breaking one's back.

On this simple and very inexpensive equipment the major part of the meals were prepared and enjoyed on a table near by surrounded by the pines.

We have one word of caution on the subject of the outdoor cooking units. Again we say STOP, THINK. Do not be carried away with enthusiasm by some of the units which contain everything but space for a piano. If you have a permanent location and may naturally do much entertaining frequently, then go the limit as to size and gadgets. If, however, you may use one occasionally and for small parties, be moderate in your ideas and avoid what may become a white elephant. The little outfit shown in Fig. 114 may not be imposing, but it will do a lot of cooking.

We heartily recommend that you consult your hardware dealer before you build anything but the simplest type of outdoor fireplace. If you build a simple unit, all you will need can be picked

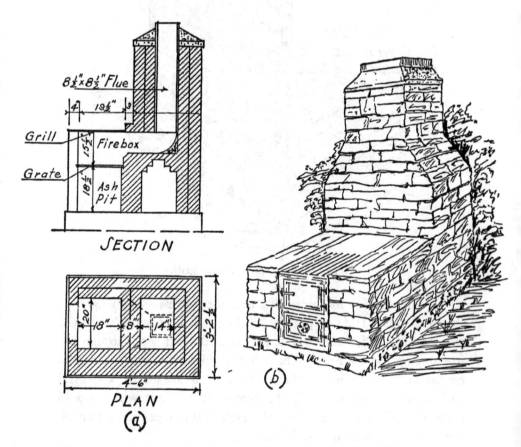

Fig. 115. Outdoor fireplace: (a) basic design, (b) elaborate unit.

up almost as salvage: a few bricks, one 24-inch length of 8″ x 8″ tile flue lining, and any old piece of grating. Some Portland cement and sand and a few hours work are all that is required.

If, however, you want a more elaborate outfit with ash pits, doors, etc., then investigate a little and you will be surprised to learn to what extent this equipment has been developed. By using one of these iron units, you need only set them in place and build the masonry work around them. There are even gadgets to be built into your unit which hold the burning charcoal in upright frames, and the steak is broiled between them like bread in an electric toaster.

If you will use your outdoor fireplace frequently and wish it to last indefinitely, you should use firebrick laid in fire-clay mortar for lining the firebox and the flue as far as the tile lining. These firebrick, which are a light buff color and slightly larger than common brick, are the only one which will withstand the destructive effect of the heat.

Shown in Fig. 115 is the basic design of a typical, more elaborate unit, which includes a firebox with door and grate, a grill top over which a sheet metal cover can be placed, and an ash pit with door and damper. The dimensioned detail drawing is shown as all brick, but stone can be used as the exposed masonry. The design is not arbitrary nor are the dimensions anything but typical.

The Picnic Table

If you are to get the full benefit of the outdoor cooking, it must be eaten within sight of the fire and that means, unless you are young and limber, a table at which to sit in comfort. The great trouble with a seat on the ground is that there is no place to put your legs. So, by all means let us have a table to go with our cooking place. You can make or purchase ready to put together a sawbuck-type table and benches which will accommodate six people and which can be dismantled after the season is over and stored in the house or garage.

Pardon me if we quote "Dunwurken" once more. A small table served for a while, but with many friends coming to spend the day, bringing their food with them, a larger table was needed. So, a table *eighteen* feet long and three feet wide was constructed, with the benches on each side built as a part of the table (Fig. 116). This size sounds absurd, but actually it was not. Set in a group of white birch and several large pines near the shore of the

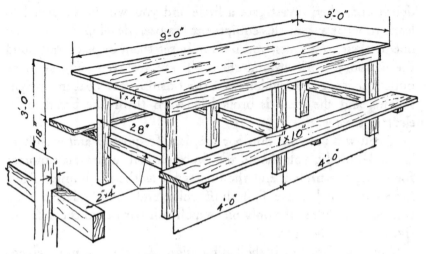

Fig. 116. Picnic table.

pool, it was dining table, writing table, and a gathering place for knitters. In the woods as it was, it was a focal point; and, being well painted, it was left outdoors permanently. That the young mother had friends in such numbers to require the large table was recompense enough for the builder.

Index